Value Investing CHECKLIST

"No matter how expert you may be, well-designed checklists can improve outcomes"
Steven Levitt.

Vivek Choudhary

Photo courtesy of Benjamin Graham

Dedicated to

You, My Grandfather, Warren Buffett & Benjamin Graham

Hope This Book Guide You To The Road Map For Success

PREFACE

You need a different checklist and mental models for different companies. I can never make it easy by saying, 'Here are three things.' You have to derive it yourself to ingrain it in your head for the rest of your life.

—Charlie Munger

The checklist is your weapon to use, approach to be successful in value investing, or any kind of investing. We cannot get success without a proper checklist, every value investor has a checklist, and without using a checklist it is not at all possible to generate a good return.

I have faced the challenges if you don't use the checklist, we cannot be right all the time, there are so many companies and it is not possible to remember each and every company ecosystem, checklist help in understanding about the company and what is important to understand.

As a value investor, I use the checklist and without a checklist, I don't invest a penny, unless the company screened by the checklist, we will never know, what information we are missing.

I hope this book wills help you in understanding the company with the help of the checklist.

Introduction

I'm a great believer in solving hard problems by using a checklist. You need to get all the likely and unlikely answers before you; otherwise it's easy to miss something important.

—Charlie Munger

This book is divided into two parts, Qualitative Analysis & Quantitative Analysis. The important of the checklist and if you don't use the checklist , what can be wrong in your investment , the importance of checklist , why a checklist is important , the benefits of using a checklist , how Warren Buffett has created enormous wealth by selecting value stock and without checklist it is not possible to know about the company. Moving forward in this book, you will learn valuable lessons from the greatest value investor like Warren Buffett, Charlie Munger, Benjamin Graham, Mohnish Pabrai, Peter Lynch, Seth Klarman, Walter Schloss, Sir John Templeton & Philip Fisher. You will learn how to use, Qualitative Analysis & Quantitative Analysis, about the value investing checklist framework, what kind of company value investors would like to invest and what kind of industry they are comfortable to invest, and you will learn, what kind of industries Warren Buffett invests. You will learn the approach to use the checklist as per value investing process principal, where you need to stop and not to use the checklist, In the Qualitative Analysis checklist you will learn about the business ecosystem, about product portfolio, who are the suppliers, about the competition in the industry, where company geographically operate in, what is the competence of management, about the franchise value, barrier to entry and durable competitive advantage.

In Quantitative Analysis you will learn about the portfolio diversification, risk and return of the portfolio , In risk, you will learn about the stock risk such as margin of safety and corporate governance or fraud, how leverage destroys value to the shareholders, moving forward you will learn about macroeconomics risks such as business recession and inflation risk, how you can avoid such risk and last you will learn about Value Investor Discipline Approach a way to be a successful value investor, the last but not the least, you will learn best quotes by Benjamin Graham from the intelligent investor.

"A man may die, nations may rise and fall, but an idea lives on. Ideas have endurance without death."
—John F. Kennedy

Are you ready to be a value investor? Such as you want to be in winning team with extraordinary investors like Warren Buffett and that looks to be a very good team to be in.

About the Author

Vivek Choudhary is a Value Investor & Entrepreneur who has over 20 years of experience in investment and entrepreneurship. Involve in diversify business Commodities, Manufacturing, Hotel & Automobiles.

He earned MBA in finance & Marketing at IIPM, MDP in Strategic Market Planning at IIM, Equity Research Analyst at BSE Institute, Value Investing at Stanford University Continue studies, and Entrepreneurship Essential & Leading with Finance at HBX Harvard Business School & Value Investing at

Columbia Business School, Business Lesson Cohort at Harvard Business School Online.

He is passionate about Value Investing and invests globally. His hobby is reading. He reads everyday value investing books and finance books.

He admires his Hero Mr. Warren Buffett Chief Executive Officer of Berkshire Hathaway – He follows his footprint of Value Investing. For him reading and studying are like compounding, it will help him in achieving his passion.

He wrote the book

- **Value Investing & Behavioral Finance**

- **Stock Investing & Financial Statement Analysis**

- **Value Investing - Legendary Graham & Dodd Valuation**

- **Value Investing CHECKLIST**

- **Billionaires Mind – Blue Print of Entrepreneurship**

- **Why Investors fail in Stock market**

CONTENTS

Preface	III
Introduction	IV

CHECKLIST

1.	The Checklist	4
2.	Importance of Checklist	17
3.	Benefits to Use Checklist	21
4.	Risk of Not Using Checklist	44
5.	Famous Value Investor Checklist	51
	• Charlie Munger	51
	• Warren Buffett	59
	• Benjamin Graham	63
	• Mohnish Pabrai	66
	• Peter Lynch	70
	• Seth Klarman	76
	• Walter Schloss	78
	• Sir John Templeton	83
	• Philip Fisher	87

QUALITATIVE & QUANTITATIVE ANALYSIS

6.	Qualitative & Quantitative Analysis	91
7.	Company Type	101
8.	Industry Type	105

CONTENTS

9. Approach to Use Checklist	113
10. Qualitative Analysis	117
11. Business Analysis	119
12. Product Analysis	168
13. Customer Analysis	192
14. Supplier Analysis	210
15. Competitors Analysis	215
16. Industry Analysis	227
17. Geographical Analysis	250
18. Management Analysis	260
19. Franchise Value Analysis	300
• Durable Competitive Advantage	302
• Barrier to entry	310
20. Quantitative Analysis	314
21. Portfolio Diversification	316
22. Financial Analysis & Valuation	326
23. Risk	356
• Stock Risk	357
• Macroeconomics Risk	370
24. Value Investing Discipline Approach	376
25. The Intelligent Investor Ben Graham Quotes	393

CHECKLIST

"My weapon of choice as a stock picker is research; it's critical for me to understand a company's value before laying down a dime"

Michael James Burry

In December 2018, Professor Bill Simon, co-founder of the Value Investing Program, had the honor to meet super-investor Warren Buffett at his office in Omaha, Nebraska.

BERKSHIRE HATHAWAY INC.
3555 FARNAM STREET, SUITE 1440
OMAHA, NEBRASKA 68131
TELEPHONE (402) 346-1400
FAX (402) 346-3375

WARREN E. BUFFETT, CHAIRMAN

December 3, 2019

Mr. William E. Simon, Jr.
11100 Santa Monica Boulevard, #1910
Los Angeles, CA 90025

Dear Bill:

    It's good to hear from you. And it's particularly good to hear the news about the naming of your program after Ben Graham.

    Ben was the best teacher I ever had. He made things come alive in the classroom in many ingenious ways, some of which I shamelessly stole from him to use myself.

    Ben was about as generous as anyone I've ever met. He constantly did things for other people with absolutely no expectation of reciprocal behavior.

    Keep spreading the gospel.

                             Best regards,

                             Warren E. Buffett

WEB/db

1

The Checklist

A checklist is a type of job aid used to reduce failure by compensating for potential limits of human memory and attention. It helps to ensure consistency and completeness in carrying out a task. A basic example is the "to do list". A more advanced checklist would be a schedule, which lays out tasks to be done according to time of day or other factors. A primary task in checklist is documentation of the task and auditing against the documentation.

A pilot of a DC-10 consulting his checklist

In aviation, a pre-flight checklist is a list of tasks that should be performed by pilots and aircrew prior to takeoff. Its purpose is to improve flight safety by ensuring that no important tasks are forgotten. Failure to correctly conduct a preflight check using a checklist is a major contributing factor to aircraft accidents.

Following a checklist would have shown that the gust lock was engaged on the Gulfstream IV crash on May 31, 2014. The National Transportation Safety Board downloaded data from the aircraft's recorder and found it was a habit: 98% of the previous 175 takeoffs were made with incomplete flight-control checks. The National Business Aviation Association analyzed 143,756 flights in 2013-2015 by 379 business aircraft and only partial flight-control checks were done before 15.6% of the takeoffs and no checks at all on 2.03% of the flights.

Boeing Model 299 aka B-17 "Flying Fortress"

According to researcher and writer Atul Gawande, the concept of a pre-flight checklist was first introduced by management and engineers at Boeing Corporation following the 1935 crash of the prototype Boeing B-17 (then known as the Model 299) at Wright Field in Dayton, Ohio, killing both pilots. Investigation found that the pilots had forgotten to disengage the crucial gust locks (devices which stop control surfaces moving in the wind while parked) prior to take-off. Life magazine published the resulting lengthy and detailed B-17 checklist in its 24 August 1942 issue.

A checklist is a list of items you need to verify, check or inspect. Checklists are used in every imaginable field — from building inspections to complex medical surgeries. Using a checklist allows you to ensure you don't forget any important steps.

You might not think that checklists have a role in the workplace. Often used for simple tasks like creating a grocery list or packing for a vacation, checklists aren't often thought of as a tool for increasing productivity and efficiency at work. But the power of checklists has been proven time and time again across a variety of professions and industries.

It doesn't matter how many times you've performed a task or how much training and experience you have in your role, checklists reduce the likelihood of important steps or tasks getting overlooked and help you feel confident that you've completed your work expertly.

"A checklist is no substitute for thinking"

Warren Buffett

"Charlie Munger is possibly without peer when it comes to the checklist of atypical investment factors he considers and his deep fluency in the diverse disciplines from which they are drawn"

Peter Kaufman

"It is also essential for a thinking man to assemble his skills into a checklist that he routinely uses. Any other mode of operation will cause him to miss much that is important"

Charlie Munger

"Before I make the final decision to buy any stock, I turn to my checklist in a last-ditch effort to prevent my unreliable brain from overlooking any potential warning sign that I might have missed"

Guy Spier

"Boeing just doesn't sit around in a room and come up with the checklist for take-offs. That has been created over 60-70 years of failures that have caused things to make the checklist. Our investment checklist was designed the same way. I looked at mistakes I made since the time I invested and I looked at mistakes that other people made that I respect like Warren Buffett and Charlie Munger, LongLeaf Partners and so on. When I look at mistakes, I would figure

out what was the reason the investment lost money and was that reason visible at the outset? Was it visible before the investment was made? And, in most cases it's extremely obvious"

Mohnish Pabrai

"The only antidote for being an absolute klutz due to the presence of a man with a hammer syndrome is to have a full kit of tools. You don't have just a hammer. You've got all the tools. And you've got to have one more trick. You've got to use those tools checklist-style, because you'll miss a lot if you just hope that the right tool is going to pop up unaided whenever you need it. But if you've got a full list of tools, and go through them in your mind, checklist-style, you will find a lot of answers that you won't find any other way."

Charlie Munger

"Why are checklists so effective? We think we're very smart; we take shortcuts, especially in investing. We get euphoric about all the money we're going to make and we are just a mix of rationality and emotions. We see a great undervalued business, we ask ourselves a bunch of questions, but we don't go through a systematic process of looking at every nook and cranny to figure out whether we got it right or not"

Mohnish Pabrai

"We're just starting a process now, it's funny I have it in my hand. This is a pilot's checklist for a certain type of plane. And what we're starting to institute at our firm is for every function, including the investment function, to have a daily checklist"

Bruce Berkowitz

"Investing and the checklist. Not Rocket Science. Pretty obvious. Start with the stuff we've learned from Graham, Buffet, Munger, Klarman, Fisher, Templeton etc .. margin of safety, moats, simple businesses .. make a real Checklist. Examine all your mistakes that led to permanent loss of capital – the plane crashed. Add to the checklist"

Mohnish Pabrai

"In investing too, the real purpose of a checklist is to serve as a survival tool, based on the haunting remembrance of things past"

Guy Spier

"My checklist is.. is it cheap?, is it a good business?, who is running it?, and what did I miss?. I go through all the checklist. When I go to 'what did I miss?' .. it is hugely important to understand psychology and human cognition"

Li Lu

"We believe there are questions to which every responsible capital allocator should know the answer, so we've developed an investment committee memo framed to address all of our core investment values. It's not a brainless exercise of box checking, but meant to ensure that the analysis gets done in the way that we've learned over time should produce high quality results"

James Chrichton

"No wise pilot, no matter how great his talent and experience, fails to use a checklist."

Charlie Munger

"Any student of value investing is well aware of the various behavioural biases to which investors are subject, but the sad reality is that awareness doesn't preclude you from succumbing to them. Every item on our checklist is meant to remind us of previous lessons learned and expose any biases we may have on a particular investment"

Christopher Begg

"The power of simple checklists should not be under estimated"

James Montier

"One of my key investing tools is a checklist of 98 or so items that help me avoid bad stock picks (most gleaned from mistakes the very best investors on the planet have made). My list was copied from the famed checklist the Federal Aviation Administration mandates to keep airline crashes to a minimum" -Monish Pabrai

"If you're trying to analyze a company without using an adequate checklist, you may make a very bad investment"

Charlie Munger

"We have multiple checklists and processes in place to improve how we think and make decisions"

Ken Shubin Stein

"We're big believers in checklists, which are the best tools available to reduce preventable human errors" Joel Hirsch

"The checklist has prevented many investments that may not have been prevented otherwise. It is one of those things where it doesn't take much effort, but delivers a huge reward, and I like that"

Mohnish Pabrai

"...all investors can benefit by keeping an investment journal and using checklists in doing their research. These two very simple tools not only will help keep people focused on their goals and sticking with their strategy, but they will also help them avoid mistakes out of impulse. They will also protect investors from some of the cognitive biases to which we are all subject. In the checklist, it's possible to put not only the steps necessary to do the research as well as lists of mistakes or problems that occurred in the past and should be avoided, but also a list of cognitive biases. This allows the investor to check with him or herself and to think about whether there are forces at play that may be activating some cognitive biases, and if so, to consider those."

Ken Shubin Stein

"My good friend, Guy Spier, observed that both of us have a pre-investment checklist, but no in-flight checklist. The pre-investment checklist has proven invaluable. However, it is not enough to just keep up with ongoings in existing investments in an ad hoc manner. It is important to periodically run and re-run the in-flight checklist."

Mohnish Pabrai

"I'm a great believer in solving hard problems by using a checklist. You need to get all the likely and unlikely answers before you; otherwise it's easy to miss something important."

Charlie Munger

"The checklist we have got created in a very holistic manner in the sense that I did not just add questions on the checklist on a blue sky basis. I looked at the mistakes either I made or other great investors made and I asked if it was obvious before the investment was made that it would not work. In many cases it was obvious. Then I asked what is the question that should have been asked before this investment was made? For example, when Warren Buffett bought Dexter Shoes the question is, "Can it be impacted by cheap labour in China?," or for US Airways, "Can unions have an impact" or "Does the structure of the airline industry ... ?

These questions were ad hoc, but later when I created all the questions and I started to categorize them into different buckets, what surprised me is that they fell very nicely into about five different categories. There's quite a few questions related to leverage that cause problems for companies. There's a number of questions related to moats, sustainable advantage, brands, etc., so that was another category. There was whole category on management ownership which has a bunch of questions. When we looked at the management and ownership section there's a number of questions, some related to the size of the ownership stake how are they compensated, are interests aligned, what's the past track record, how long has the team been together, those kinds of things. There's a number of questions that come up in that section that are absolutely fundamental. In fact, many times that is the section where I end up having to go back and do more research because I end up not knowing the answer to many of those questions the first time I run it. Usually those are the ones that I tend to naturally miss and go back and figure out after the fact. Capital allocation is fundamental - there's a whole bunch of checklist questions on that as well" Mohnish Pabrai

"You need a different checklist and different mental models for different companies. I can never make it easy by saying, 'Here are three things'. You have to derive it yourself to ingrain it in your head for the rest of your life"

Charlie Munger

"I'm a prolific maker of lists, and the more trouble I had in the early 1990s, the more I attacked it and dealt with it by making lists and checking off items as we accomplished them"

Sam Zell "

"Both Warren and I feel it's our moral duty to be as rational as we can possibly be. A lot of people who are brilliant in some ways tend to make these utterly asinine decisions in other ways. We both tend to collect the asininities of the world in a kind of checklist. And we try to avoid everything on the checklist."

Charlie Munger

A checklist, when used properly, is an assurance that a particular piece of information has been inspected. As each item on the checklist is ticked off, the person doing the research is verifying that each area is in correct checked?

Every business have their own set of checklist to avoid any kind of error and to accomplish the desired result , the checklist is a approach to get positive result , business with automobiles have different checklist to repair the car , that approach use for avoid any type of car accident , while doctor operating a surgery, The WHO Surgical Safety Checklist was developed after extensive consultation aiming to decrease errors and adverse events, and increase teamwork and communication in surgery. The 19-item checklist has gone on to show significant reduction in both morbidity and mortality and is now used by a majority of surgical providers around the world. "Planning ahead can help ensure you have a successful procedure and heal faster with a smooth recovery."

The Surgical Safety Checklist

In 2009, the World Health Organization (WHO) published the Surgical Safety Checklist (SSC) as part of their Safe Surgery Saves Lives campaign. The checklist was adapted from the field of aviation, where checklist use is standard practice. In aviation, checklists were developed in response to a crash involving an experienced pilot operating a new airplane with features that were significantly different from previous models. Shortly after takeoff, the plane stalled and crashed. An investigation revealed that the pilot had forgotten to perform one of the steps necessary for takeoff. In response, the checklist was created to prevent future avoidable disasters.

With more than 200 million operations performed annually, the WHO recognized the importance of addressing surgical safety when the checklist was introduced. The purpose of the checklist was to help operating room (OR) teams remember important details that may be missed during an operation. In addition, it served as a tool to encourage teamwork and communication. In a sense, the WHO came to the same conclusion that the plane crash investigation team had: even highly skilled OR teams need tools to help them achieve optimal results. The initial WHO SSC was piloted at eight diverse hospitals around the world and contained 19 items that were to be addressed at defined time points during the operation .The items included in the SSC are aimed at preventing uncommon but serious errors by reminding the team to confirm patient identity, surgical site, and other important characteristics such as co-morbid conditions or anticipated complications. Results from the initial prospective, sequential, time-series observational study showed significant reductions in complications, in-hospital mortality, rates of unplanned reoperation, and surgical site infection (SSI) compared to pre-checklist rates.

2
Importance of Good Checklist

Simply put, a checklist is a list of items for consideration. They can come in several forms, like a list of questions or actions to be carried out. They can be accompanied by check boxes that can be ticked off when that list item has been completed. People accept the results of a completed checklist as reliable and true. Thus, it is used as a memory aid or a job tool to make sure all issues have been considered.

The human brain is said to be capable of holding 4.7 million books in memory. And yet, there is no lack of documented failures in our history. So, why do people still fail, even though we are capable of holding a great amount of information and use a considerable number of skills? According to philosophers, we fail for 2 reasons: ignorance and ineptitude. We fail, firstly, because we do not have the information to perform a task. We fail also because, although we have the information, we are unable to apply it consistently and correctly. The real problems are getting the information and methods in our brain, and managing them effectively once they are inside.

Getting information in our brain to help us succeed is a problem of effort and attention. A psychologist who won a Nobel Prize tells of 2 systems in our brain. System 1 is a fast system that lets us function with minimal effort. We use this system automatically to do things that feel natural and intuitive. System 2 is a slow system that requires conscious, deliberate thought that takes much effort. We use this when making big decisions and solving problems. Instinctively, we prefer to use System 1, and that is why our brain loves checklists. Checklists are familiar and concise.

The other reason we fail is because the great amount of information in our head becomes unmanageable sometimes. People with complex jobs hold an enormous amount of knowledge and experience. These highly trained, highly skilled people are usually also the hardworking people with important or critical responsibilities. Over time, they become prone to make mistakes when the need to apply these knowledge and experience comes. This is where a simple checklist can make them better at their jobs without having to spend more time than necessary.

Using a checklist in the workspace can save lives in the operating room, can prevent a building from collapsing, or stop an innocent person from going to jail. Checklists can improve performance in the job and help people achieve more consistent results. They are explicit reminders of the minimum necessary steps. They are methods of verification, and they support a discipline toward higher performance.

Checklists are designed carefully to ensure basic checks are always completed before performing an important task.

Picking a winning stock that can give consistent returns for many years requires a lot of analysis and research. However, you can simplify the research process if you have an investment checklist.

Having a reliable checklist for picking stocks can reduce the chances of missing an important detail that you should have studied before investing in the stock. As Charlie Munger, Vice-Chairman of Berkshire Hathaway has famously quoted:

"No wise pilot, no matter how great his talent and experience, fails to use a checklist."

Charlie Munger

It's true that picking a winning stock required a tremendous amount of research. However, having an investment checklist of questions to ask before investing in stock significantly reduce the chances of investing in fundamentally weak stocks. Moreover, you can easily eliminate over 90% of the companies that don't meet your checklist.

We know that all investors have biases, it's a function of human nature. When it comes to investing those biases can lead to sub-optimal returns, or worse, the permanent loss of capital. Many of the Investment Masters have turned to basic 'checklists' to help improve investment results. Charlie

Munger, Warren Buffett's partner and one of the world's greatest investors, couldn't have been more definitive when he said: *"If you're trying to analyze a company without using an adequate checklist, you may make a very bad investment"*.

"The risk that matters most is the risk of permanent loss." Howard Marks

" ...in terms of building checklists, there is no question that the place to go is past mistakes. Not only one's own past mistakes, but also to look at other investors' past mistakes and see what those mistakes were." Guy Spier

There are thousand and thousand companies listed in the stock exchange, picking the one that can make you rich is like finding a needle in a huge mountain of companies. In order to make things easier, you must start by preparing a list of businesses that you really understand. Warren Buffett calls it circle of competence.

By understanding the business, you will be able to make better projections about the business's future growth potential and how its earnings are going to look like in the coming years. This will help you in understanding if the business in question is worth investing or not.

3

Benefits to Use Checklist

"The stock investor is either right or wrong because others agreed or disagreed with him; he is right because his facts and analysis are right."

— Benjamin Graham, The Intelligent Investor

Important is that they catch mental flaws of memory and attention and thoroughness inherent in all of us. Our brains are designed to arrive at answers quickly by taking shortcuts. As Mohnish Pabrai notes, "when you see the lion, you run. You don't process your options, you just run". Our in-built biases can be useful sometimes, but also dangerous at other times.

Checklists help us cope with the limits of our memory - we can only retain a few things at a time but the limit is not necessarily the gold standard for what it takes to get things done. Checklists also help us to counter biases that might get in the way while selecting the stock to invest.

When you purchase stocks, you turn out to be shareholders of the business. This gives you a privilege to vote at the shareholder's meeting and enables you to get any benefits that the organization assigns to its owners—these benefits are alluded to as profits. When you buy a stock, you aren't ensured anything. Many stocks don't pay profits, profiting just by expanding in esteem and going up in price—which won't not occur.

Stocks give moderately high potential returns. Obviously, there is a cost for this potential: you should accept the danger of losing a few or the greater part of your investment. The primary objective of investing is to ensure that every person is able to meet his or her future financial objectives. Rise in inflation makes it inadequate for individuals to simply earn and save some part of their incomes. To meet the price increases due to inflation, investments become important. The stock market is one of the oldest and most popular investment avenues due to several benefits of investing in stocks.

Compared to other investment products like bonds and fixed deposits, stock investing provides investors an excellent possibility of making greater returns in comparatively shorter time periods. Adhering to the stock market basics, such as planning the trade, using stop-loss and take-profit triggers, doing the research and due diligence, and being patient can significantly mitigate the risks inherent to stock investing and maximize the returns on share market investments.

Even if an investor acquires a single share in a company, he acquires a portion of ownership in the company. This ownership, in turn, provides investors the right to vote and offer his contribution in the strategic movement of the business.

There are certain companies or business houses and sectors which we love to track and at times imagine if we had the opportunity to run that company or business. But being a retail investor with limited financial capacity that might not be possible. However, we can partner the same business by buying the shares of the company and becoming part owner of the company we love.

What shareholders actually own are shares issued by the corporation; and the corporation owns the assets held by a firm. So, if you own 33% of the shares of a company, it is incorrect to assert that you own one-third of that company; it is instead correct to state that you own 100% of one-third of the company's shares. Shareholders cannot do as they please with a corporation or its assets. A shareholder can't walk out with a chair because the corporation owns that chair, not the shareholder. This is known as the "separation of ownership and control."

Owning stock gives you the right to vote in shareholder meetings, receive dividends (which are the company's profits) if and when they are distributed, and it gives you the right to sell your shares to somebody else.

If you own a majority of shares, your voting power increases so that you can indirectly control the direction of a company by appointing its board of directors. This becomes most apparent when one company buys another: the acquiring company doesn't go around buying up the building, the chairs, the employees; it buys up all the shares. The board of directors is responsible for increasing the value of the corporation, and often does so by hiring professional managers, or officers, such as the Chief Executive Officer, or CEO.

For most ordinary shareholders, not being able to manage the company isn't such a big deal. The importance of being a shareholder is that you are entitled to a portion of the company's profits, which, as we will see, is the foundation of a stock's value. The more shares you own, the larger the portion of the profits you get. Many stocks, however, do not pay out dividends, and instead reinvest profits back into growing the company. These retained earnings, however, are still reflected in the value of a stock. If the company grows and becomes more valuable, the share is worth more – so your investment is worth more too.

Understanding how Warren Buffett selects winning stocks starts with analyzing the investment philosophy of the company he is most closely associated with, Berkshire Hathaway. Berkshire has a long-held and public strategy when it comes to acquiring shares. The company should have consistent earning power, a good return on equity (ROE), capable management, and be sensibly-priced.

Buffett belongs to the value investing school, popularized by Benjamin Graham. Value investing looks at the intrinsic value of a share rather than focusing on technical indicators, such as moving averages, volume, or momentum indicators. Determining intrinsic value is an exercise in understanding a company's financials, especially official documents such as earnings and income statements.

There are several things worth noting about Buffett's value investing strategy. To guide him in his decisions, Buffett uses several key considerations to evaluate the attractiveness of a possible investment.

Let's go through the important points of benefit to use checklist as follow: -

- Earn Higher Returns
- Right Investment
- The Safe Way
- Not to lose your capital
- For your success
- Approach to achieve the return
- Long term investment
- Measure Risk of your Investment
- Peace of mind
- No herd mentality

Earn Higher Returns

In order to grow your money, you need to put it in a place where it can earn a high rate of return. The higher the rate of return, the more money you will earn. Investment vehicles tend to offer the opportunity to earn higher rates of return than savings accounts. Therefore, if you want the chance to earn a higher return on your money, you will need to explore investing your money. Checklist if a tool you can use to accomplish the high return from your investment. If you buy shares in larger, long-established companies you'll probably get dividends, but you might not get rapid growth. Shares that pay regular dividends are good for getting an income or the dividends can be reinvested to grow your capital.

Right Investment

Selecting a right stock to invest, when you have used the tool of checklist, then your chance of success is very high, you are in a right direction. The right shares can help you grow your wealth.

Let see example of warren buffet about the right investment can create miracles and wonders...

Warren Buffett bought more than $1 billion of Coca-Cola (KO) shares in 1988, an amount equivalent to 6.2% of the company, making it the largest position in his portfolio at the time. It remains one of Berkshire Hathaway's biggest holdings today, the stock market crash of 1987 had created attractive valuations, as all types of stocks were sold off with little regard to fundamentals. Coca-Cola is the dominant company in the beverage industry and has large food holdings as well. Further, Coca-Cola's iconic name and global reach created a moat around its core soft drink product, so Buffett did not have to worry a competitor would come and take away its market share. Coca-Cola is Berkshire

Hathaway's third-largest holding, more than 30 years after it first joined the portfolio.

Buffett first started buying shares of Coca-Cola in 1988, not long after the famous Black Monday stock market crash in 1987. By the end of 1989, he had purchased 23.35 million shares worth $1.8 billion.

See's Candy is one of Buffett's more interesting investments because not a lot of people expected it to succeed. Buffett bought See's way back in 1972. See's needed a buyer after its patriarch, Laurance See, passed away. The company thought they were going to under but managed to stay afloat. Buffett paid in year 1972 was $25 million and now the return is $1.32 billion.

Buffett walked into See's in 1972. His favorite See's candies became their chocolate walnut fudge and peanut brittle. His investment partner, Charlie Munger, was also with him. They both fell in love with the company, calling it a "dream business."

Warren Buffett's flagship investment firm, Berkshire Hathaway, in year 1970 paid $2 per share and now return is $280 per share, is itself one of Buffett's most legendary investments. It was unique from his other ventures because it became his investment vehicle for acquiring and purchasing companies. Buffett first purchased the stock for $12 per share.

Berkshire, at that time, was a textile company, not an investment firm. Buffett shut down the company and totally retooled it. He acquired insurance companies through Berkshire Hathaway, as well as a range of other businesses, such as Fruit of the Loom, Heinz, Dairy Queen, and more.

Berkshire also provides insurance, and that gives it a large source of cash. Buffett is a "hands off" investor, only getting involved when companies are about to crumble, such as paint producer Benjamin Moore, which Buffett had to swoop in on.

These are the benefit of using checklist, it is a tool an approach to make wealth like Warren and Charlie, some facts of their investment with return that will make you believe, this tool create real billions of dollars .

Goldman Sachs

Year: 2008
Investment: $5 billion
Return: $5.64 billion + 13 million free shares of stock

Bank of America

Year: 2011
Investment: $5 billion
Return: $14.2 billion

Freddie Mac

Year: 1988
Investment: $4 per share
Return: $70 per share

Burlington Northern Santa Fe

Year: 2009
Investment: $44 billion
Return: $93 billion

See's Candy

Year: 1972
Investment: $25 million
Return: $1.32 billion

Coca-Cola

Year: 1988
Investment: $1.3 billion
Return: $19 billion

Berkshire Hathaway

Year: 1970
Investment: $2 per share
Return: $280 per share

Petrochina

Year: 2002
Investment: $488 million
Return: $3.6 billion

BYD

Year: 2008
Investment: $230 million
Return: $1.8 billion

Wells Fargo

Year: 1995
Investment: $290 million
Return: $27 billion

The Intelligent Investor Book Bible of Investing

Year: 1949
Investment: $5
Return: $88 billion

Apple

Year: 2016

Investment: $100 per share

Return: $220 per share

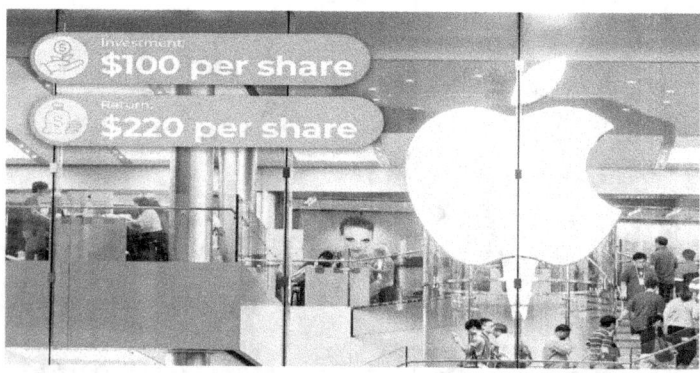

Moody's Corporation

Year: 2001

Investment: $248 million

Return: $3.45 billion

American Express

Year: 1965
Investment: $1.28 billion
Return: $14.45 billion

You might be wondering why Buffett's own company doesn't follow his advice. After all, Berkshire Hathaway was built on investing in individual companies, and its portfolio contains billions of dollars of stock investments in companies including Wells Fargo, American Express, and Coca-Cola.

It's a portfolio built on a philosophy called value investing, which was pioneered by Benjamin Graham, Buffett's mentor and professor at Columbia Business School. Value investing ignores swings in the markets and focuses on a company's intrinsic value. Buffett and his team look for companies that have a competitive advantage, great management, and a higher true value than the current stock price.

If you wanted to pick stocks, value investing would be a fine strategy to follow. Still, keep in mind that Buffett and his investment team manage billions of dollars in assets and have the ability to make massive investments and influence the operations of the companies in the Berkshire Hathaway portfolio. Individual investors are typically working with thousands of dollars and do not have the time, assets, or expertise to mimic Buffett's success.

Keep in mind also that individual investors, unlike a huge institutional investor like Berkshire Hathaway, are less able to handle the big losses that come with investing in the market. And make no mistake: those inevitable losses will come.

Warren buffet choose right stock to invest using his investment checklist tool, everyone has their own tool and, in this book, we will learn what tool value investor use and we will apply same principal to achieve our investment return.

The Safe Way

Just as the fast lane and the slow lane on the highway eventually will get you to the same place, there are quick and slow ways to double your money. If you prefer to invest it safe, bonds can be a less hair-raising journey to the same destination, if you take benefit of the checklist, you are in the safe side of your investment, you don't have to take worry, what market is going to be, you selecting is based on your checklist.

"An investment operation is one which, upon thorough analysis, promises safety of principal and an adequate return. Operations not meeting these requirements are speculative." — Benjamin Graham, the Intelligent Investor

Not to lose your capital

You are not investing in the stock market to lose your investment, for this using checklist, will safely guard your capital for not losing your money, loss of capital is their mistake many investor makes due to poor knowledge in investment world, not using any kind of checklist.

Due to the way stocks are traded, investors can lose quite a bit of money if they don't understand how fluctuating share prices affect their wealth. In the simplest sense, investors buy shares at a certain price and can then sell the shares to realize capital gains. However, if the share price drops dramatically, the investor will not realize a gain.

If the investor uses the checklist, they will not act irrational way such as another type of loss is somewhat less painful and harder to quantify but still very real. You might have bought $10,000 of a hot growth stock, and one year later, after some ups and downs, the stock is very close to what you paid for it.

You might be tempted to tell yourself "Well, at least I didn't lose anything." But that's not true. You tied up $10,000 of your money for a year and you received nothing in return. If you had bought a certificate of deposit instead, you would have earned at least a little bit of interest during that year.

For your success

Proper research should always be undertaken before investing in stocks. But that is rarely done. Investors generally go by the name of a company or the industry they belong to. This is, however, not the right way of putting one's money into the stock market. Never invest in a stock. Invest in a business instead. And invest in a business you understand. In other words, before investing in a company, you should know what business the company is in.

Historically it has been witnessed that even great bull runs have shown bouts of panic moments. The volatility witnessed in the markets has inevitably made investors lose money despite the great bull runs.

However, the investors who put in money systematically, in the right shares and held on to their investments patiently have been seen generating outstanding returns. Hence, it is prudent to have patience and follow a disciplined investment approach besides keeping a long-term broad picture in mind.

There's nothing wrong with hoping for the 'best' from your investments, but you could be heading for trouble if your financial goals are based on unrealistic assumptions, to avoid such issue to arise make sure you use the checklist, you will see the success.

"If we buy the business as a business and not as a stock speculation, then it becomes personal. I want it to be personal.

– Phil Town

Approach to achieve the return

The checklist is the only approach to achieve the return, you have expected from your invested, in the investment world, there are few people who understand importance of a checklist and use this *effective tool to create wealth for a long horizon.*

"The ability to focus attention on important things is a defining characteristic of intelligence."

– Robert J. Shiller

Long term investment

The checklist will make your long-term investment worth, those who don't use it, there return can be vanish in few months or year, the return cannot be sustainable. Long-term investments may not be as exciting, but they tend to be a lot less risky. And if you choose wisely, you could still benefit from the odd dividend from time to time. By investing for the long-term, you are committing to your investments, and history has shown that this strategy can pay off handsomely.

One of the major benefits of long-term investing is the ability to make substantial gains through compound interest.

For the long-term investor, compound interest is basically free money. Each year, all being well, you will receive some sort of return on your initial investment. Re-invest this and you will increase the amount of interest which you can receive the following year. Each year, by continuing to re-invest your interest you are growing your capital, and the longer you do this the more money you can make. For example, if you invested $1000 in year one and took a return of 10%, you would have increased your capital to $1100. By the end of year two, that 10% would be worth %110. Reinvest this and by year three 10% would mean $121.

By simply reinvesting your annual interest, within three years you would have made an overall return of more than 20% on your original investment.

"An investment in knowledge pays the best interest." - Benjamin Franklin

When it comes to investing, nothing will pay off more than educating yourself. Do the necessary research, study, and analysis before making any investment decisions.

A thousand dollars invested with Warren Buffett since 1965 would be worth more than $27 million today, while the comparable amount for the S&P 500 is roughly $200,000, it is not possible they warren buffet have not used checklist, he uses to tool to analyse and research the right stock, which is within his circle of competence.

The overall return of Berkshire Hathaway's stock from 1965 to 2019; during this same period, the S&P 500 returned just 19,784%.

Measure Risk of your Investment

When you have done proper analysis of the business then you don't have to worry about what other are saying, your risk will be always in your control. Your individual investments can typically be summed up in two words: "risk" and "reward." The general rule of thumb is the greater the potential reward, the greater the risk, but that rule doesn't always hold true in reverse order greater risk doesn't necessarily translate into greater potential reward. Sometimes greater risk is just greater risk with little potential reward. Risk isn't a bad thing. But you need to understand what kind of risks you are willing to take with your investment dollars, and how to reduce unacceptable levels of risk. Risk can only reduce by your understanding of the company.

How much you know the company *"you must thoroughly analyze a company, and the soundness of its underlying businesses, before you buy its stock; you must deliberately protect yourself against serious losses; you must aspire to "adequate," not extraordinary, performance."*

— Benjamin Graham, The Intelligent Investor

Peace of mind

Maximum number of investors worried about their investment daily. *"On the other hand, investing is a unique kind of casino—one where you cannot lose in the end, so long as you play only by the rules that put the odds squarely in your favor."*

— Benjamin Graham, The Intelligent Investor

"And back in the spring of 1720, Sir Isaac Newton owned shares in the South Sea Company, the hottest stock in England. Sensing that the market was getting out of hand, the great physicist muttered that he "could calculate the motions of the heavenly bodies, but not the madness of the people." Newton dumped his South Sea shares, pocketing a 100% profit totaling £7,000. But just months later, swept up in the wild enthusiasm of the market, Newton jumped back in at a much higher price—and lost £20,000 (or more than $3

million in today's money). For the rest of his life, he forbade anyone to speak the words "South Sea" in his presence."

― Benjamin Graham, The Intelligent Investor

When you have done your research and used your entire checklist and choose the stock to invest, you enjoy the peace of mind and happiness.

No to herd mentality

A good value investor never get trap in the herd mentality because he has done his work so properly and used all his checklist to find a value company. Herd instinct in finance is the phenomenon where investors follow what they perceive other investors are doing, rather than their own analysis. In other words, an investor exhibiting herd instinct will gravitate toward the same or similar investments based almost solely on the fact that many others are buying the securities.

The term has been derived from the natural instinct of a number of sheep walking together in a herd so as to avoid falling into the pitfalls of danger.

Herding behavior in the stock market can take three forms. Information-based herding happens when everyone reacts the same way to announced information. Reputation-based herding is caused by a respected investor or major trading house taking a specific trading stance. Compensation-based herding occurs when certain conditions prompt large institutional money managers to take profits, generally to protect fund earnings before year-end reporting. These behaviors create large volume in certain stocks or sectors that are popular institutional portfolio investments, prompting those watching to react quickly.

4

Risk of Not Using Checklist

"Rule number one: Don't lose money. Rule number two: Don't forget rule number one."

- Warren Buffett

"Risk comes from not knowing what you're doing."

– Warren Buffett

Without a checklist, you cannot study a company and your investment is in a risk, you need to ask yourself, is that your investment is screened by your checklist and deep analysis of quantitative and qualitative research or just depend on the luck .In an investor context, risk is the amount of uncertainty an investor is willing to accept in regard to the future returns they expect from their investment. Risk tolerance, then, is the level of risk an investor is willing to have with an investment - and is usually determined by things like their age and amount of disposable income.

"If you don't study any companies, you have the same success buying stocks as you do in a poker game if you bet without looking at your cards."

-Peter Lynch

Risk is the possibility of something bad happening. Risk involves uncertainty about the effects/implications of an activity with respect to something that human's value, often focusing on negative, undesirable consequences. Different practice areas of risk management have used many different definitions. Although it is often used in different contexts, risk is the possibility that an outcome will not be as expected, specifically in reference to returns on investment in finance. However, there are several different kinds or risk, including investment risk, market risk, inflation risk, business risk, liquidity risk and more. Generally, individuals, companies or countries incur risk that they may lose some or all of an investment.

"The most realistic distinction between the investor and the speculator is found in their attitude toward stock-market movements. The speculator's primary interest lies in anticipating and profiting from market fluctuations. The investor's primary interest lies in acquiring and holding suitable securities at suitable prices. Market movements are important to him in a practical sense, because they alternately create low price levels at which he would be wise to buy and high price levels at which he certainly should refrain from buying and probably would be wise to sell. It is far from certain that the typical investor should regularly hold off buying until low market levels appear, because this may involve a long wait, very likely the loss of income, and the possible missing of investment opportunities. On the whole it may be better for the investor to do his stock buying whenever he has money to put in stocks, except when the general market level is much higher than can be justified by well-established standards of value. If he wants to be shrewd he can look for the ever-present bargain opportunities in individual securities. Aside from forecasting the movements of the general market, much effort and ability are directed on Wall Street toward selecting stocks or industrial groups that in matter of price will "do better" than the rest over a fairly short period in the future. Logical as this endeavor may seem, we do not believe it is suited to the needs or temperament of the true investor—particularly since he would be competing

with a large number of stock-market traders and first-class financial analysts who are trying to do the same thing. As in all other activities that emphasize price movements first and underlying values second, the work of many intelligent minds constantly engaged in this field tends to be self-neutralizing and self-defeating over the years. The investor with a portfolio of sound stocks should expect their prices to fluctuate and should neither be concerned by sizable declines nor become excited by sizable advances. He should always remember that market quotations are there for his convenience, either to be taken advantage of or to be ignored. He should never buy a stock because it has gone up or sell one because it has gone down. He would not be far wrong if this motto read more simply: "Never buy a stock immediately after a substantial rise or sell one immediately after a substantial drop."

— Benjamin Graham, The Intelligent Investor

Despite having advantages for not using any checklist, there are a lot of things that you need to bring in consideration when it comes to buying stocks. There are different types of risk associated with investing in stocks. The biggest risk is that the prices are always fluctuating. There is no obvious pattern when it comes to prices of the stock so the risk of losing your money is always high.

Your poor Decisions Could Cost to Loss of Entire Capital: People usually end up making bad decision when they see a stock price going down, as they hope it will be high again after sometime. However, when the prices instead of increasing continue to go down, investors realize they have made a poor decision but by then it is way too late.

If you are not using the checklist then you are gambling in the stock market. Given Buffett's objective is to own companies whose earnings will be higher in the future, his primary concern is Business Risk; how will a companies' earnings manifest themselves over time?

"Should we conclude that the risk in owning a piece of a company - its stock - is somehow divorced from the long-term risk inherent in its business operations? We believe this conclusion makes no sense and that equating beta with investment risk also makes no sense." Warren Buffett

"When we look at businesses, we try to think of what can go wrong with them. We try to look for businesses that are good businesses now, and we think about what can go wrong with them. If we think there's a lot that can go wrong with them, we just forget it. We are not in the business of assuming a lot of risk in businesses."

Warren Buffett

"We think of business risk in terms of what can happen — say five, 10, 15 years from now — that will destroy, or modify, or reduce the economic strengths that we perceive currently exist in a business." Warren Buffett

Warren call checklist as a filter One of Buffett's most powerful risk mitigation and prevention tools are his Filters. (in other words warren use checklist).

"We do care about being right about the economic characteristics of the business, and that's one thing we think we've got certain filters that tell us in certain cases that we know enough to assess." Warren Buffett

"We have a bunch of filters we've developed in our minds over time. We don't say they're perfect filters. We don't say that those filters don't occasionally leave things out that should get through. But they're very efficient." Warren Buffett

Every investment needs an edge and it's impossible to have an edge if you don't understand an investment or other people have a better understanding than you. Buffett's first filter is understanding what he owns and it relies on a strong appreciation for the boundaries of what he knows and what he doesn't - his circle of competence.

"Different people understand different businesses. And the important thing is to know which ones you do understand and when you're operating within what I call your "circle of competence." Warren Buffett

If a potential investment falls outside of that circle or he won't be able to get it within that circle it is discarded immediately. Buffett doesn't venture outside of the circle.

"The first filter we probably put it through is whether we think — and we know instantly — whether it's a business we're going to understand, and whether it's a business that — if it passes through that, it's whether a company can have a sustainable edge." Warren Buffett

"We do have filters, and sometimes those filters are very irritating to people who check in with us about businesses, because we really can say in ten seconds or so "no" to 90 percent-plus of all the things that come in, simply because we have these filters. We have some filters in regard to people, too." Warren Buffett

Buffett doesn't compromise his filters, they're black and white. He doesn't raise his discount rate to overcome his risk concerns, the filters work as a strict go/no-go valve.

"We look at riskiness, essentially, as being sort of a go/no-go valve in terms of looking at the future businesses. In other words, if we think we simply don't know what's going to happen in the future, that doesn't mean it's necessarily risky, it just means we don't know. It means it's risky for us. It might not be risky for someone else who understands the business." Warren Buffett

"Don't worry about risk the way it is taught at Wharton. Risk is a go/no go signal for us - if it has risk, we just don't go ahead." Warren Buffett

Only in fairy tales are emperors told they're naked.

With stockbrokers often rewarded for activity, not successful investments, it's critically important to make sure you believe that what you're doing is right. Chasing others' opinions may seem logical, but investors like Munger and Buffett often succeed by going against the grain. Big Berkshire investments such as Coca-Cola (NYSE:KO), and more recently Petrochina (NYSE:PTR), were largely ignored by the masses when they were first made.

5

Famous Value Investor Checklist

Charlie Munger

Charles Thomas Munger (born January 1, 1924) is an American investor, businessman, former real estate attorney, and philanthropist. He is vice chairman of Berkshire Hathaway, the conglomerate controlled by Warren Buffett; Buffett has described Munger as his partner. Munger served as chairman of Wesco Financial Corporation from 1984 through 2011. He is also chairman of the Daily Journal Corporation, based in Los Angeles, California, and a director of Costco Wholesale Corporation.

The great thing about checklists is they provide an extra layer of stability. We are only human, so we cannot remember every single mistake or piece of investment advice ever received in our minds alone.

What's Munger's secret?

He has spent his life studying the best ideas across a wide range of disciplines.

This deliberate practice helped Munger identify a set of "mental models." Munger reckons that if you understand about 80 or 90 of these models, you'll know enough to have the world figured out.

Munger's advice is to be a "learning machine." All investors need to learn and relearn basic principles. And that means they must read and think constantly. Munger believes the "psychology of human misjudgment" is by far the most critical area in mental models. Ironically, Munger disdains most of academic psychology. That's because academics teach and research the wrong things.

We all recognize universal emotions, like fear and greed. The same is true for, say, envy. But good luck finding an academic treatise on any of these topics. Munger says he has never even seen the word envy in the index of an introductory psychology textbook.

95-year-old Munger would like the world to remember him more as a thinker than as an investor. Still, most of us are more curious about the investment philosophy that turned him into a billionaire.

Munger is a big fan of using checklists in decision making. Pilots use checklists to improve their performance. Surgeon Atul Gawande wrote a book on the importance of lists in the operating room. Munger believes that all investors should use checklists too.

Like his mental models, Munger's investing checklist is not original. Instead, he derives it from investment pioneer Benjamin Graham's principles of value investing.

1. **Risk**—all investment evaluations should begin by measuring risk, especially reputational Incorporate an appropriate margin of safety. Avoid dealing with people of questionable character, insist upon proper compensation for risk assumed, always beware of inflation and interest rate

exposures and avoid big mistakes; shun permanent capital loss.

2. **Independence**— "Only in fairy tales are emperors told they are naked"

Objectivity and rationality require independence of thought, remember that just because other people agree or disagree with you doesn't make you right or wrong—the only thing that matters is the correctness of your analysis and judgment.

Mimicking the herd invites regression to the mean (merely average performance)

3. **Preparation**— "The only way to win is to work, work, work, work, and hope to have a few insights"

Develop into a lifelong self-learner through voracious reading; cultivate curiosity and strive to become a little wiser every day, more important than the will to win is the will to prepare, develop fluency in mental models from the major academic disciplines.

If you want to get smart, the question you have to keep asking is "why, why, why?"

4. **Intellectual humility**—acknowledging what you don't know is the dawning of wisdom, stay within a well-defined circle of competence, Identify and reconcile disconfirming evidence and resist the craving for false precision, false certainties, etc.

Above all, never fool yourself, and remember that you are the easiest person to fool.

5. **Analytic rigor**—Use of the scientific method and effective checklists minimizes errors and omissions, determine value apart from price; progress apart from activity; wealth apart from size, it is better to remember the obvious than to grasp the esoteric.

Be a business analyst, not a market, macroeconomic, or security analyst, consider totality of risk and effect; look always at potential second order and higher-level impacts. Think forwards and backwards—invert, always invert.

6. **Allocation**—Proper allocation of capital is an investor's number one job. Remember that highest and best use is always measured by the next best use (opportunity cost), good ideas are rare—when the odds are greatly in your favor, bet (allocate) heavily.

Don't "fall in love" with an investment—be situation-dependent and opportunity-driven

7. **Patience**—Resist the natural human bias to act, "Compound interest is the eighth wonder of the world" (Einstein); never interrupt it unnecessarily, avoid unnecessary transactional taxes and frictional costs; never take action for its own sake and be alert for the arrival of luck.

Enjoy the process along with the proceeds, because the process is where you live.

8. **Decisiveness**—when proper circumstances present themselves, act with decisiveness and conviction. Be fearful when others are greedy, and greedy when others are fearful, opportunity doesn't come often, so seize it when it does, opportunity meeting the prepared mind: that's the game.

9. **Change**—live with change and accept un-removable complexity. Recognize and adapt to the true nature of the world around you; don't expect it to adapt to you and continually challenge and willingly amend your "best-loved ideas"

Recognize reality even when you don't like it—especially when you don't like it

10. **Focus**—Keep things simple and remember what you set out to do, remember that reputation and integrity are your most valuable assets—and can be lost in a heartbeat. Guard against the effects of hubris and boredom. Don't overlook the obvious by drowning in minutiae, be careful to exclude unneeded information or slop: "A small leak can sink a great ship"

Face your big troubles; don't sweep them under the rug.

The framework is called the Four Filters, and it first appeared in the 1977 Letters to Shareholders in this form.

"We select our marketable securities in much the same way we would evaluate a business for acquisition in its entirety. We want the business to be (1) one that we can easily understand, (2) with favorable long-term prospects, (3) operated by honest and competent people, and (4) available at an attractive price."

1: Develop an understanding of the business.

Warren Buffett said it perfectly. "Seek whatever information will further your understanding of the business."

Charlie is a huge proponent of developing checklists to help him make better decisions, for each company, he develops a checklist to keep him on track. The reason for a different checklist is that every company is different and have different guidelines to follow.

Charlie developed a system of "latticework of mental models" to help him sort through his thoughts and ideas. He used these models to help him think better.

2: Does the company have a durable competitive advantage?

A durable competitive advantage refers to a moat, according to Harvard Business School professor Michael Porter. According to Berkshire parlance the business itself is the castle, and the value of the castle will be determined by the strength of the moat.

3: Is there management in place with integrity and talent?

For Munger and Buffett, management is part of the moat that they create with their businesses. Because they only have 20 people on staff at the home office, they must rely on their managers to maintain their investments.

They have two criteria for their managers.

1. **Capital Allocation** – This is the primary management activity at Berkshire, the Capital allocation is job number one. One of the managers of Berkshire's reinsurance company, Ajit Jain, who according to Buffett "has created tens of billions of dollars in value for this company with nothing but his brains and hard work."

2. **Compensation Systems** – At Berkshire, because most of the managers that work for them are already rich, they have devised other compensation systems to entice talent to their businesses. They select management that loves what they do so much that it outweighs the financial aspects of the job.

4: A business with an attractive price with a margin of safety.

Anyone who wants to understand Munger needs to understand that when you invest, you are buying a piece of that business, not just a stock or a piece of paper but an actual piece of the business. You need to treat it like you are an owner of the business, which you are. Looking at it as a business owner gives you a different perspective on your purchase.

Charlie is a firm believer in what Benjamin Graham teaches which this is.

"An investment operation is one which, upon thorough analysis, promises safety of principal and an adequate return. Operations not meeting these requirements are speculative."

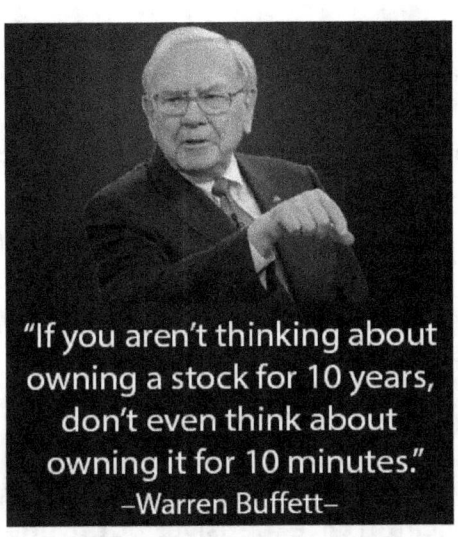

Warren Buffett

Warren Edward Buffett born August 30, 1930 is an American investor, business tycoon, and philanthropist, who is the chairman and CEO of Berkshire Hathaway. He is considered one of the most successful investors in the world and has a net worth of US$88.9 billion as of December 2019, making him the fourth-wealthiest person in the world.

Warren Buffett spoke about the checklist he uses to analyze investments at the 1998 Berkshire Hathaway annual meeting.

Responding to a shareholder who asked for his thoughts on the checklist process, Buffett layed out the steps he uses to assess the potential investments for the Berkshire portfolio:

"The criteria for selecting a stock is really the criteria for looking at a business. We are looking for a business we can understand. That means they sell a product that we think we understand, or we understand the nature of the competition, what could go wrong with it over time. And then when we find that business, we try to figure out whether the economics of it means the earning power over the next five, or 10, or 15 years is likely to be good and getting better or poor and getting worse. But we try to evaluate that future stream. And then we try to decide whether we're getting in with some people that we feel comfortable being in with. And then we try to decide what's an appropriate price for what we've seen up to that point."

As the Oracle of Omaha went on to explain, this checklist is not very complicated or expensive, but it does the job quite well.

Simple is best

At its core, the checklist is designed to help Buffett stay away from investments that he doesn't understand and that look expensive. The list does not have to be particularly extensive for an investor to meet this goal. After laying out the simple points above, Buffett handed the microphone over to his right-hand man at Berkshire, Charlie Munger, who gave his thoughts on making investment decisions:

"Yeah. If finance were -- when finance is properly taught, it should be taught from cases where the investment decision is easy. And the one I always cite is the early history of National Cash Register Company, and that was created by a fanatic who bought all the patents, and had the best sales force, and the best production plants. He was a very intelligent man and passionately dedicated to the cash register business. And of course, the cash register business was a godsend to retailing when cash registers were invented...If you read an early annual report prepared by Patterson, who was CEO of National Cash Register, an idiot could see that this was a talented fanatic. Very favorably located, and that, therefore, the investment decision was easy."

Buffett restricts his investments to businesses he can easily analyze. After all, if a company's operational philosophy is ambiguous, it's difficult to reliably project its performance. For this reason, Buffett did not suffer significant losses during the dot-com bubble burst of the early 2000s due to the fact that most technology plays were new and unproven, causing Buffett to avoid these stocks

Buffett's management tenets help him evaluate the track records of a company's higher-ups, to determine if they've historically reinvested profits back into the company, or if they've redistributed funds to back shareholders in the form of dividends. Buffett favors the latter scenario, which suggests a company is eager to maximize shareholder value, as opposed to greedily pocketing all profits.

In the financial measures silo, Buffett focuses on low-levered companies with high profit margins. But above all, he prizes the importance of the economic value added (EVA) calculation, which estimates a company's profits, after the shareholders' stake is removed from the equation. In other words, EVA is the net profit, minus the expenditures involved with raising the initial capital.

In this category, Buffett seeks to establish a company's intrinsic value. He accomplishes this by projecting the future owner's earnings, then discounting them back to present-day levels. Furthermore, Buffett generally ignores short-term market moves, focusing instead on long-term returns. But on rare occasions, Buffett will act on short-term fluctuations, if a tantalizing deal presents itself. For example, if a company with strong fundamentals suddenly drops in price from $50 per share to $40 per share, Buffet might acquire a few extra shares at a discount.

Benjamin Graham

Benjamin Graham May 9, 1894 – September 21, 1976 was a British-born American investor, economist, and professor. He is widely known as the "father of value investing", and wrote two of the founding texts in neoclassical investing: Security Analysis (1934) with David Dodd, and The Intelligent Investor (1949). His investment philosophy stressed investor psychology, minimal debt, buy-and-hold investing, and fundamental analysis, concentrated diversification, buying within the margin of safety, activist investing, and contrarian mindsets.

Benjamin Graham the father of Value Investing has been an inspiration for many of today's most successful businesspeople like *Warren Buffett*. Ben Graham's checklist guided us with his practical thoughts about stock market and the psychology of investors.

He had a very simple theory for differentiating Investing from Speculating as he knew the psychology of investors in Wall Street, who actually calls themselves as Investors but mostly were just speculators.

Ben Graham's Checklist for investing had just three simple steps, whenever it comes to investing, he suggested doing the thorough analysis, there must be safety of principal and to have an adequate return.

Thorough Analysis: When it comes to investment in stocks, you must do a thorough analysis of the underlying business of that particular stock.

Safety of Principal: You must check the credibility of the underlying business and protect yourself against serious losses.

Adequate Return: You must aspire to "adequate", not extraordinary returns on investment.

Benjamin Graham Deep Value Checklist is a value investing strategy based on rules suggested by legendary investor, Benjamin Graham, who wrote The Intelligent Investor. The strategy focuses on building portfolios of both large and small value stocks. It involves a 10-point checklist of valuation ratios and financial measures. Ben Graham regarded the most important of those measures to be earnings yield, dividend yield and for total debt to be less than book value. Ben Graham wrote: "Try to buy groups of stocks that meet some simple criterion for being undervalued - regardless of the industry and with very little attention to the individual company.

Societe Generale back tested the strategy to 1992 and found that the group of stocks scoring 9 and 10 on the list returned 37.1% and 48.7% per year respectively. Ben Graham devised the Deep Value Checklist late in his life as a much more systematic approach than his other value investing strategies.

Here is the original checklist consisting of ten items.

1. An earnings-to-price yield at least twice the AAA bond rate.

2. P/E ratio less than 40% of the highest P/E ratio the stock had over the past 5 years.

3. Dividend yield of at least 2/3 the AAA bond yield.

4. Stock price below 2/3 of tangible book value per share.

5. Stock price below 2/3 of Net Current Asset Value (NCAV).

6. Total debt less than book value.

7. Current ratio great than 2.

8. Total debt less than 2 times Net Current Asset Value (NCAV).

9. Earnings growth of prior 10 years at least at a 7% annual compound rate.

10. Stability of growth of earnings in that no more than 2 declines of 5% or more in yearend earnings in the prior 10 years are permissible.

Mohnish Pabrai

Pabrai worked with Tellabs between 1986–91, first in its high speed data networking group, and then in 1989, joined its international subsidiary, working in international marketing and sales.

In 1991 he started his IT consulting and systems integration company, TransTech, Inc. with about US$30,000 from his own 401(k) account and US$70,000 from credit card debt. He sold the company in 2000 to Kurt Salmon Associates for US$20 million. Today he is the managing partner of the Pabrai Investment Funds (a family of hedge funds inspired by Buffett Partnerships), which he founded in 1999.

In 2019, Pabrai expanded his US holdings by tripling his holding of Micron Technology. Pabrai also invested in 4.12 million shares of Ohio-based GrafTech International Ltd., a graphite electrodes and petroleum coke manufacturer. Found very strange was how you can have an entire industry which does not function with a solid framework. To me, it is like people doing brain surgery by just 'winging it'.

That is how I saw mutual funds work – they were just winging it, or they come up with any nuance or 'flavor of the day' they want to pursue.

I had a thought that if novices like me simply adopted Buffett's approach and invested in the equity markets with a concentrated portfolio, etc. that I was likely to do better than most of the industry professionals.

So, I said it was worth testing this hypothesis out. I was lucky at the time in 1994; I had about $1 million in cash. I had just sold some assets of my business and I decided to go ahead and manage that in a Buffett-style concentrated portfolio, buying things I understood, etc. That is how I got into value investing.

Pabrai's long-only equity fund has returned a cumulative 517% net to investors vs. 43% for the S&P 500 Index since inception in 2000. An out-performance of 1,103%.

His Checklist

1. Focus on buying an existing business.
2. Buy simple businesses in industries with an ultra-slow rate of change.

3. Buy distressed businesses in distressed industries.
4. Buy businesses with a moat.
5. Bet heavily when the odds are overwhelmingly in your favour.
6. Buy businesses at big discounts to their underlying intrinsic value.
7. Look for low-risk, high-uncertainty business.

'Would you prefer to be the greatest lover in the world and be known as the worst, or would you prefer to be the worst lover and be known as the greatest?' And [Warren Buffett] said, 'If you know how to answer that correctly, then you have the right internal yardstick.'

"I put the checklist in place, in 2008 till today, we have made I think more than 30 different investments in the last five years or so. We only have so far, we invested about $200 million. We've already exited a bunch of positions and we've exited with about $500 million on those positions, and we only lost money on two investments. And the total amount of money we lost from those two investments is less than 5 or 6 million dollars. And I think a large part of that is the checklist significantly brought down the error rate"

He also saw that most of the mistakes made by the guru investors fell into five groups.

1. **Valuation**
2. **Leverage**
3. **Management and Ownership**
4. **Moats**

5. Personal Biases

"The checklist that I created came out of looking at mistakes made by great investors. The single biggest reason why investments don't work out for investors is leverage. The second biggest reason has to do with a misunderstanding of the comparative advantage of the moat. Then you get to management and ownership and other issues. You might get too environmental or unions and labor and that sort of things. The three really big things are — leverage, moats, and management, probably in that order."

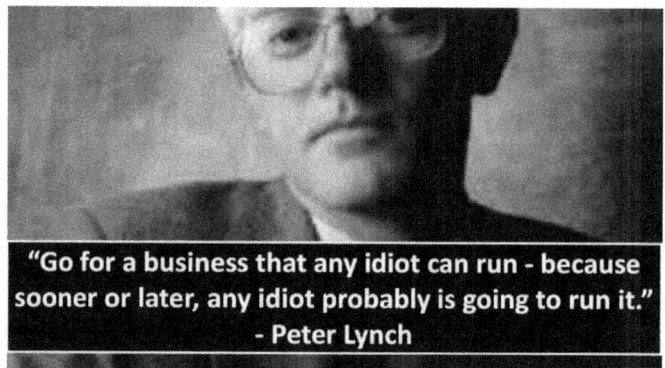

Peter Lynch

In the early 1980s, a young portfolio manager named Peter Lynch was becoming one of the most famous investors in the world, and for a very understandable reason – when he took over the Fidelity Magellan mutual fund in May of 1977 (his first job as a portfolio manager), the assets of the fund were $20 million. He proceeded to turn it into the largest mutual fund in the world, outperforming the market by a mind-boggling 13.4% per year annualized!

Stocks in General

- The P/E ratio, Is it high or low for this particular company and for similar companies in the industry.

- The percentage of institutional ownership. The lower is the better.

- Whether insiders are buying and whether the company itself is buying back its own shares, both are positive signs.

- The record of earnings growth to date and whether the earnings are sporadic or consistent.

- Whether the company has a strong balance sheet or a weak balance sheet (debt-to-equity ratio) and how it's rated for financial strength.

- The cash position. With $16 net cash, I know Ford is unlikely to drop below $16 a share. That's the floor on the stock.

Slow Growers

- Since you may buy these for the dividends (why else would you own them?) you want to check to see if the dividends have always been paid, and whether they are routinely raised.

- When possible, find out what percentage of earnings are being paid out as dividends. If it's a low percentage, then the company has a cushion in hard times. It can earn less money and still retain the dividend. If it's a high percentage, then the dividend is riskier.

Stalwarts

- These are big companies that aren't likely to go out of business. The key issue is price, and the P/E ratio will tell you whether you are paying too much.

- Check for possible diversifications that may reduce the earnings in the future.

- Check the company's long term growth rate, and whether it has kept up the same momentum in recent years.

- If you plan to hold the stock forever, see how the company has fared during the previous recessions and market drops.

Cyclical

- Keep a close watch on inventories, and the supply-demand relationship. Watch for new entrants into the market, which is usually a dangerous development.

- Anticipate a shrinking P/E multiple over time as a business recovers and investors look ahead to the end of the cycle, when peak earnings are achieved.

- If you know your cyclical, you have an advantage in figuring out the cycles. (For instance, everyone knows there are cycles in the auto industry. Eventually there are going to be three or four up years to follow three or four down years. There always are. Cars get older and they have to be replaced. People can put off replacing cars a year or two longer than expected, but sooner or later they are back in the dealerships. The worse the slump in the auto industry, the better the recovery.

Fast Grower

- Investigate whether the product that's supposed to enrich the company is a major part of the company's business.

- What the growth rate in earnings has been in recent years. (My favourites are the ones in the 20 to 25 percent range. I'm wary of companies that seem to be growing faster than 25 percent. Those 50 percent are usually found in hot industries, and you know what that means.)

- That the company has duplicated its success in more than one city or town, to prove the expansion will work.

- That the company still has room to grow.

- Whether the stock is selling at a P/E ratio at or near the growth rate.

- Whether the expansion is speeding up (three new motels last year and five this year). For stock companies which sales are primarily "one-shot" deals—as opposed to razorblades which customers have to keep on buying—a slowdown in growth can be devastating.

- That few institutions own the stock and only a handful of analysts have ever heard of it. With fast growers on the rise, this is a big plus.

Turnarounds

- Most importantly, can the company survive a raid by its creditors? How much cash does the company have? How much debt?

- What is the debt structure, and how long can it operate in the red while working out its problems without going bankrupt?

- If it's bankrupt already, then what's left for the shareholders?

- How is the company supposed to be turning around? Has it rid itself of unprofitable divisions?

- Is the business coming back?

- Are costs being cut? If so, what will the effect be?

Asset Plays

- What's the value of the assets? Are there any hidden assets?

- How much debt is there to detract from these assets?

- Is the company taking on new debt, making the assets less valuable?

- Is there a raider in the wings to help shareholders reap the benefits of the assets?

Seth klarman

Another area where investors struggle is trying to define what constitutes a good business. Someone once defined the best possible business as a post office box to which people send money. That idea has certainly been eclipsed by the creation of subscription Web sites that accept credit cards. Today's most profitable businesses are those in which you sell a fixed amount of work product—say, a piece of software or a hit recording—millions and millions of times at very low marginal cost. Good businesses are generally considered those with strong barriers to entry, limited capital requirements, reliable customers, low risk of technological obsolescence, abundant growth possibilities, and thus significant and growing free cash flow.

—Seth Klarman, *Security Analysis, Preface to the Sixth Edition: The Timeless Wisdom of Graham and Dodd*

Some important point for a checklist he mentions

- Strong barriers to entry
- Limited capital requirements
- Reliable customers
- Low risk of technological obsolescence
- Abundant growth possibilities
- Significant and growing free cash flow

walter schloss

Walter J. Schloss was an American investor, fund manager, and philanthropist. He was a well-regarded value investor, as well as a notable disciple of the Benjamin Graham School of investing.

What kind of stocks does Walter Schloss look at for investments?

- We look for stocks that are depressed (Schloss liked to comb the paper for stocks hitting 52-week lows)

- Why are they depressed?

- Are they selling below book value?

- Is good will in book value?

- What has been the high and low over the last 10 years?

- Does the company have any cash flow?

- Does the company have any net income?

- How has the company done over the last 10 years?

- What is the company's debt load?

- What kind of industry are they in?

- What are their profit margins?

- How are their competitors doing?

- Is this company doing poorly compared to its competitors?

Investing Wisdom Shared by Waltor Schloss

- When it comes to investing, my suggestion is to first understand your strengths and weaknesses, and then devise a simple strategy so that you can sleep at night.

- I don't like stress and prefer to avoid it; I never focus too much on market news and economic data. They always worry investors.

- You have to invest the way that's comfortable for you.

- Try not to let your emotions affect your judgment. Fear and greed are probably the worst emotions to have in connection with the purchase and sale of stocks.

- I think investing is an art, and we tried to be as logical and unemotional as possible. Because we understood that investors are usually affected by the market, we could take advantage of the market by being rational. As Graham said, 'The market is there to serve you, not to guide you!'

- I like Ben's analogy that one should buy stocks the way you buy groceries not the way you buy perfume.

- The ability to think clearly in the investment field without the emotions that are attached to it is not an easy undertaking. Fear and greed tend to affect one's judgment.

- Don't buy on tips or for a quick move. Let the professionals do that, if they can.

- Remember that a share of stock represents a part of a business and is not just a piece of paper.

- Prefer stocks over bonds. Bonds will limit your gains and inflation will reduce your purchasing power.

- Listen to suggestion from people you respect. This doesn't mean you have to accept them. Remember it's your money and generally it is harder to keep money than to make it. Once you lose a lot of money it is hard to make it back.

- Most look at earnings and earnings potential, well I can't get into that game.

- I used the same investment approach I used at Graham-Newman finding net-net stocks. It was all about capital preservation because I had to serve in the best interests of my investors. Many of them were not wealthy, and they needed me to generate returns that would allow them to cover their living expenses.

- I try to protect myself from permanent loss of capital by investing in stocks that are depressed.

- When you buy a depressed company, it's not going to go up right after you buy it, believe me.

- I like to buy companies with very little debt so it has a margin of safety.

- I like to buy basic businesses not high flyers that sell at huge multiples.

- I'm not very good at judging people. So, I found that it was much better to look at the figures rather than people.

- We don't own stocks that we'd never sell. I guess we are a kind of store that buys goods for inventory (stocks) and we'd like to sell them at a profit within 4 years if possible.

- Remember the word compounding, for example, if you can make 12% a year and reinvest the money back, you will double your money in 6 years, taxes excluded. Remember the rule of 72. Your rate of return into 72 will tell you the number of years to double your money.

- You never really know a stock until you own it.

On common stocks March 10, 1994

Walter & Edwin Schloss Associates, L.P.
52 VANDERBILT AVENUE • NEW YORK NY 10017
(212) 370-1844

Factors needed to make money in the stock market

1. Price is the most important factor to use in relation to value.

2. Try to establish the value of the company. Remember that a share of stock represents a part of a business and is not just a piece of paper.

3. Use book value as a starting point to try and establish the value of the enterprise. Be sure that debt does not equal 100% of the equity. (Capital and surplus for the common stock).

4. Have patience. Stocks don't go up immediately.

5. Don't buy on tips or for a quick move. Let the professionals do that, if they can. Don't sell on bad news.

6. Don't be afraid to be a loner but be sure that you are correct in your judgment. You can't be 100% certain but try to look for weaknesses in your thinking. Buy on a scale and sell on a scale up.

7. Have the courage of your convictions once you have made a decision.

8. Have a philosophy of investment and try to follow it. The above is a way that I've found successful.

9. Don't be in too much of a hurry to sell. If the stock reaches a price that you think is a fair one, then you can sell but often because a stock goes up say 50%, people say sell it and button up your profit. Before selling try to reevaluate the company again and see where the stock sells in relation to its book value. Be aware of the level of the stock market. Are yields low and P-E ratios high. If the stock market historically high. Are people very optimistic etc?

10. When buying a stock, I find it helpful to buy near the low of the past few years. A stock may go as igh as 125 and then decline to 60 and you think it attractive. 3 years before the stock sold at 20 which shows that there is some vulnerability in it.

11. Try to buy assets at a discount than to buy earnings. Earnings can change dramatically in a short time. Usually assets change slowly. One has to know much more about a company if one buys earnings.

12. Listen to suggestions from peole you respect. This doesn't mean you have to accept them. Remember it's your money and generally it is harder to keep money than to make it. Once you lose a lost of money it is hard to make it back.

13. Try not to let your emotions affect your judgment. Fear and greed are probably the worst emotions to have in connection with the purchase and sale of stocks.

14. Remember the work compounding. For example, if you can make 12% a year and reinvest the moneyback, you will double your money in 6 yrs, taxes excluded. Remember the rule of 72. Your rate of return into 72 will tell you the number of years to double your money.

15. Prefer stocks over bonds. Bonds will limit your gains and inflation will reduce your purchasing power.

WJS

16. Be careful of leverage. It can go against you.

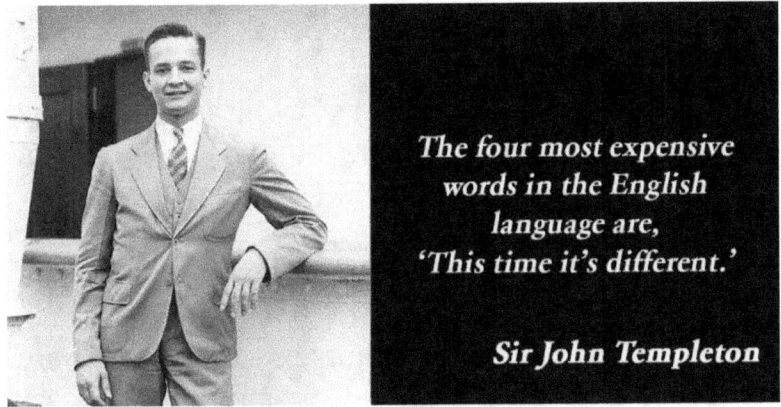

Sir John Templeton

- Valuation Factors Price-earnings record

    Look for a share priced exceptionally low relative to its 5 to 10 years growth prospects.

- Price to book ratio

    Adjusting book value to replacement value and if the ratio is less than one then the assets of the company are greater than the price paid.

- Share price to sales ratio

    A low figure might indicate that the market is not sufficiently allowing for the potential of profit margins on sales to improve.

- Share price to cash flow multiple

    A low multiple is often a sign of undervaluation.

- Share price to liquidation value

    There are a number of ways in which value can be generated for shareholders if the assets are lowly priced not least a takeover.

- Business Factors Competitive advantages

    Have competitive advantages that are hard to replicate, is the undisputed low-cost producer, is the technological leader or have the strongest brand.

- Profit margin on sales

    Have the widest profit margins and the most rapidly increasing profits.

- Market share

    A strong position often produces high earning power.

- Financial strength

    Is it well capitalized? Is there sufficient equity capital? Too little equity capital can mean excess debt and more risk or restricted growth.

- Management Factors Long-range plans of senior executive

    What are the executives' long-term plans?

- Return on capital employed

    A high figure means that additional money used in the business such as retained earnings will probably generate high shareholder value.

Learning to invest like John Templeton is accessible because of his willingness to share. In 1993, he published 16 Rules for Investment Success. The following checklist allows us to fully understand and implement the principles underpinning his investment philosophy:

- Invest for maximum total real (after-inflation) return.

- Invest – don't trade or speculate.

- Remain flexible and open-minded about types of investments.

- Buy low.

- When buying stocks, search for bargains among quality stocks.

- Buy value, not market trends or economic outlook.

- Diversify. In stocks and bonds, as in much else, there is safety in numbers.

- Do your homework or hire wise experts to help you.

- Aggressively monitor your investments.
- Don't panic.
- Learn from your mistakes.
- Begin with a prayer.
- Outperforming the market is a difficult task.
- An investor who has all the answers doesn't even understand all the questions.
- There's no free lunch.
- Do not be too fearful or negative too often.

> "If the job has been correctly done when a common stock is purchased, the time to sell it is – almost never."
>
> – Philip Fisher

Philip Fisher

Philip Fisher was an American stock investor best known for his top selling book "Common stocks and uncommon profits" which was originally published in 1958.

Mr. Fisher began his investing career in 1928 as a securities analyst with the Anglo-London Bank in San Francisco. Later, he started his own money management firm, Fisher & Company, in 1931 which he managed for nearly 70 years till his retirement in 1999.

"I sought out Phil Fisher after reading his "Common Stocks and Uncommon Profits". When I met him, I was impressed by the man and his ideas. A thorough understanding of a business, by using Phil's techniques ... enables one to make intelligent investment commitments."
— Warren Buffett

Here is Philip Fisher's 15 points checklist to look into common stocks before investing.

1. Does the company have products or services with sufficient market potential to make possible a sizable increase in sales for at least several years?

2. Does the management have a determination to continue to develop products or processes that will still further increase total sales potentials when the growth potentials of currently attractive product lines have largely been exploited?

3. How effective are the company's research and development efforts in relation to its size?

4. Does the company have an above- average sales organization?

5. Does the company have a worthwhile profit margin?

6. What is the company doing to maintain or improve profit margins?

7. Does the company have outstanding labor and personnel relations?

8. Does the company have outstanding executive relations?

9. Does the company have depth to its management?

10. How good are the company's cost analysis and accounting controls?

11. Are there other aspects of the business, somewhat peculiar to the industry involved, which will give the investor important clues as to how outstanding the company may be in relation to its competition?

12. Does the company have a short-range or long-range outlook in regard to profits?

13. In the foreseeable future will the growth of the company require sufficient equity financing so that the larger number of shares then outstanding will largely cancel the existing stockholders' benefit from this anticipated growth?

Qualitative & Quantitative Analysis

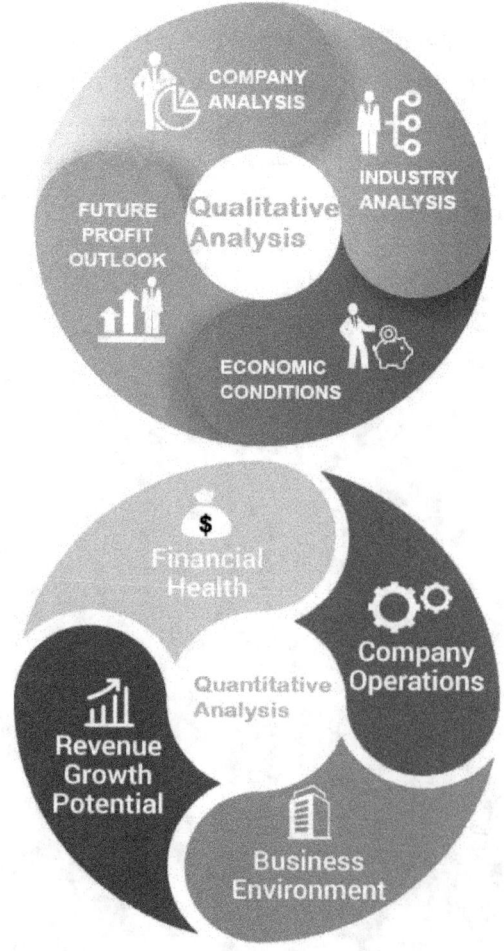

6
Qualitative & Quantitative Analysis

Qualitative data analysis is based on classification of objects (participants) according to properties and attributes whereas quantitative analysis is based on classification of data based on computable values. Qualitative analysis is subjective whereas quantitative is objective.

The distinction between qualitative and quantitative approaches is similar to the difference between human and artificial intelligence. Quantitative analysis uses exact inputs such as profit margins, debt ratios, earnings multiples, and the like. These can be plugged into a computerized model to yield an exact result, such as the fair value of a stock or a forecast for earnings growth. Of course, for the time being, a human has to write the program that crunches these numbers, and that involves a fair degree of subjective judgment. Once they are programmed, though, computers can perform quantitative analysis in fractions of a second, while it might take even the most gifted and highly-trained human's minutes or hours.

Qualitative analysis, on the other hand, deals with intangible, inexact concerns that belong to the social and experiential realm rather than the mathematical one. This approach depends on the kind of intelligence that machines (currently) lack, since things like positive associations with a brand, Management trustworthiness, customer satisfaction, competitive advantage and cultural shifts are difficult, arguably impossible, to capture with numerical inputs.

Qualitative Analysis

Qualitative analysis uses subjective judgment based on non-quantifiable information, such as management expertise, industry cycles, and strength of research and development and labor relations. Qualitative analysis contrasts with quantitative analysis, which focuses on numbers found in reports such as balance sheets. The two techniques, however, will often be used together to examine a company's operations and evaluate its potential as an investment opportunity.

Admittedly, gathering data for qualitative analysis can be difficult. Fortune 500 CEOs are not known for sitting down with retail investors for a chat or showing them around the corporate headquarters. In part, Warren Buffett can use qualitative analysis so effectively because people are willing to give him access to their time and information.

The rest of us have to sift through news reports and companies' filings to get a sense of managers' records, strategies and philosophies. The management discussion and analysis (MD&A) section of a company's 10-K filing and quarterly earnings conference calls provide a window into strategies and communication styles. Clear, transparent communication and coherent strategies are useful. Buzzwords, evasiveness and short-termism, not so much.

Quantitative Analysis

Quantitative analysis (QA) is a technique that seeks to understand behavior by using mathematical and statistical modeling, measurement, and research. Quantitative analysts aim to represent a given reality in terms of a numerical value.

Quantitative analysis is employed for several reasons, including measurement, performance evaluation or valuation of a financial instrument, and predicting real-world events, such as changes in a country's gross domestic product (GDP).

While quantitative analysis serves as a useful evaluation tool, it is often combined with the complementary research and evaluation tool of qualitative analysis. It is common for a company to use quantitative analysis to evaluate figures such as sales revenue, profit margins, or return on assets (ROA).

Neither qualitative nor quantitative analysis is inherently better. Many analysts consider them together.

Qualitative Analysis

There are four key fundamentals that analysts always consider when regarding a company. All are qualitative rather than quantitative. They include:

The business model: What exactly does the company do? This isn't as straightforward as it seems. If a company's business model is based on selling fast-food chicken, is it making its money that way? Or is it just coasting on royalty and franchise fees?

Competitive advantage: A company's long-term success is driven largely by its ability to maintain a competitive advantage—and keep it. Powerful competitive advantages, such as Coca Cola's brand name and Microsoft's domination of the personal computer operating system, create a moat around a business allowing it to keep competitors at bay and enjoy growth and profits. When a company can achieve a competitive advantage, its shareholders can be well rewarded for decades.

Management: Some believe that management is the most important criterion for investing in a company. It makes sense: Even the best business model is doomed if the leaders of the company fail to properly execute the plan. While it's hard for retail investors to meet and truly evaluate managers, you can look at the corporate website and check the resumes of the top brass and the board members. How well did they perform in prior jobs? Have they been unloading a lot of their stock shares lately?

Corporate Governance: Corporate governance describes the policies in place within an organization denoting the relationships and responsibilities between management, directors and stakeholders. These policies are defined and determined in the company charter and its bylaws, along with corporate laws and regulations. You want to do business with a company that is run ethically, fairly, transparently, and efficiently. Particularly note whether management respects shareholder rights and shareholder interests. Make sure their communications to shareholders are transparent, clear and understandable. If you don't get it, it's probably because they don't want you to.

It's also important to consider a company's industry: customer base, market share among firms, industry-wide growth, competition, regulation, and business cycles. Learning about how the industry works will give an investor a deeper understanding of a company's financial health.

Quantitative Analysis

Financial statements are the medium by which a company discloses information concerning its financial performance. Followers of fundamental analysis use quantitative information gleaned from financial statements to make investment decisions. The three most important financial statements are income statements, balance sheets, and cash flow statements.

The Balance Sheet

The balance sheet represents a record of a company's assets, liabilities and equity at a particular point in time. The balance sheet is named by the fact that a business's financial structure balances in the following manner:

$$Assets = Liabilities + Shareholders \backslash Equity$$

Assets represent the resources that the business owns or controls at a given point in time. This includes items such as cash, inventory, machinery and buildings. The other side of the equation represents the total value of the financing the company has used to acquire those assets. Financing comes as a result of liabilities or equity. Liabilities represent debt (which of course must be paid back), while equity represents the total value of money that the owners have contributed to the business - including retained earnings, which is the profit made in previous years.

The Income Statement

While the balance sheet takes a snapshot approach in examining a business, the income statement measures a company's performance over a specific time frame. Technically, you could have a balance sheet for a month or even a day, but you'll only see public companies report quarterly and annually.

The income statement presents information about revenues, expenses and profit that was generated as a result of the business' operations for that period.

Statement of Cash Flows

The statement of cash flows represents a record of a business' cash inflows and outflows over a period of time. Typically, a statement of cash flows focuses on the following cash-related activities:

Operating Cash Flow (OCF): Cash generated from day-to-day business operations

Cash from investing (CFI): Cash used for investing in assets, as well as the proceeds from the sale of other businesses, equipment or long-term assets

Cash from financing (CFF): Cash paid or received from the issuing and borrowing of funds

The cash flow statement is important because it's very difficult for a business to manipulate its cash situation. There is plenty that aggressive accountants can do to manipulate earnings, but it's tough to fake cash in the bank. For this reason, some investors use the cash flow statement as a more conservative measure of a company's performance.

To be a good value investor, while using your checklist, there are three characters of Qualitative vs. Quantitative Analysis Horizon. What you need to do as a value investor in this picture you may check.

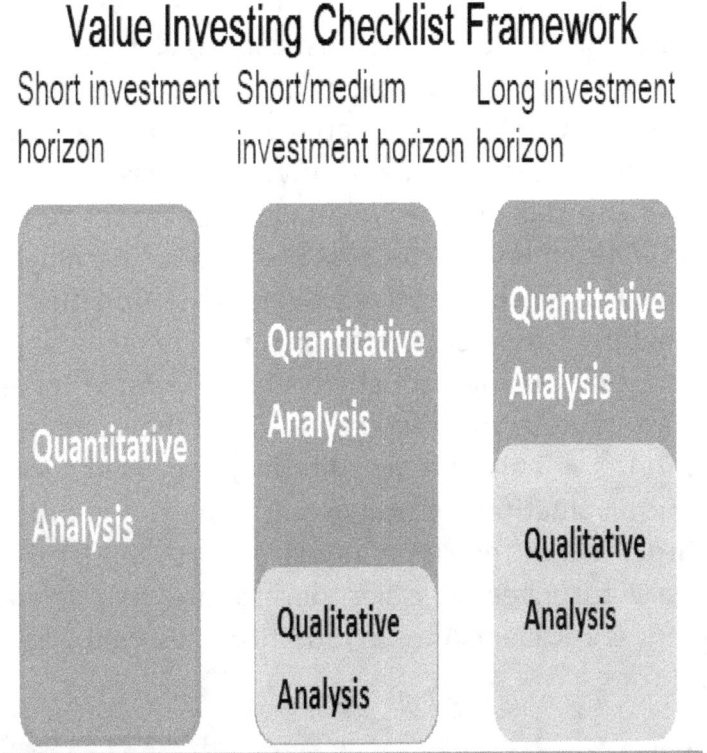

In value investing we use 50 % Qualitative and 50 % Quantitative Analysis.

Qualitative Analysis is for the long term horizon, approach to analyse the connection between the economic and positioning of the company, and the valuation approach whereas the Quantitative Analysis emphasizes statistical regularities in data.

Algo Trading, that's mostly about qualitative analysis, about the very short-term horizon. Quantitative investment instead combines some aspects of qualitative analysis, some particular assessment of the statistical regularities in the data, but mostly it's about quantitative analysis as well. Instead, the Value Investing approach combines both qualitative analysis and quantitative analysis in equal measure. We use this qualitative analysis, because we need to make an assessment of the sustainability of earnings, of the sustainability of competitive advantages. And that will require qualitative assessment to things like technological disruption, or what is the probability that a competitor may come in, and contest the market in which the company is operating. But it will also be quantitative, because of course we will do firm valuation, we will use firm metrics in order to compare firms within the same industry by looking at things like inventory turnover, or sales per square foot if we're dealing with a retailer. And in addition, we will look at industry metrics.

We would like to see to what extent the revenue shares are stable throughout a certain period of time for that particular industry and their study.

7

Company Type

Type of company as per Value Investing

1. Value Company
2. Growth Company

Value Investing Companies

Value Company
High Gross Margin, Operating Margin Net Margin
Stable Earning
Predictable Earning

Growth Company
Low Gross Margin, operating margin & Net Margin
Growth in Earning 10% for 5 years

Warren Buffet invests in both type and other value investor also like to invest in both type of company, in modern value investing consider in investing in the both type of the company.

Growth stocks are considered stocks that have the potential to outperform the overall market over time because of their future potential, while value stocks are classified as stocks that are currently trading below what they are really worth and will, therefore, provide a superior return. Which category is better? The comparative historical performance of these two sub-sectors yields some surprising results.

Value Company

There are two type of company value investor like warren buffet like; the first type of company is Value Company that enjoys barriers to entry, and has sustainable competitive advantage and sustainable earning and fat gross margin, operating margin and net profit margin such as Coca Cola, Apple.

Growth Company

The second type company which value investor invest in a growth company and in this they check the growth year to year and they might not have fat margin but still enjoy competitive advantage and have barrier to entry such as Amazon.

The concept of a growth stock versus one that is considered to be undervalued generally comes from the fundamental stock analysis. Growth stocks are considered by analysts to have the potential to outperform either the overall markets or else a specific sub segment of them for a period of time.

Growth stocks can be found in small-, mid- and large-cap sectors and can only retain this status until analysts feel that they have achieved their potential. Growth companies are considered to have a good chance for considerable expansion over the next few years, either because they have a product or line of products that are expected to sell well or because they appear to be run better than many of their competitors and are thus predicted to gain an edge on them in their market.

Value stocks are usually larger, more well-established companies that are trading below the price that analysts feel the stock is worth, depending upon the financial ratio or benchmark that it is being compared to. For example, the book value of a company's stock may be $25 a share, based on the number of shares outstanding divided by the company's capitalization. Therefore, if it is trading for $20 a share at the moment, then many analysts would consider this to be a good value play.

Stocks can become undervalued for many reasons. In some cases, public perception will push the price down, such as if a major figure in the company is caught in a personal scandal or the company is caught doing something unethical. But if the company's financials are still relatively solid, then value-seekers may see this as an ideal entry point, because they figure that the public will soon forget about whatever happened and the price will rise to where it should be. Value stocks will typically trade at a discount to either the price to earnings, book value or cash flow ratios.

Value investing is about buying a company for a market price below the intrinsic value of the business. According to Buffett, this is the only way to truly invest, since paying a price above the estimated value -- usually hoping to sell it for an even higher price -- should be considered speculation. Growth is one of the variables you need to consider when estimating that intrinsic value. Growth can be a major part of the company's value, or it can be a less crucial driver -- it depends on the particular business. Growth can also sometimes be negative in terms of value -- this happens when a company puts money to work in ultimately unprofitable growth initiatives. In his letter to Berkshire Hathaway (NYSE:BRK.A) (NYSE:BRK.B) shareholders in 1992, Buffett wrote:

Most analysts feel they must choose between two approaches customarily thought to be in opposition: "value" and "growth." Indeed, many investment professionals see any mixing of the two terms as a form of intellectual cross-dressing.

We view that as fuzzy thinking (in which, it must be confessed, I myself engaged some years ago). In our opinion, the two approaches are joined at the hip: Growth is always a component in the calculation of value, constituting a variable whose importance can range from negligible to enormous and whose impact can be negative as well as positive.

8

Industry Type

Type of Industry as per Value Investing

Predictable Product Predictable Profit

Type of Business

Consumer Monopoly

Unique Product
Unique Services
Supply Based
- *Patents*
- *Regulatory Licenses*
- *Cost advantage/Economic of Scale*

Demand Based
- *Network Switching Cos*
- *Habits*
- *Search*

Commodity Type

Not a Barrier to Entry
- *Brands Based*
- *First Mover advantage*

Industry -
Metals – Silver, Gold, Platinum, and Copper.
Energy – Crude oil, Natural gas, Gasoline, and Heating oil.
Agriculture – Corn, Beans, Rice, Wheat, etc.,
Livestock and Meat – Eggs, Pork, Cattle, etc.,
Automobiles

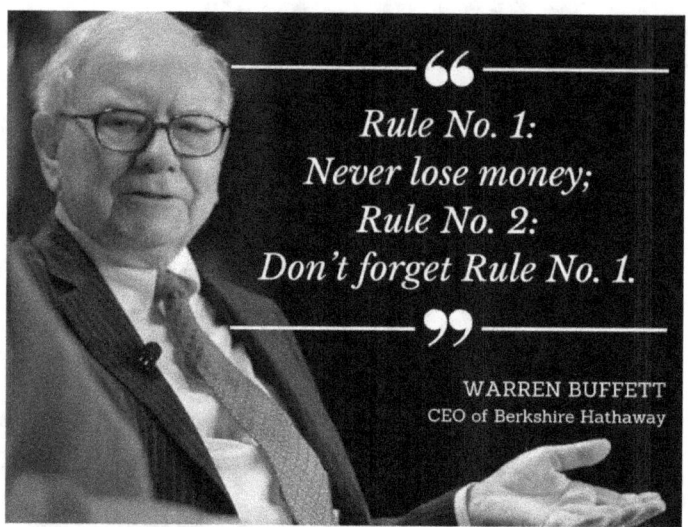

A commodity-type business is a business that sells a product whose price is the single most important motivation factor in the consumer's buy decision. Commodity businesses constantly underperform vs consumer monopolies. A consumer monopoly is a company selling a product that requires a consumer to return over and over again that controls the marketplace with their brand or quality. Think of a company like Coca-Cola.

1. Does the business have an identifiable consumer monopoly?

2. Are the earnings of the company strong and showing an upward trend?

3. Is the company conservatively financed?

4. Does the business consistently earn a high rate of return on shareholder's equity?

5. Does the business get to retain its earnings?

6. How much does the business have to spend on maintaining current operations?

7. Is the company free to reinvest retained earnings in new business opportunities, expansion of operations, or share repurchases? How good of a job does management do of this?

8. Is the company free to adjust prices to inflation?

9. Will the value added by retained earnings increase the market value of the company?

Consumer Monopoly

A monopoly refers to when a company and its product offerings dominate a sector or industry. Monopolies can be considered an extreme result of free-market capitalism in that absent any restriction or restraints, a single company or group becomes large enough to own all or nearly all of the market (goods, supplies, commodities, infrastructure, and assets) for a particular type of product or service. The term monopoly is often used to describe an entity that has total or near-total control of a market.

Monopolies typically have an unfair advantage over their competition since they are either the only provider of a product or control most of the market share or customers for their product. Although monopolies might differ from industry-to-industry, they tend to share similar characteristics that include:

- High or no barriers to entry: Competitors are not able to enter the market, and the monopoly can easily prevent competition from developing their foothold in an industry by acquiring the competition.

- Single seller: There is only one seller in the market, meaning the company becomes the same as the industry it serves.

- Price maker: The Company that operates the monopoly decides the price of the product that it will sell without any competition keeping their prices in check. As a result, monopolies can raise prices at will.

- Economies of scale: A monopoly often can produce at a lower cost than smaller companies. Monopolies can buy huge quantities of inventory, for example, usually a volume discount. As a result, a monopoly can lower its prices so much that smaller competitors can't survive. Essentially, monopolies can engage in price wars due to their scale of their manufacturing and distribution networks such as warehousing and shipping that can be done at lower costs than any of the competitors in the industry.

Buffett seeks out consumer monopolies selling products in which there is no effective competitor, either due to a patent or brand name or similar intangible that makes the product unique. Investors can seek these companies by identifying the manufacturers of products that seem indispensable. Consumer monopolies typically have high profit margins because of their unique niche; however, simple screens for high margins may simply highlight firms within industries with traditionally high margins.

Consumer Monopoly companies are such as Apple, Visa, MasterCard, Coca Cola.

Commodity Type

"Commodity businesses are not good businesses at the end of the day: they're capital intensive, the products don't have any differentiation, and returns tend to be lower over time. We've decided that we would only get involved in commodity businesses if we can identify the low-cost producer, the commodity is priced below the cost of production, and the balance sheet is clean."

Commodity Business Characteristics:

Sells generic product or service where price is the most important motivating factor in the consumer's decision to buy.

Airlines, Gas/Oil, Paper, Automobile Manufacturers.

Monopolies vs. Commodities Warren Buffett seeks first to identify an excellent business and then to acquire the firm if the price is right. Buffett is a buy-and-hold investor who prefers to hold the stock of a good company earning 15% year after year over jumping from investment to investment with the hope of a quick 25% gain. Once a good company is identified and purchased at an attractive price, it is held for the long-term until the business loses its attractiveness or until a more attractive alternative investment becomes available.

Buffett seeks businesses whose product or service will be in constant and growing demand. In his view, businesses can be divided into two basic types:

Commodity-based firms, selling products where price is the single most important factor determining purchase. Buffett avoids commodity-based firms. They are characterized with high levels of competition in which the low-cost producer wins because of the freedom to establish prices. Management is key for the long-term success of these types of firms.

Consumer monopolies, selling products where there is no effective competitor, either due to a patent or brand name or similar intangible that makes the product or service unique.

While Buffett is considered a value investor, he passes up the stocks of commodity-based firms even if they can be purchased at a price below the intrinsic value of the firm. An enterprise with poor inherent economics often remains that way. The stock of a mediocre business treads water.

How do you spot a commodity-based company? Buffett looks for these characteristics:

The firm has low profit margins (net income divided by sales);

- The firm has low return on equity (earnings per share divided by book value per share);
- Absence of any brand-name loyalty for its products;
- The presence of multiple producers;
- The existence of substantial excess capacity;
- Profits tend to be erratic; and
- The firm's profitability depends upon management's ability to optimize the use of tangible assets.

Buffett seeks out consumer monopolies. These are companies that have managed to create a product or service that is somehow unique and difficult to reproduce by competitors, either due to brand-name loyalty, a particular niche that only a limited number companies can enter, or an unregulated but legal monopoly such as a patent.

Consumer monopolies can be businesses that sell products or services. Buffett reveals three types of monopolies:

Businesses that make products that wear out fast or are used up quickly and have brand-name appeal that merchant must carry to attract customers. Nike is a good example of a firm with a strong brand name demanded by customers. Any store selling athletic shoes must carry Nike products to remain competitive. Other examples include leading newspapers, drug companies with patents, and popular brand-name restaurants such as McDonald's.

Communications firms that provide a repetitive service that manufacturers must use to persuade the public to buy the manufacturer's products. All businesses must advertise their items, and many of the available media face little competition. These include worldwide advertising agencies, magazine publishers, newspapers, and telecommunications networks.

Businesses that provide repetitive consumer services that people and businesses are in constant need of. Examples include tax preparers, insurance companies, and investment firms.

9

Approach to use Checklist

First we need to understand by using the qualitative checklist about the details in depth analysis of the business, what company do? , who are the customers, suppliers and in which market company operate?, importance of the management and their role in operating company, do company enjoy the barrier to entry and have a durable competitive advantage, once we will go through all the details about the company and if we able to understand the ecosystem how company operate and it comes within our circle of competence then only we will move forward to quantitative analysis.

If our answer is no in the qualitative analysis, we will not explore the quantitative analysis of the business.

Lessons from an investing legend

Former Fidelity fund manager Peter Lynch shares some of his secrets to success.

How should individual investors approach picking stocks?

Peter Lynch: Stocks aren't lottery tickets. Behind every stock is a company. If the company does well, over time the stocks do well, and vice versa. You have to look at the company—that's what you research. That's what we do at Fidelity, and that's what I do.

How can an average investor get an edge?

Peter Lynch: Ask yourself: Can I analyze the company? Everybody has a good idea of what McDonald's does. But it's hard to analyze biotechnology companies or computer software companies. So, ask yourself: Do you know something about the company? What can you add to the math? Do you have an edge?

You could be an interventional cardiologist and you put in a heart pump. You say, wow, this really is an incredible breakthrough, preventing shock, providing hemodynamic support. You're actually in the operating room, seeing this breakthrough way ahead of most people. That's an edge. You need an edge on something.

What do you look for when shopping for stocks to buy?

Wal-Mart was in only 15% of the United States when they were a 10-year-old public company. All they did for the next 30 years was go from 15% to 100%. The stock went up 50-fold. They had a great formula, and they just rolled with it in the United States.

How do you think about the economy's impact on stocks?

Lynch: I think if you spent over 13 minutes a year on economics, you've wasted over 10 minutes. I mean, it's not helpful. Everybody wants to predict the future, and I've tried to call the 1-800 psychic hotlines. It hasn't helped. The only thing I would look at is what's happening right now.

What's the biggest mistake you see individual investors making?

Lynch: the public's careful when they buy a house, when they buy a refrigerator, when they buy a car. They'll work hours to save a hundred dollars on a roundtrip air ticket. They'll put $5,000 or $10,000 on some zany idea they heard on the bus. That's gambling. That's not investing. That's not research. That's just total speculation.

What do you need to become a great investor?

Lynch: In the stock market, the most important organ is the stomach. It's not the brain.

On the way to work, the amount of bad news you could hear is almost infinite now. So the question is: Can you take that? Do you really have faith that 10 years, 20 years, 30 years from now common stocks are the place to be. If you believe in that, you should have some money in equity funds.

It's a question of what's your tolerance for pain. There will still be declines. It might be tomorrow. It might be a year from now. Who knows when it's going to happen? The question is: Are you ready—do you have the stomach for this?

Most people do really well because they just hang in there.

One of Buffett's hallmark investment strategies is an investing in quality. This means that he invests in companies that have well-known, well-regarded products that add value to the consumer and the economy. The companies he inverts money in are usually household names, which is to say that they have both strong market penetration and brand recognition.

Many less successful investors are drawn to companies and industries that they know little or nothing about. They assume that the less they know, the more likely it is that the investment will be a success, as though it will succeed based on some unexplained mystery factor. Quality – not mystery – makes a company a long-term winning investment.

10

Qualitative Analysis

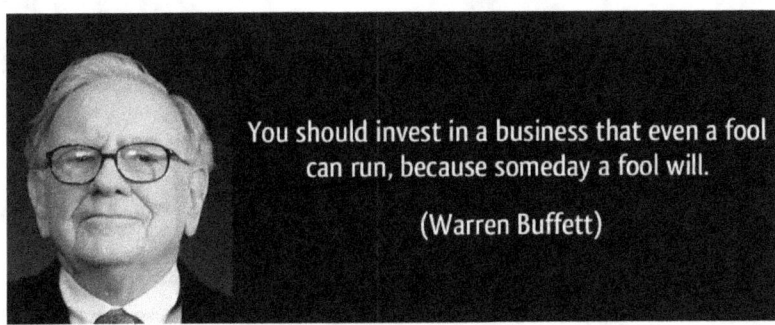

A business is defined as an organization or enterprising entity engaged in commercial, industrial, or professional activities. Generally, a business begins with a business concept (the idea) and a name. Depending on the nature of the business, extensive market research may be necessary to determine whether turning the idea into a business is feasible and if the business can deliver value to consumers.

Businesses most often form after the development of a business plan, which is a formal document detailing a business's goals and objectives, and its strategies of how it will achieve the goals and objectives. Business plans are almost essential when borrowing capital to begin operations. A corporation is a business in which a group of people acts together as a single entity; most commonly, owners of a corporation are shareholders who exchange consideration for the corporation's common stock.

A company may describe its business by communicating the industry in which it operates. For example, the real estate business, advertising business, or mattress production business are industries in which a business can exist.

"Time is the friend of the wonderful business, the enemy of the mediocre."

-Warren

Qualitative Analysis

- BUSINESS
- PRODUCT
- SUPPLIER
- COMPETITORS
- INDUSTRY
- GEOGRAPHY
- MANAGEMENT
- FRANCHISE VALUE
- DURABLE COMPETATIVE ADVANTAGE
- BARRIER TO ENTRY

11

Business Analysis

"Never invest in a business you can't understand."

– Warren Buffett

One need to ask our self about the business we are selecting before investing, this business is good, do we understand this business, with the help of the checklist we will understand about ecosystem how this business work. Business provides goods and services to satisfy wants and needs.

1. What does business do? (Goods or services)

While starting the qualitative analysis, first we need to ask our self, what business company do what kind of product they sell or what kind of services they render?

Like Warren Buffett hold different companies from goods to services such as Apple are in selling of goods business and are in repairing of electronic and apple cloud, in services business, like Coca Cola are in selling of goods business and J P Morgan and Goldman Sachs are in Service business.

You have to understand business in two prospect good and services, whichever you choose it supposed to be within your circle of competence.

Definition of Goods: -

- Physical product
- Tangible in nature
- Homogeneous
- It has inventory
- Example – Car, Aeroplane, Pizza, Soft Drink.

Definition of Services: -

- Intangible in nature
- A process
- Heterogeneous
- No inventory
- Example - Software, Education.

Warren Buffett doesn't invest in stocks; he buys businesses. He's not interested in the stock price; he's more interested in the "business" of a business.

When the dot com bubble began, the dot-com bubble (also known as the dot-com boom, the tech bubble, and the Internet bubble) was a stock market bubble caused by excessive speculation in Internet-related companies in the late 1990s, a period of massive growth in the use and adoption of the Internet. Between 1995 and its peak in March 2000, the Nasdaq Composite stock market index rose 400% only to fall 78% from its peak by October 2002, giving up all its gains during the bubble.; many entrepreneurs and companies were jumping to start their own web-based business but Warren Buffett refused to budge because he doesn't understand the technology industry. He only understands financial service businesses and he has stuck to this industry.

"If you understood a business perfectly and the future of the business, you need very little in the way of a margin of safety."

— Warren Buffett

There is a major difference between goods and services based on both tangible as well as intangible factors. Goods are basically objects or products which have to be manufactured, stored, transported, marketed and sold. Lays chips, BMW, Adidas are some companies manufacturing goods.

Services on the other hand are output of individuals and they can be a collective or individualistic action or performance by an individual. For example, a barber or chartered accountants are giving individual services. Airlines on the other hand have airplanes which are a product but travelling by airplanes is a service (airlines are one of the most competitive service sectors today).

2. What is the product portfolio?

A product portfolio is the collection of all the products or services offered by a company. Product Portfolio can be defined as the compilation of products and services offered by the company to the target market. It comprises of all the set of products offered right from the ones that were launched and offered during the inception of the brand to the ones that are launched currently along with ones that are in the pipeline.

A product portfolio is comprised of all the products which an organization has. A product portfolio may comprise of different categories of products, different product lines and finally the individual product itself. Products Portfolio management is one of the most crucial elements of the entire business strategy as it helps the company to attain its overall business objectives and plan the future line of products accordingly.

It works as a significant tool for the corporate financial planning of the firm and also for the investors conducting the equity research analyzing the return on investments.

The thorough analysis of the Product Portfolio can provide the management of the company with crucial information such as stock type, growth prospects of the brand, products that are high on profit margins, income contribution by each and every product offered to the market, market share of every product, operational risks, and market leadership.

Apple Product Portfolio

Johnson & Johnson

Powdered and Liquid Beverages

Nutrition and Health Science

PetCare

Milk products and Ice cream

Prepared dishes and cooking aids

Nestle

3. How does business generate revenue?

In accounting, revenue is the income that a business has from its normal business activities, usually from the sale of goods and services to customers. Revenue is also referred to as sales or turnover. Some companies receive revenue from interest, royalties, or other fees. Revenue may refer to business income in general, or it may refer to the amount, in a monetary unit, earned during a period of time.

We need to look company revenue breakup such as this revenue comes from selling a range of services, such as iCloud storage services, Apple Music subscriptions, and AppleCare warranties. According to Apple, there are over 450 million paid subscriptions on Apple's platform. In 2010, Apple's services business revenue generated only $5.2 billion in revenue.

- Apple sells smart phones, personal computers, tablets, wearable's and accessories, and services.

- iPhones are Apple's biggest source of revenue by product, and the Americas is the largest revenue generator among its geographic regions.

- Apple's high-margin services business is one of the company's fastest growing sources of revenue.

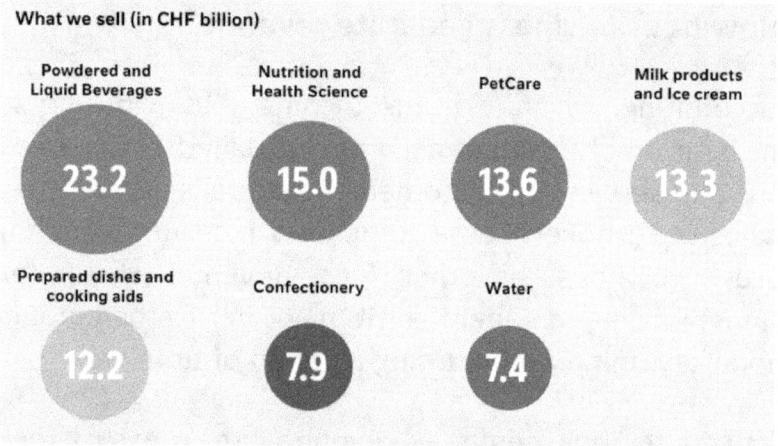

Nestle

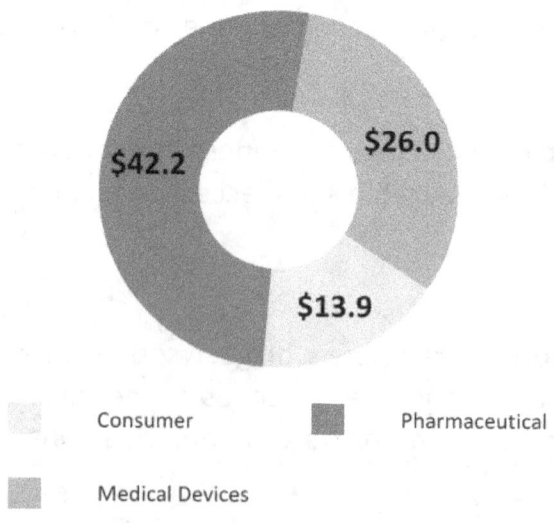

Johnson & Johnson's

4. What is the percentage of revenue from each segment of product portfolio?

In each segment at what percentage of revenue is contributing to the total business net revenue.

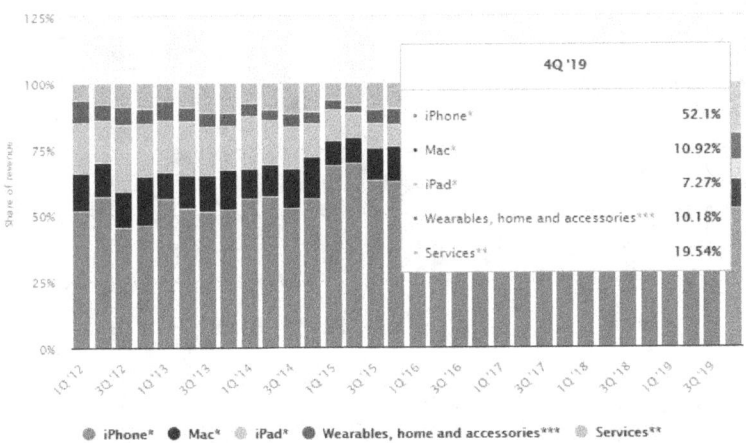

Apple Inc

It is very good understanding to analyse which product contribution highest revenue in percentage as such in Apple Inc., we can see iPhone is contributing to 52.1% compare with MAC 10.92%, earlier Apple Inc. was knowing as the personal computer making company as by the time, there is big changes as now apple is in Smartphone, services, computer, smart watch and accessories.

80% of the profit Apple Inc makes from iPhone, and apple 52% revenue comes from iPhone sale , that the way Apple make money .

Zone AMS
In millions of CHF

	2018*	2019	Proportion of total sales (%)
United States and Canada	20 540	22 719	68.5%
Latin America and Caribbean	10 435	10 435	31.5%
Powdered and Liquid Beverages	4 057	5 473	16.5%
Milk products and Ice cream	6 991	7 291	22.0%
Prepared dishes and cooking aids	5 541	5 604	16.9%
Confectionery	2 718	2 514	7.6%
PetCare	8 783	9 370	28.3%
Nutrition and Health Science	2 885	2 902	8.7%
Total sales	30 975	33 154	
Underlying trading operating profit	6 496	6 998	21.1%
Trading operating profit	6 053	6 159	18.6%
Capital additions	7 356	1 804	5.4%

Nestle

Income Before Tax by Segment

Income before tax by segment of business were as follows:

(Dollars in Millions)	Segment Sales		Percent of Segment Sales	
	2019	2018	2019	2018
Consumer	13,898	13,853	14.8%	16.7
Pharmaceutical	42,198	40,734	20.9	30.9
Medical Devices	25,963	26,994	28.1	16.3
Total [1]	82,059	81,581	22.1	23.6
Less: Net expense not allocated to segments [2]				
Earnings before provision for taxes on income	82,059	81,581	21.1%	22.1

Johnson & Johnson

5. What is the Gross Margin and Operating Margin from each product portfolio?

You need to check both the margin to understand, what is the highest and lowest margin in each product line. Margin is one of the major factors that company make money, to be in a sustainable position, company margin needs to be growing or sustainable.

Gross profit margin and operating profit margin are two metrics used to measure a company's profitability. The difference between them is that gross profit margin only figures in the direct costs involved in production, while operating profit margin includes operating expenses like overhead. Both metrics are important in assessing the financial health of a company.

JC Penney earned only $3 million in operating income after earning $2.67 billion in revenue. Although gross profit margin appeared healthy at 38%, after taking out expenses and SG&A, operating profit margin tells a different story. The disparity between the numbers shows the importance of using multiple financial metrics in analyzing the profitability of a company.

Some company won't share product wise gross profit margin such as Apple Inc, in this case refer to total revenue gross profit as I have shown in Nestle for year 2017, 2018 and 2019.

Nestle Operating Margin by Product Line

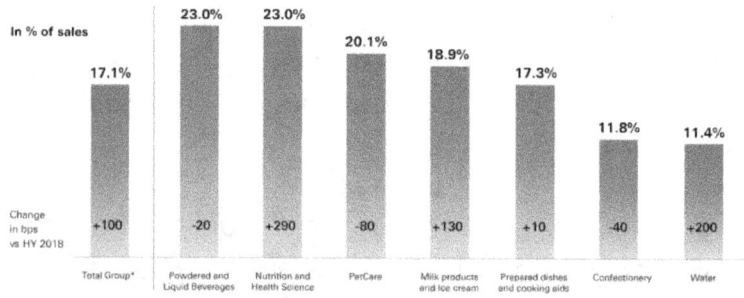

Nestle

Nestle Gross Profit Margin

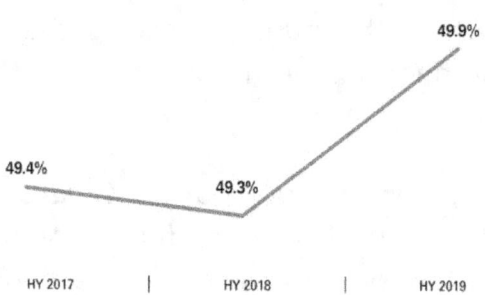

Nestle

6. What are the Gross Margin and Operating Margin and net profit margin from over all combined revenue?

We need to look at the company income statement and from there, we can able to calculate the margin, this margin is very impotent as, this three-margin state that what is the current and what was the financial margins, company is maintaining for the operating of the business.

We have to look at the margin should be stable and sustainable and keep maintaining, all product has different margin and margin can be different as per the country, they are operating, so this is only approach to understand company fundamental status.

Gross margin and operating margin are two fundamental profit metrics used by investors, creditors, and analysts to evaluate a company's current financial condition and prospects for future profitability. The two margins differ in regard to the specific costs and expenses included in their calculations and the different purposes they serve in providing a company with information for analysis.

Gross margin, also called gross profit margin, represents the percentage of total revenue a company has left over above costs directly related to production and distribution. The percentage figure is calculated by subtracting those costs from the total revenue figure and then dividing that sum by the total revenue figure. For gross margin, the higher the percentage, the more is retained on each dollar of sales by the company. On the other hand, if a company's gross margin is falling, it may look to find ways to cut labor costs, lower costs on acquiring materials or even increase prices.

Operating margin additionally subtracts all overhead and operational expenses from revenues, indicating the amount of profit the company has left before figuring in the expenses of taxes and interest. For this reason, operating margin is sometimes referred to as EBIT, or earnings before interest and tax.

Net profit margin is one of the most important indicators of a company's financial health. By tracking increases and decreases in its net profit margin, a company can assess whether current practices are working and forecast profits based on revenues. Because companies express net profit margin as a percentage rather than a dollar amount, it is possible to compare the profitability of two or more businesses regardless of size.

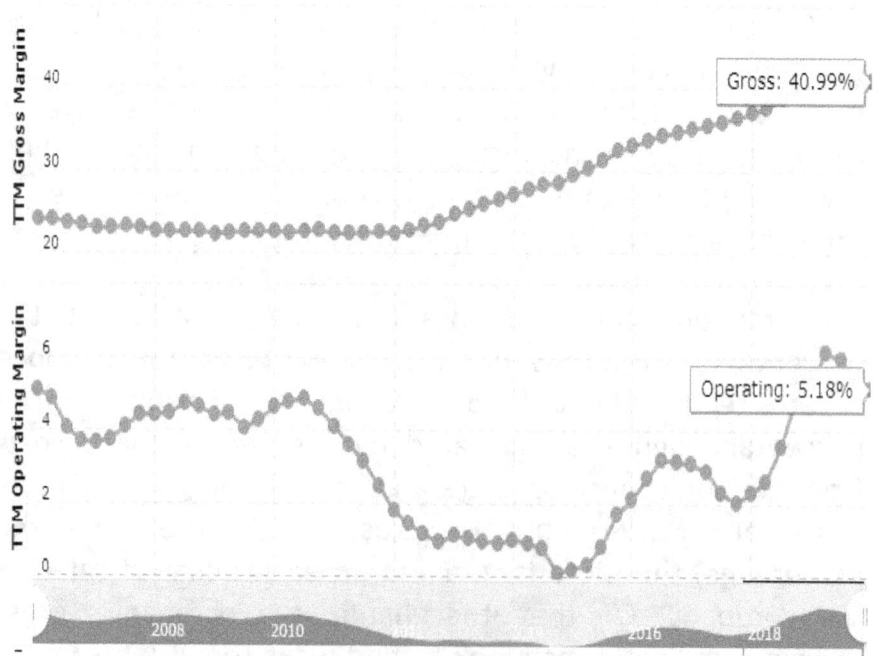

Amazon Gross Profit Margin & Operating Profit Margin

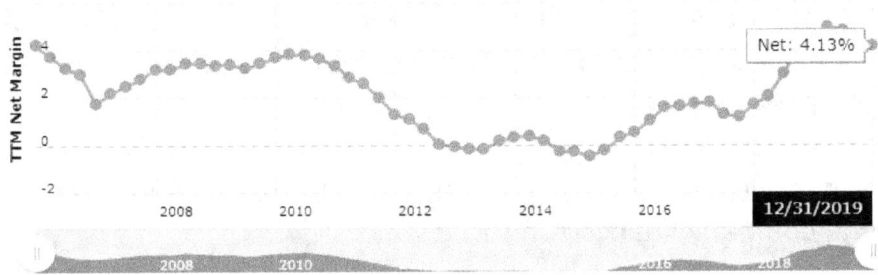

Amazon Net Profit Margin

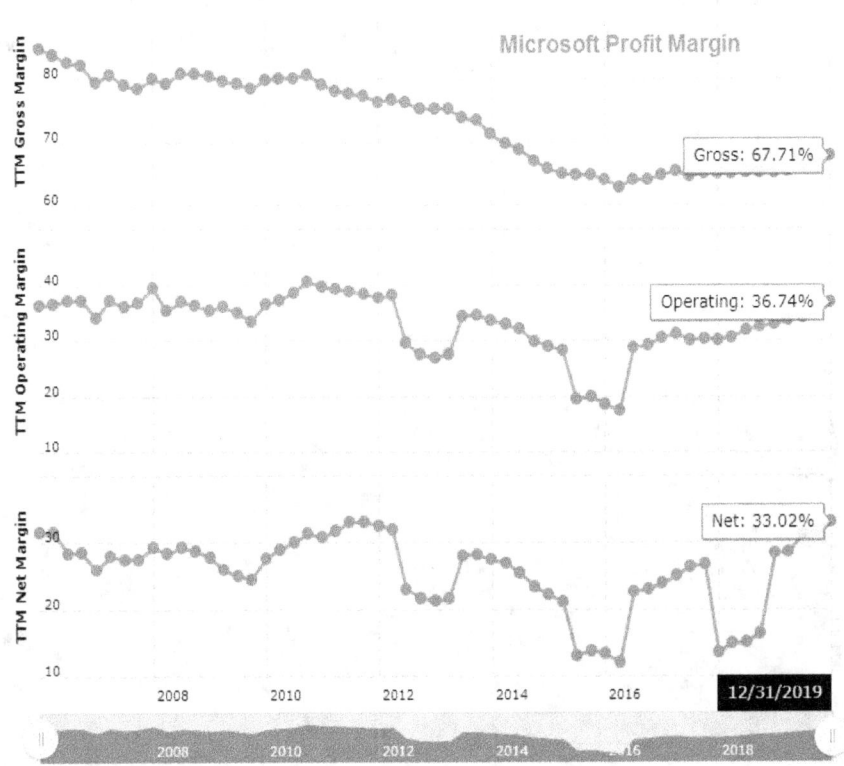

Microsoft Gross Profit, Operating Profit & Net Profit Margin

7. Business gross margin, operating margin and net profit margin from last five or ten years sustainable, growth or decline?

When we look at that margin, we can able to judge, about the company life cycle in three ways

- Is the company growing and it looking good to me to buy?
- Is the company sustainable in cyclical phase?
- Due to high competition, or not able to performance that reflect in the decrease in margin, no competitive advantage.

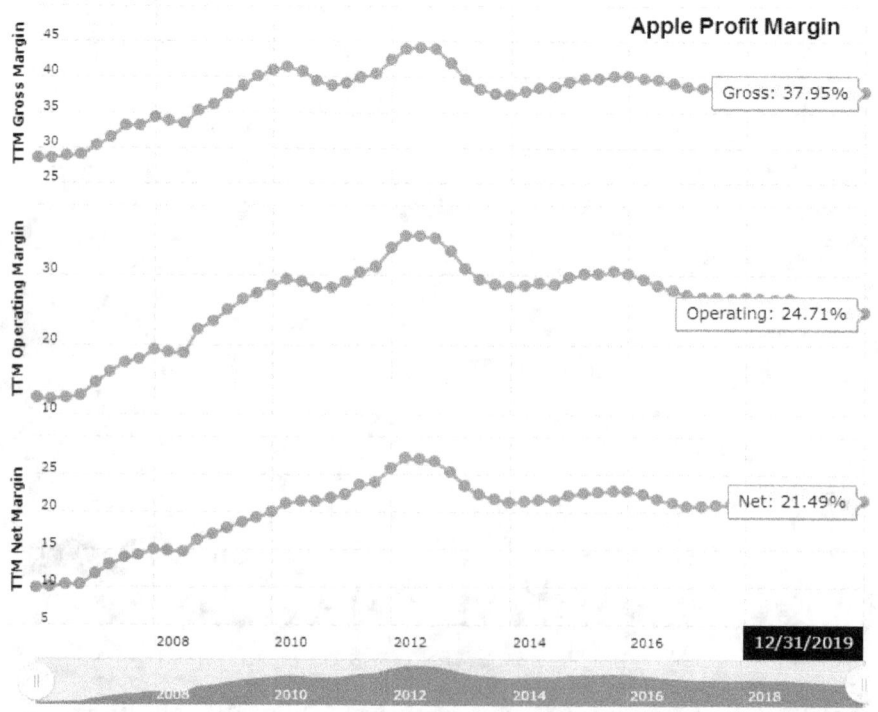

Apple Inc Gross Profit, Operating Profit & Net Profit Margin

Apple in fiscal year 2008 Gross Profit Margin 28%, Operating Profit margin was 12% & Net Profit Margin was 10 %, and now after ten years there is an increase in margin and we can see the margin is now sustainable as 2019 Gross Profit Margin 38%, Operating Profit margin was 25% & Net Profit Margin was 22 %.

This kind of details we need to check before making any investment in the company. An upward trend means that profit has generally increased over time in the short or long run. A downward profitability trend means profits are declining. Recognizing problems early in profitability trends gives you a better chance to address revenue and cost issues in play.

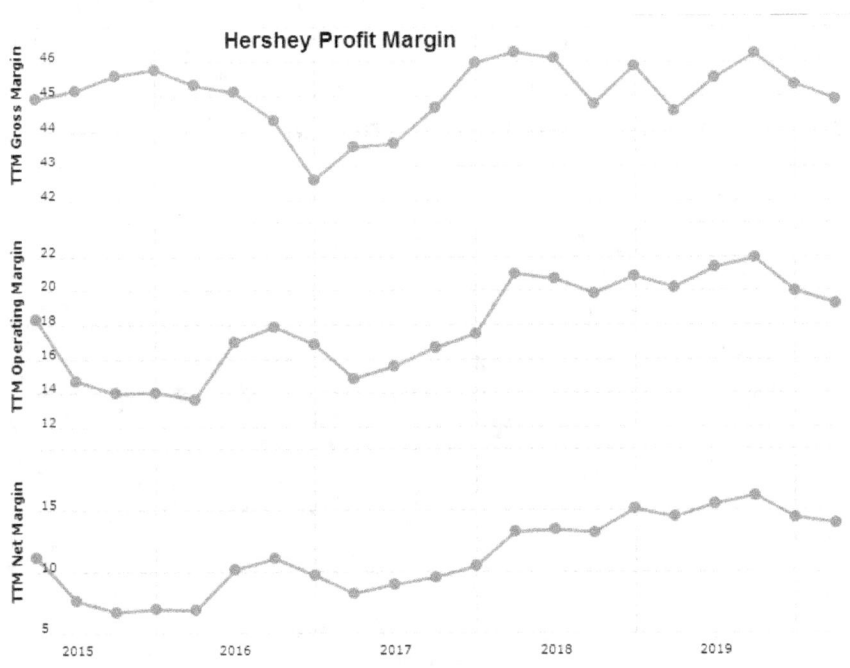

Hershey Margin Upward Trend

Trend charts are graphical representations of data arranged in a time sequence. It shows a trend line that displays the general pattern of change. Using the chart to observe net profit trends over a given period of time allows you to identify favorable and unfavorable trend changes. To maintain uniformity and accuracy of comparison, the net profit figures used must have similar time periods, such as months to months, quarters to quarters and years to years.

The general direction of change in net profit over the period of time covered by the net profit trend analysis indicates your profitability progress. A stable trend indicates that although profitability did not deteriorate, no significant progress was made over the years. An increasing trend is seen as favorable while a decreasing one is unfavorable. An increasing trend indicates that profits are rising and operational efficiency may be improving. A decreasing trend is a sign of poor performance and may indicate upcoming losses.

8. What is the overall revenue growth rate?

Revenue Growth Rate is an indicator of how well a company is able to grow its sales revenue over a given time period. While the revenue is an actual number, the revenue growth rates simply compare the current sales figures with different years.

It indicates that at what percentage company is growing in year-on-year basis, it will give you a good picture that how each product sale has been in increasing such as when Apple inch launch iPhone, due to big success, the revenue jump and apple starting making more revenue due to the new launch, so when we will see the growth in revenue, we need to ask some important question as: -

- The story behind the growth in revenue
- Any new product launches
- Same product reinvented
- New geographical operating has started

This kind of questing you need to ask and look for the reason for the growth of the revenue. Revenue growth is the increase (or decrease) in a company's sales from one period to the next. Shown as a percentage, revenue growth illustrates the increases and decreases over time identifying trends in the business.

The formula for calculating revenue growth is:

$$\frac{\text{Current Year Revenue} - \text{Prior Year Revenue}}{\text{Prior Year Revenue}}$$

(in billion U.S. dollars)

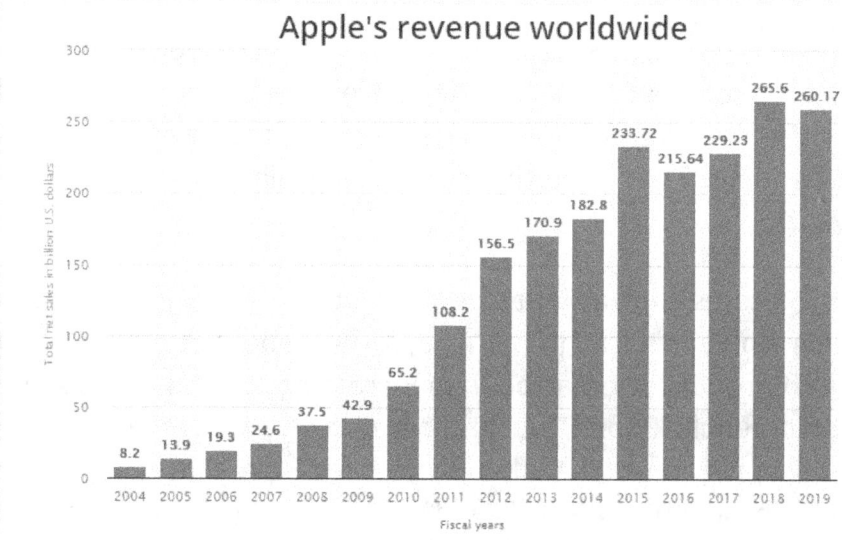

How much growth is reasonable? It depends on the company, the industry, and the economic situation. A growth rate of 10 percent a year, sustained over time, is remarkably good.

In millions	Sep-28-19	Sep-29-18	Sep-30-17	Sep-24-16	Sep-26-15	Sep-27-14	Sep-28-13	Sep-29-12
Revenues	2,60,174	2,65,595	2,29,234	2,15,639	2,33,715	1,82,795	1,70,910	1,56,508
Revenue growth	-2.00%	15.90%	6.30%	-7.70%	27.90%	7.00%	9.20%	44.60%

Apple Inc Revenue Year to Year Growth & Degrowth

9. What is the revenue growth rate in each product line?

Knowing the growth rate is very important; to get in depth understanding of the clear view, look for product things, while answering this question.

- **Where is the revenue coming from?**
- **Which product sale is increasing?**
- **Which product sale is shrinking?**
- **Which product is stable?**
- **Which product is going to be discontinued?**

Product lining is offering several related products for sale individually. Unlike product bundling, where several products are combined into one group, which is then offered for sale as units, product lining involves offering the products for sale separately. A line can comprise related products of various sizes, types, colors, qualities, or prices. Line depth refers to the number of subcategories a category has. Line consistency refers to how closely relate the products that make up the line are. Line vulnerability refers to the percentage of sales or profits that are derived from only a few products in the line of Amazon.

AMAZON PRODUCT LINE SALE	Year Ended December 31,		
	2017	2018	2019
Net Sales:			
Online stores (1)	$ 108,354	$ 122,987	$ 141,247
Physical stores (2)	5,798	17,224	17,192
Third-party seller services (3)	31,881	42,745	53,762
Subscription services (4)	9,721	14,168	19,210
AWS	17,459	25,655	35,026
Other (5)	4,653	10,108	14,085
Consolidated	$ 177,866	$ 232,887	$ 280,522

Apple Inc

Products and Services Performance Beginning in the first quarter of 2019, the Company classified the amortization of the deferred value of Maps, Siri and free iCloud services, which are bundled in the sales price of iPhone, Mac, iPad and certain other products, in Services net sales. Historically, the Company classified the amortization of these amounts in Products net sales consistent with its management reporting framework. As a result, Products and Services net sales for 2018 and 2017 were reclassified to conform to the 2019 presentation.

The following table shows net sales by category for 2019, 2018 and 2017 (dollars in millions):

	2019	Change	2018	Change	2017
Net sales by category:					
iPhone [1]	$ 142,381	(14)%	$ 164,888	18 %	$ 139,337
Mac [1]	25,740	2 %	25,198	(1)%	25,569
iPad [1]	21,280	16 %	18,380	(2)%	18,802
Wearables, Home and Accessories [1][2]	24,482	41 %	17,381	36 %	12,826
Services [3]	46,291	16 %	39,748	22 %	32,700
Total net sales	$ 260,174	(2)%	$ 265,595	16 %	$ 229,234

One of the key areas which cannot be avoided by the value investor, product is the heart of the business and as a value investor we need to know, what is the story of the product line and what was the status and what is the status and what will be the status.

10. From last five to ten years, what is the status of net profit and at what percentage net profit is increasing or shrinking?

Net profit is the life blood of the business, is there is no profit then there is no business and business will be vanished, so while selecting a good business, it is very important to understand about whole picture where this profit is coming from and what is the status, we need to ask some important questing while evaluation a business.

- What is the profit look like in last five to 10 years?
- Is profit in upward trend?
- Sustainable profit growth?
- Shrinking profit yearly?

Apple Net Profit Growth

YEAR	Net Profit	Growth
2012	41	
2013	37	-9.8%
2014	39	5.4%
2015	53	35.9%
2016	45	-15.1%
2017	48	6.7%
2018	59	22.9%
	3.71%	7.67%
CAGR RETURN	3.71%	
AVERAGE RETUN	7.67%	

Apple Net Profit

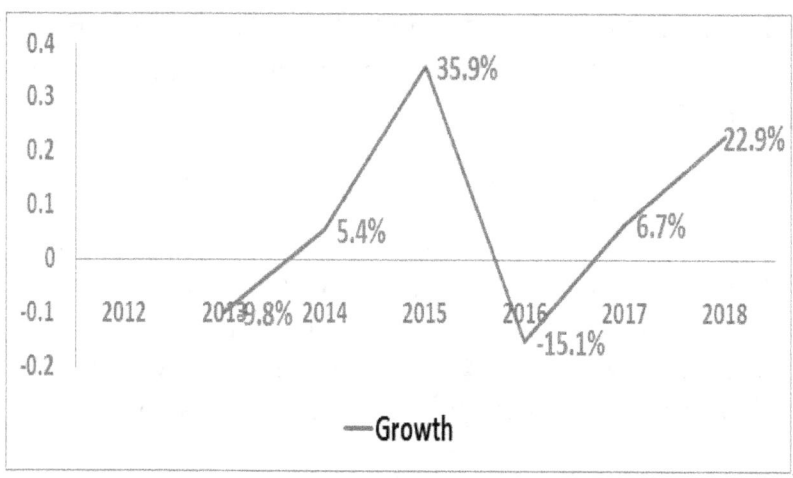

Apple Net profit Status

There is a growth in the net profit as per CAGR is 3.71% and if you do average it is 7.67%.

Net profit is one of the vital ingredients to approach for the successful in business.

11. Which segment is growing and shrinking?

To understand this, we need to deep dive in the breakup of the revenue to get the clear picture, if you see the example of Apple Inc, we have analysis in four parts:

- Growth in Segment – iPhone & Other Product.
- Sustainable Segment – Services
- Shrinking Segment - Mac
- Decline Segment – iPod

Fraction of Sales by Segment

Segment	2013	2014	2015	2016	2017	2018
iPhone	53%	56%	66%	63%	62%	63%
iPad	19%	17%	10%	10%	8%	7%
Mac	13%	13%	11%	11%	11%	10%
iPod	3%	1%				
Services	9%	10%	9%	11%	13%	7%
Other Products	3%	3%	4%	5%	6%	6%
Total	100%	100%	100%	100%	100%	100%

Apple Inc

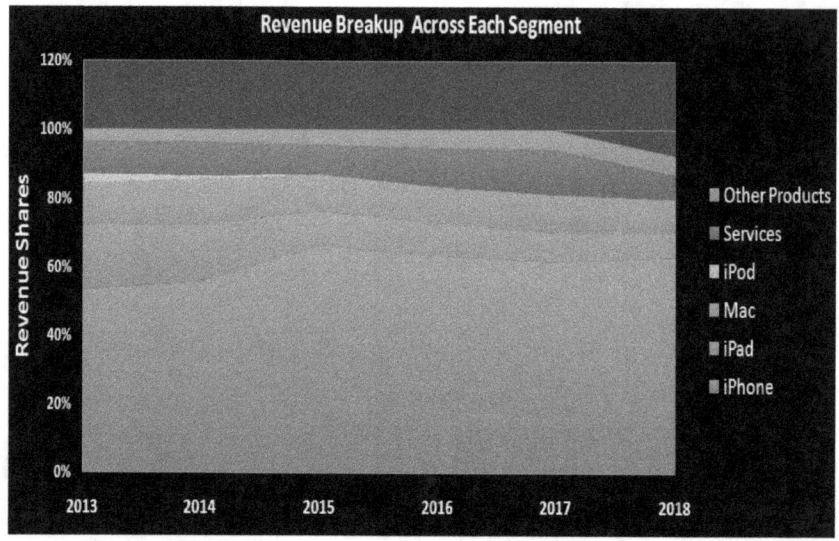

Apple used to be a computer manufacturing company but they starting diversify the company product in different segment as well as the industry.

When you are projecting revenue of apple, you don't take shrinking segment and decline segment because, it will be vanished in five to ten years, or the contribution in the revenue will be very less and what will be known as "All that glitters is not gold".

Many Wall Street analyst get trap to understand the ecosystem, they projection is very high. Your analysis should be based on real facts and figure.

"You only have to do a very few things right in your life so long as you don't do too many things wrong." Warren Buffett

12. Growth by Synergy or Organic growth?

Organic growth is the process by which a company expands on its own capacity. In an organic growth strategy, a business utilizes all of its resources – without the need to borrow – to expand its operations and grow the company. Organic growth is ultimately often more difficult to come by because it takes longer and it usually requires a shift in how the company operates. Still, organic growth is arguably better in the long term because it prevents the loss of a company as an independent entity

Organic growth is important because it demonstrates that a business is capable of earning more and expanding its market share year over year. Note that organic growth is especially significant when it's the result of the reinvestment of the company's earnings — as opposed to external investments — into its development. However, there are several potential challenges:

Growth by Synergy

By comparison, is accomplished by using resources or growth opportunities outside of a company's own means. It includes things like taking loans and entering into mergers and acquisitions.

Growth through acquisition refers to acquisitions of one company by another. It can be merger or taking over of control. ... In this growth through acquisition strategy the policies made by consent prevails and both work as one entity. In a downstream acquisition process, one firm acquires the other to expand its business.

For example, when Proctor & Gamble Company acquired Gillette in 2005, a P&G news release cited that "the increases to the company's growth objectives are driven by the identified synergy opportunities from the P&G/Gillette combination. The company continues to expect cost synergies of approximately $1 to $1.2 billion...and an increase in the annual sales run-rate of about $750 million by 2008.

Apple growth is by Acquisition and by the Organic growth, apple acquire lots of company to make their product better and enhanced.

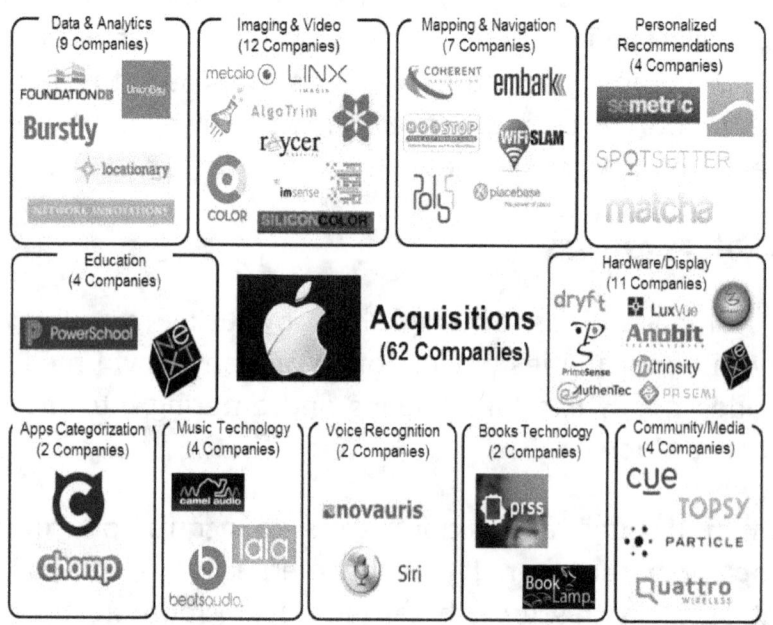

"2019 was another year of strong progress. Key operating and financial metrics improved significantly for a second consecutive year. Our organic growth reached 3.5%. Real internal growth accelerated to 2.9% for the full year, the highest level in the last six years."

-Nestle Annual Report Statement

Group sales (in CHF)	Organic growth*	Real internal growth*
92.6 billion	**3.5%**	**2.9%**

Nestle

Boosting organic growth through fast innovation ,an engaged generation of consumers is driving a new food ideology, with trends toward more natural and organic foods, plant-based proteins and simpler, healthier ingredients. They expect brands to provide experiences beyond the product, be authentic and act as a force for good – both socially and environmentally. These forces have led us to redefine our approach to new product development with shorter innovation cycles and faster launches. During 2019, we shortened timelines of fundamental research projects by 30% on average. Fifty key fast-track projects made the journey from idea to launch within 12 months. In total, we introduced around 1400 new products worldwide and reformulated 4000 products to improve nutritional value. Starbucks. The rapid launch of our Starbucks portfolio is a prime example of how we aim to act with urgency and speed to maximize growth opportunities. Within six months of acquiring the license, we successfully launched the first wave *of new products. In 2019, we launched 29 Starbucks products into more than 40 countries and generated incremental sales of more than CHF 300 million. Plant-based food. We believe that plant-based products should be delicious, offer a better nutritional profile and have a lower environmental footprint compared to meat. Through our strong innovation capacity, we developed our Garden Gourmet Incredible Burger in one year and launched it successfully in 10 European countries during 2019.*

-Nestle Annual Report Statement

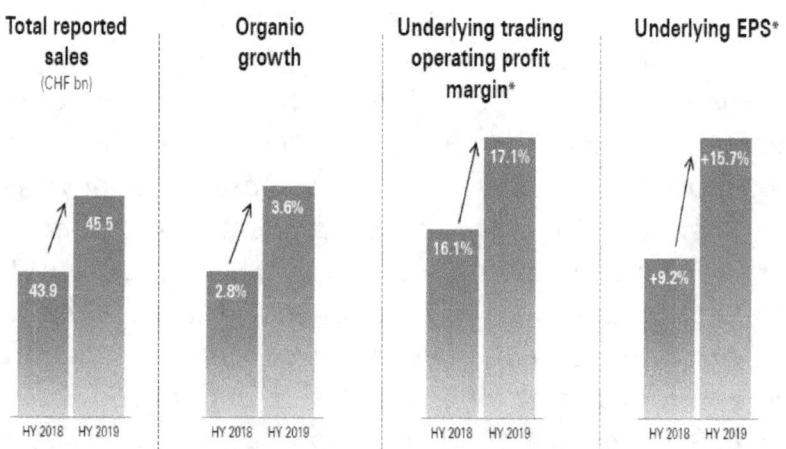

Nestle Organic Growth

13. Does the business simple or too complex to fully understand?

Look for a business that you understand and comfortable to hold the shares and reap for the profit, rather wonder what will happen to the business and their product.

The business should be within in your circle of competence, you should not have any second thought, when you buy a business.

"I would take one industry at a time and develop an expertise in half a dozen... If I were looking at an insurance company or a paper company, I would put myself in the frame of mind that I just inherited that company, and it was the only asset that my family was ever going to own."

"You should invest in a business that even a fool can run, because someday a fool will." "Don't sweat the math."

"You don't need a rocket scientist," to be a shrewd and successful investor.

"If calculus were required, I'd have to go back to delivering papers. I've never seen any need for algebra. Essentially, you're trying to figure out the value of a business. It's true that you have to divide by the number of shares outstanding, so division is required."

"Whether you made the right purchase or not would depend on the future earning ability of that enterprise, and then relating that to the price you are being asked for the asset."

- *Warren*

Words from Warren Buffett

- For example, he purchased See's Candies with long-time business partner Charlie Munger in 1972 and spent more than $1 billion on Coca-Cola stock in 1988 — both of which turned out to be good bets he still owns today.

- "Put together a portfolio of companies whose aggregate earnings march upward over the years, and so also will the portfolio's market value," Buffett wrote in his 1996 letter to shareholders. "If you aren't willing to own a stock for 10 years, don't even think about owning it for 10 minutes."

- "What an investor needs are the ability to correctly evaluate selected businesses. Note that word 'selected': You don't have to be an expert on every company, or even many. You only have to be able to evaluate companies within your circle of competence.

  "The size of that circle is not very important; knowing its boundaries, however, is vital."

- In his 1986 letter to shareholders, Buffett laid out the different aspects he and Munger were looking for in new companies, including "simple businesses." He even went so far as to say that "if there's lots of technology, we won't understand it."

- More specifically, Buffett's model states that it's inadvisable to invest in a business where you cannot predict whether the company will have a long-term (20+ years or more) competitive advantage.

- In his 2007 letter, Buffett expands on his thinking about which kinds of businesses he prefers to invest in. "A truly great business must have an enduring 'moat' that protects excellent returns on invested capital," he writes, "The dynamics of capitalism guarantee that competitors will repeatedly assault any business 'castle' that is earning high returns."

- When Buffett invests, he is not looking at the innovative potential of the company or, in a vacuum, its growth potential. He is looking for a competitive advantage.

- "The key to investing is not assessing how much an industry is going to affect society, or how much it will grow," he writes "But rather determining the competitive advantage of any given company and, above all, the durability of that advantage."

- In 1999, when Wall Street analysts were extolling the virtues of virtually every dotcom stock on the market, Buffett was seeing a repeat of an earlier time: the invention of the automobile.

- When the car was first invented, a naive investor might have thought that virtually every automobile stock was guaranteed to succeed. At one point, there were 2,000 separate car brands just in the United States. Of course, those didn't all last.

- "If you had foreseen, in the early days of cars, how this industry would develop, you would have said,

'Here is the road to riches,'" Buffett writes. "So what did we progress to by the 1990s?" he asks. "After corporate carnage that never let up, we came down to three US car companies."

- He observes that the airplane industry suffered similarly. While the technological innovation was even more impressive than the car, the industry as a whole could be said to have failed most of its investors. By 1992, the collection of all airline companies produced in the United States had produced a total of no profits whatsoever.

- His conclusion about dotcom stocks at the time was simple: there will be a few winners, and an overwhelming majority of losers.

- Correctly picking the winners requires understanding which companies are building a competitive advantage that will be defensible over the very long term. During the dotcom boom, that meant understanding how the infrastructure of the web would change over the next several decades — an impossible task for any observer at the time.

- Buffett prefers to keep it simple, as he makes clear in his 1996 letter.

What we learn from the warren buffet statement is that if you buy poor company, there is no chance you will ever make any penny. A good selection of a company can makes you wealthy; make sure your selection should be without any bias.

14. Do you think you can predict the earning?

To predict the earning, you don't need big stock screen terminal, and lots of graph, all you need is an understanding about the company, how business work, once you will able to answer this question, how business work, do business enjoy barrier to entry and have durable competitive advantage, your chance to be successful is very high, the reason I am saying because, what we learn from the value investor is that "Investment is most intelligent when it is most business-like." --Benjamin Graham.

"Actually, Wall Street thinks just as the Greeks did. The early Greeks used to sit around for days and debate how many teeth a horse has. They thought they could figure it out by just sitting there, instead of checking the horse. "

— Peter Lynch

"Understand the nature of the companies you own and the specific reasons for holding the stock"

— Peter Lynch

"You are neither right nor wrong because the crowd disagrees with you. You are right because your data and reasoning are right."

-Warren Buffett

"Stop trying to predict the direction of the stock market, the economy, interest rates, or elections."

-Warren Buffett

"Buy companies with strong histories of profitability and with a dominant business franchise."

-Warren Buffett

There are a variety of investment styles to choose from. Warren Buffett has become known as one of the savviest investors by using a simple approach. Buffet's elementary probability approach keeps his investing analysis simple: he focuses on transparent companies with a wide moat that is easy to understand and logical in their progression.

However, Buffett is also known for his deep value approach which he perfected through his study and work with Benjamin Graham. His value approach combined with a simplified understanding of companies limits the investable universe for Berkshire's portfolio to companies with low P/Es, high levels of cash flow, and sustained earnings.

It took Warren Buffet some time to evolve the right investment philosophy for him, but once he did, he stuck to his principles. By definition, companies with a durable competitive advantage generate an excess return on capital and their competitive advantage acts like a moat around a castle. The "moat" ensures the continuity of excess return on capital for the company because it decreases the probability of a competitor eating into the company's profitability.

"People calculate too much and think too little."

— Charles T. Munger

15. Do you understand how the company generates sales incurs expenses and produces profits?

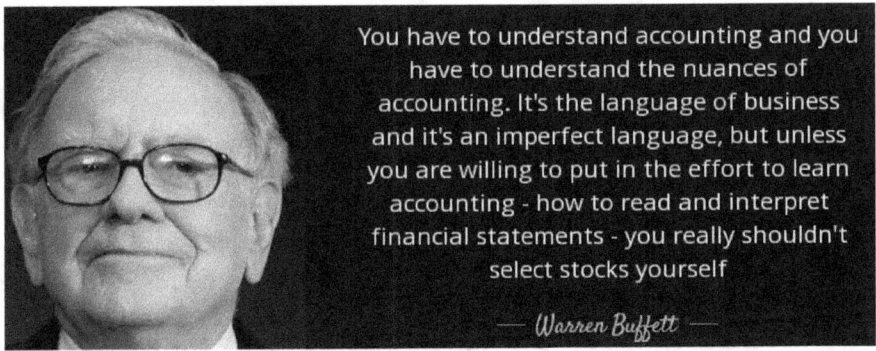

You have to understand accounting and you have to understand the nuances of accounting. It's the language of business and it's an imperfect language, but unless you are willing to put in the effort to learn accounting - how to read and interpret financial statements - you really shouldn't select stocks yourself

— Warren Buffett —

Accounting or accountancy is the measurement, processing, and communication of financial and non-financial information about economic entities such as businesses and corporations. Accounting, which has been called the "language of business", measures the results of an organization's economic activities and conveys this information to a variety of users, including investors, creditors, management, and regulators. Practitioners of accounting are known as accountants. The terms "accounting" and "financial reporting" are often used as synonyms.

- Investors who know how to calculate and analyze a corporate profit margin gain insight into a company's current effectiveness in generating profits and its potential to generate future profits.

- The three-key profit-margin ratios investors should analyze when evaluating a company are gross profit margins, operating profit margins, and net profit margins.

- Companies with large profit margins frequently have a competitive advantage over other companies in their industry.

- Understanding a company's margin ratios can be a starting point for further analysis to decide if a company would be a good investment option.

There are three important margin to know looking at the income statement such as:

- **Gross Profit Margin**

    Gross Profit Margin = (Sales - Cost of Goods Sold)/Sales

- **Operating Profit Margin**

    Operating Profit Margin = EBIT/Sales

- **Net Profit Margin**

    Net Profit Margins = Net Profits after Taxes/Sales

Accounting skills help you to understand about company financial information.

The language of accounting explains a business's financial situation: how much money it brings in, how much its assets are worth, how much it owes. The language of finance takes the data that accountants develop and uses it to project the future: How will the company's value grow? What will the rate of return be for its investors? How should the company allocate capital? Economics is the language for discussing the underlying bedrock principles of how buying and selling works: supply and demand, consumer preferences, price elasticity.

In business, there are three main "languages" – accounting, finance, and economics. While there are many other disciplines in business, such as marketing, human resources, operations, etc., it's the core principles and terminology behind accounting, finance, and economics that drive decisions across businesses. In this guide, we will break down the language of business in simple terms.

Accounting

Within any business, the accounting language is critical to understand, yet far too few people properly understand it.

Companies produce three main financial statements:

- Balance sheet
- Income statement
- Cash flow statement

Finance

Once you have a solid understanding of the accounting language, it's equally important to understand the language of finance. Accounting is backward-looking, while finance is forward-looking and therefore critical to decision-making processes at companies.

- Assessing value
- Looking into the future
- Rates of return
- Allocating capital

Economics

It's one thing to making a financial forecast using financial methods, but it's another entirely to make sure that forecast is supported by a sound understanding of supply and demand, consumer preferences, price sensitivity.

- Supply and demand (and equilibrium)
- Consumer preferences
- Indifference curves
- Substitutes
- Price elasticity

If you can understand the language of business then you can understand the whole business ecosystem and your chance to be successful will be very high.

16. Business is consumer monopoly or commodity type?

Value investor look for a business which is consumer monopoly, consumer loves the brands and company must have consumer captive power. The consumer loyalty is very important such as you may find in Coca Cola, KFC, Pizza Hut, same on other hand if you see airlines and automobiles company, they cannot have any consumer loyalty, they only play in the market due to their cheap price, customer is not interested, which brands of airline they are using, all they are interested in paying cheap to travel in a flight.

The investor is well-known for his income and value approaches to investing, and his portfolio reflects his ideology. As of Dec. 31, 2019, the Berkshire Hathaway portfolio had a value of approximately $194.91 billion. The portfolio's greatest weights were in Apple (AAPL), Bank of America Corp (BAC), and Coca-Cola Company (KO). Combined, these three companies totalled 56% of the equity holdings.

As a percentage of equity investments, Berkshire Hathaway is most heavily invested in the financial sector at 38%, followed by 26% in technology, and 15% in consumer defensive. Other sectors in the portfolio include industrials, consumer cyclical, health care, energy, communication services, basic materials, and real estate. Warren buffer Portfolio

- Financial 45.5% - Bank of America
- Information Technology 26.8% – Apple Inc
- Consumer staples 14.9%- Coca -Cola

BERKSHIRE HATHAWAY FINANCIAL SECTOR HOLDINGS

Bank of America Corp	11.4%
American Express Company	7.7%
Wells Fargo & Co	5.1%
JPMorgan Chase & Co	3.2%
Moody's Corporation	2.7%
U.S. Bancorp	2.5%
Bank of New York Mellon Corp	1.4%
Goldman Sachs Group Inc	1.1%
Visa Inc	0.97%
Mastercard Inc	0.67%
PNC Financial Services Group	0.48%
M&T Bank Corporation	0.31%
Synchrony Financial	0.26%
Globe Life	0.23%

Source: Berkshire Hathaway, Form 13F, as of Dec. 31, 2019

Many investor and analyst makes mistake in not knowing what they are doing and why they are selecting the stock, all they can do it to make rosy picture.

"Selling your winners and holding your losers is like cutting the flowers and watering the weeds."

– Peter Lynch

How much money you will make determine by the stock you select to invest, your selection is not only based on the free cash flow or yearly earnings growth rate, but understanding what kind of business you are entering in and how long will it make you to earn the good return.

Suppose you invest your money in automobiles such as Renault and Nissan Automobiles Company, let understand, how any investor can easily destroy his capital and become beggar.

Groupe Renault is a French multinational automobile manufacturer established in 1899. The company produces a range of cars and vans, and in the past has manufactured trucks, tractors, tanks, buses/coaches, aircraft and aircraft engines, and autorail vehicles.

Suppose you have invested in fiscal year 1994 for 27.22 EUR and today still you keep the stock in 2020, can you imagine what is the stock price after 26 years is 18.26 EUR

Let see now the Nissan Car Company

Nissan Motor Co., Ltd., usually shortened to Nissan, is a Japanese multinational automobile manufacturer headquartered in Nishi-ku, Yokohama. The company sells its cars under the Nissan, Infiniti, and Datsun brands with in-house performance tuning products labelled.

Suppose you have invested in fiscal year 2000 for 480 JPY and today still you keep the stock in 2020, can you imagine what is the stock price after 20 years is 370 JPY.

If you have invested in this both companies, you would have made zero money, don't get rosy by the logo design and the slogan or impressive vision Statement Company make, this doesn't work in commodity type business, don't get flow by this beautiful picture, all you need to invest in simple and business where you can easily predict the earning for fifteen or twenty years.

Lesson to be learn by both the company

- Poor economics of the business
- Fraud Management

- To create synergies Renault and Nissan Renault buying 36.8 percent of Nissan's stock, while Nissan promised to buy Renault's stock when it had the financial power to do so. After almost falling to bankruptcy in 2001, Nissan made a comeback and purchased a 15 percent of Renault stock. Afterward, Renault increased its share in Nissan stock to 44.4 percent.

- The profitable business venture of Renault Nissan alliance could break, thanks to the political struggles between France and Japan. So, if France doesn't agree to relinquish some power of the partnership to Nissan than this collaboration might just end. This struggle started when Japan felt that the ownership favors the French giant. If we were talking about this in 1999, then this would make sense.

But in 2019, Nissan is accounting for most of the combined capitalization for this Renault Nissan alliance.

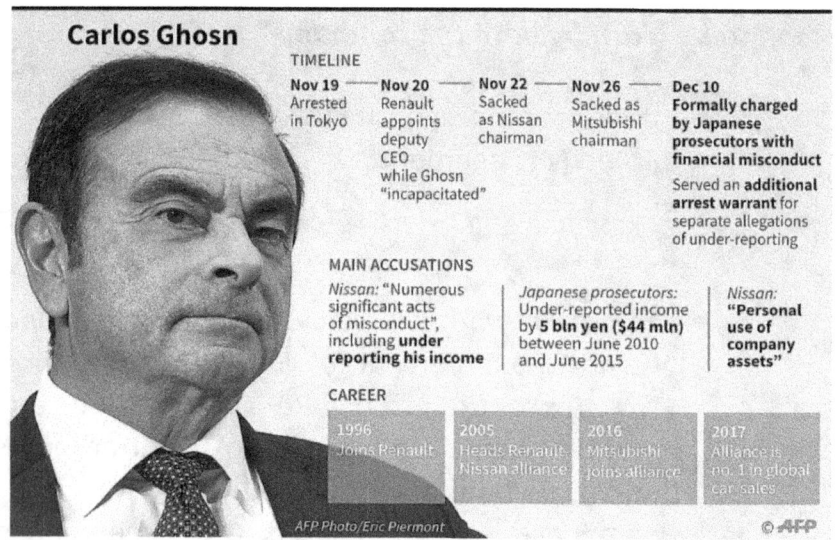

This case study what we learn: -

- Nissan was in bankruptcy.
- Renault acquire Nissan share to make more profit that never worked.
- Chairman scandal and fraud.

Peter Lynch said in the speech year 1994 that "if you want a piece of crap like that you will never make money and people buy this junk all the time, he made money in Dunkin donuts" he made 15 times of money in Dunkin donuts".

17. Is the past history has been good?

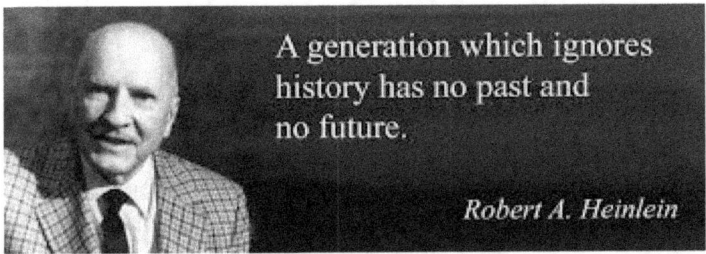

Studying history is important because it allows us to understand our past, which in turn allows us to understand our present. ... Studying history can provide us with insight into our cultures of origin as well as cultures with which we might be less familiar, thereby increasing cross-cultural awareness and understanding. One can study history because it allows one to exercise their critical thinking skills. These critical thinking skills are important for all areas in life, academic and otherwise.

What past history can teach you in buying a stock?

- You can make money
- You can lose money

Let see some example

Not performing proper due diligence when buying General Reinsurance

Multiple investment tips can be garnered from Warren Buffett's acquisition of General Reinsurance. In his 2001 shareholders letter, he offered more insights on the reason Berkshire Hathaway took such a large initial hit on the purchase. This included enduring underwriting losses, overlooking the possibility of terrorist attacks and failing to realize Gen Re didn't have enough in reserve to pay losses from old policies. Berkshire Hathaway realized $800 million in losses from the latter in 2001.

The lesson here is to double-check the numbers and run them by several trusted advisors. You should always know what a worst-case scenario could cost you.

Opting not to buy Amazon stock

In a February 2017 interview with "Squawk Box," Buffett was asked why he'd never bought stock in Amazon. He admitted he didn't have a good answer.

"Obviously, I should have bought it long ago, because I admired it long ago," he said. "But I didn't understand the power of the model as I went along. And the price always seemed to more than reflect the power of the model at that time. So, it's one I missed big time."

Warren Buffett's investments never include businesses he doesn't understand, which is both good and bad. Backing companies blindly is not a smart move, but shying away from them isn't wise, either. Partnering with someone whose strengths differ from yours can help you avoid missing out on great opportunities.

Warren Buffett used to sell Coca –Cola and Washington post at the age of six and thirteen, we was well qualified to analyse the value of the both company, knowing the past history of company is good, he bought both the stock and made enough wealth, still he have Coca-Cola in his portfolio.

- Warren Buffett's Berkshire Hathaway bought more than $1 billion in Coca-Cola shares in 1988.

- After the stock market crash, Coca-Cola stock had been hit hard along with so many other companies.

- Buffett & Co. determined it was a good company, had great value, could withstand competition, and was poised to recover.

- Purchasing the shares of Coca-Cola marked a significant turnaround in Buffett and Berkshire Hathaway's investing philosophy.

- Today, Coca-Cola is Berkshire's third-biggest holding.

12

Product Analysis

Product analysis involves examining product features, costs, availability, quality, appearance and other aspects. Product analysis is conducted by potential buyers, by product managers attempting to understand competitors and by third party reviewers.

Product analysis can also be used as part of product design to convert a high-level product description into project deliverables and requirements. It involves all facts of the product, its purpose, its operation, and its characteristics.

No matter how well costs are driven or held down, no product can be profitable unless it sells. Therefore, all products must satisfy customer needs and wants. As all customers are different and seek different benefits from products, businesses would ideally tailor their products to satisfy each customer's wants and needs. However, for many businesses this is not achievable, so they need a way of classifying products in a structure aligned to customer segments, as defined by their needs and wants. The more flexibility a business has to configure products to different customer segments at minimal cost, the more segments they can target with the core product. Which is why it is vital to develop new products with flexibility as a key feature. Philip Kotler, an economist, devised a model that recognises customers have five levels of need, ranging from functional or core needs to emotional needs. The model also recognises that products are merely a means to satisfy customers' varying needs or wants. He distinguished three drivers of how customers attach value to a product:

Need: a lack of a basic requirement.

Want: a specific requirement of products to satisfy a need.

Demand: a set of wants plus the desire and ability to pay for the product.

Customers will choose a product based on their perceived value of it. Satisfaction is the degree to which the actual use of a product matches the perceived value at the time of the purchase. A customer is satisfied only if the actual value is the same or exceeds the perceived value. Kotler attributed five levels to products:

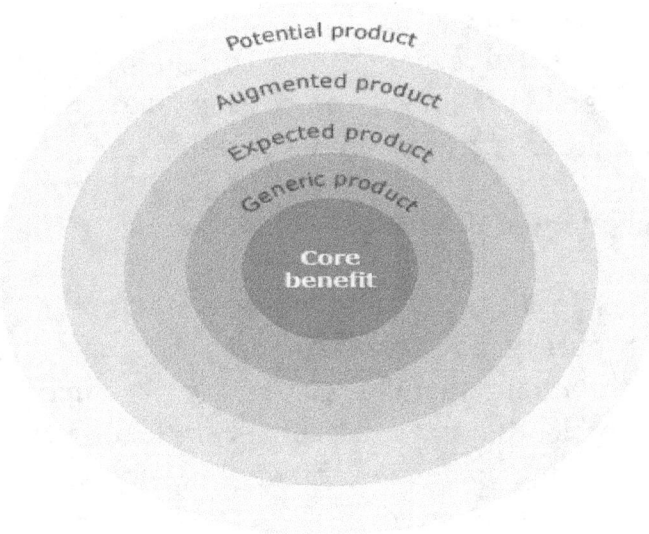

The five product levels are:

Core benefit:

The fundamental need or want that consumers satisfy by consuming the product or service. For example, the need to process digital images.

Generic product:

A version of the product containing only those attributes or characteristics absolutely necessary for it to function. For example, the need to process digital images could be satisfied by a generic, low-end, personal computer using free image processing software or a processing laboratory.

Expected product:

The set of attributes or characteristics that buyers normally expect and agree to when they purchase a product. For example, the computer is specified to deliver fast image processing and has a high-resolution, accurate colour screen.

Augmented product:

The inclusion of additional features, benefits, attributes or related services that serve to differentiate the product from its competitors. For example, the computer comes pre-loaded with a high-end image processing software for no extra cost or at a deeply discounted, incremental cost.

Potential product:

This includes all the augmentations and transformations a product might undergo in the future. To ensure future customer loyalty, a business must aim to surprise and delight customers in the future by continuing to augment products. For example, the customer receives ongoing image processing software upgrades with new and useful features.

Warren Buffett at Coca Cola shareholders meeting

This kind of product warren love to have, have moats and barrier to enjoy and enjoy customer captivity.

1. What is the product of the company, is that Goods or Services?

While you are selecting the company, you need to check, what all the product company sell, if it is product like Coca-Cola or is it a service like J P Morgan. Whichever product you select, make sure you must have understood everything about the product what company sell, as product is the heart of the company, without a good product, no company can make profit.

Warren Buffett is very specific about the selecting the product, he mentions that things he doesn't understand, he won't buy.

Some important point needs to be noted while selecting a good product as per value investor:

- A product that not change over time like Coca –Cola, or insurance.
- Look for product that customer require and again and again willing to buy.
- A product that creates value to the customer and enjoy the market share like Apple iPhone.

As investors, we have to train ourselves to assess how a company is going to do five or 10 years ahead. You want it to be continuing to do the same thing again and again.

'There are all kinds of important subjects that Charlie and I, we don't know anything about, and therefore we don't think about them. So, we have - our view about what the world will look like over the next ten years in business or competitive situations, we're just no good.

We do think we know something about what Coca-Cola's going to look like in ten years, or what Gillette's going to look like in ten years, or what Disney's going to look like in ten years, or what some of our operating subsidiaries are going to look like in ten years.

2. Is the business having only one product line or multiple product portfolios?

When you check the business product portfolio, it very important to understand some important points: -

- Like Apple have multiple product
- Airline have single product that is service
- Nestle have lots of product
- Coca-Cola has multiple product but all are in same industry.

These are the question we need to ask, while analysing a company product portfolio.

NESTLE	Brands
Powdered and liquid beverages	Nescafé, Nespresso, Coffee-Mate, Nestea
Pet care	Purina, Dog Chow, Gourmet
Confectionery	Nestle Chocolates, Kit Kat, Crunch
Prepared dishes and cooking aids	Maggi, Buitoni, DiGiorno, Hot Pockets, Lean Cuisine
Nutrition and healthcare	Cerelac, Gerber
Milk products & ice cream	Nesquick, Ovaltine, Milo, Häagen-Dazs, Dreyer's, Edy's
Water	Perrier, Poland Spring, Pure Life, San Pellegrino

Product Portfolio

Apple Product Portfolio

Product	Segment
iPhone	SmartPhone
iPad	Computer
Mac	Computer
Services	Music
Other Products	smartwatches
Services	Pay
Services	Cloud

If you see the Apple product portfolio, apple is in both segments as follows: -

- *Product*
  - *iPhone*
  - *iPad*
  - *Mac*
  - *Other Product*

- *Services*
  - *Apple Play*
  - *Cloud*
  - *Music*
  - *Repair*

3. Out of many products, is the company largely depend on single product that contribute to the revenue?

We need to check which all products are contributing maximum revenue, let see in an example.

Fraction of Sales by Segment

Segment	2013	2014	2015	2016	2017	2018
iPhone	53%	56%	66%	63%	62%	63%
iPad	19%	17%	10%	10%	8%	7%
Mac	13%	13%	11%	11%	11%	10%
iPod	3%	1%				
Services	9%	10%	9%	11%	13%	7%
Other Products	3%	3%	4%	5%	6%	6%
Total	100%	100%	100%	100%	100%	100%

iPhone is having 63% of the contribution in the total revenue, currently Apple is largely depending on iPhone sale, if the iPhone sale will shrink than Apple might be in trouble.

Nestle have a lot of product and sale in not depend on any one product like Apple, they have multiple sources of income and risk is very less.

It's more important to understand the product life cycle.

In millions of CHF Nestlé.	2019
Powdered and Liquid Beverages	
Soluble coffee/coffee systems	9 144
Other	14 077
Total sales	**23 221**
Underlying trading operating profit	5 197
Trading operating profit	4 701
Water	
Total sales	**7 391**
Underlying trading operating profit	846
Trading operating profit	667
Milk products and Ice cream	
Milk products	10 433
Ice cream	2 835
Total sales	**13 268**
Underlying trading operating profit	2 706
Trading operating profit	1 678

4. What is the product line cycle of the business?

Products, like people, have life cycles. The product life cycle is broken into four stages: introduction, growth, maturity, and decline. This concept is used by management and by marketing professionals as a factor in deciding when it is appropriate to increase advertising, reduce prices, expand to new markets, or redesign packaging.

The product introduction phase generally includes a substantial investment in advertising and a marketing campaign focused on making consumers aware of the product and its benefits. Assuming the product is successful, it enters its growth phase. Demand grows, production is increased, and its availability expands.

As a product matures, it enters its most profitable stage, while the costs of producing and marketing decline. However, it inevitably begins to take on increased competition as other companies emulate its success, sometimes with enhancements or lower prices. The product may lose market share and begin its decline.

It is a very important approach to understand, how long product will last because the product is integrated with the company revenue.

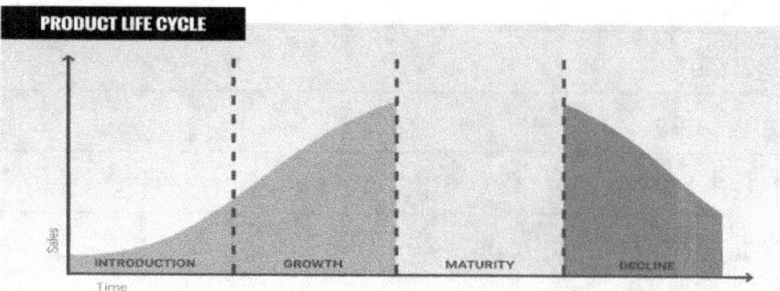

Fraction of Sales by Product Life Cycle

Segment	2013	2014	2015	2016	2017	2018
iPhone	53%	56%	66%	63%	62%	63%
iPad	19%	17%	10%	10%	8%	7%
Mac	13%	13%	11%	11%	11%	10%
iPod	3%	1%				
Services	9%	10%	9%	11%	13%	7%
Other Products	3%	3%	4%	5%	6%	6%
Total	100%	100%	100%	100%	100%	100%

Apple

Apple iPad and iPod is already lost the competitive advantage and now in the decline phase.

While analysing the product analysis, you must be sure to know the details of the product life cycle, it is very much important to predict the company financial position and earnings.

5. The product contributes largely on revenue need to be re-invented?

Digital technology is simultaneously friend and foe: highly disruptive, yet it cannot be ignored. Companies that fail to make use of it put themselves in the line of fire for disintermediation or even eradication. But digital technology is also the biggest opportunity to reposition incumbent product-making businesses by thinking about how they conceive, make, distribute and support the next generation of goods in the marketplace.

Reinventing the Product makes a stringent case for companies to rethink their product strategy, their innovation and engineering processes, and the entire culture to build the future generations of successful 'living products'.

Let take an example of Apple and Microsoft , as Apple always bring new iPhone with new fresh look and updated features so that the customer will buy a upgraded mobile phone with new price .

Same applicable with Microsoft, as they have Microsoft window, they always bring updated version and new features so that customer can use it and be with the brand, don't switch to the other brand.

Apple Card

CEO Cook spoke about the company's goal to "replace the wallet" with Apple Pay, which it says is on target to surpass 10 billion transaction in more than 40 countries. Next in the payments world for the tech giant is a brand new service called Apple Card, created in partnership with Goldman Sachs Group Inc. (GS) and MasterCard Inc. (MA). The firm says its finance arm is hyper-focused on simplicity, privacy and security. Users can sign up on the iPhone and start using the no-fee card within minutes. Instead of points, Apple is offering daily cash back on all purchases. Apple says its interest rates will be among the lowest in the industry. Also available to Apple Pay users is a swanky titanium, laser-etched bank card with no expiration, number or signature. Apple Card is slated to come to the wallet app in the US this year.

Apples News +

Apple also announced plans to integrate its Apple News platform, which it says is now the leading News app, with a new magazine service: it launched a paid Apple News Plus subscription service. The platform boasts access to over 300 magazines across a wide range of topics, including the LA Times and The Wall Street Journal. At a price of $9.99 per month with family sharing, and the first month free, Apple says customers are gaining access to over $8,000 worth of subscriptions with a highly personalized service.

6. Is the product will remain the same as now to contribute in revenue?

Value investor like to invest in the company where the product remains the same reason for that is, company sell same product for decades then only you are able to predict the earning, if the product will change, then it is not at all possible to predict the earning.

Warren Buffett buys company, that will be doing same for around more than fifty years, like Coca –Cola, it is in business of selling soft drink since May 8, 1886; 133 years ago, if you will buy a company whose product get change in some years, then it is not at all possible to make any kind of analysis.

Coca-Cola, or Coke, is a carbonated soft drink manufactured by The Coca-Cola Company. Originally marketed as a temperance drink and intended as a patent medicine, it was invented in the late 19th century by John Stith Pemberton and was bought out by businessman Asa Griggs Candler, whose marketing tactics led Coca-Cola to its dominance of the world soft-drink market throughout the 20th century.

The American Express Company, also known as Amex, is an American multinational financial services corporation headquartered at 200 Vesey Street in New York City. The company was founded in 1850 and is one of the 30 components of the Dow Jones Industrial Average. The company is best known for its charge card, credit card, and traveler's cheque businesses.

In 2016, credit cards using the American Express network accounted for 22.9% of the total dollar volume of credit card transactions in the United States. As of December 31, 2019, the company had 114.4 million cards in force, including 54.7 million cards in force in the United States, each with an average annual spending of $19,972.

Nestlé's origins date back to the 1860s, when two separate Swiss enterprises were founded that would later form Nestlé. In the following decades, the two competing enterprises expanded their businesses throughout Europe and the United States.

In 1866, Charles Page (US consul to Switzerland) and George Page, brothers from Lee County, Illinois, USA, established the Anglo-Swiss Condensed Milk Company in Cham, Switzerland. The company's first British operation was opened at Chippenham, Wiltshire, in 1873

Nestlé's products include baby food, medical food, bottled water, breakfast cereals, coffee and tea, confectionery, dairy products, ice cream, frozen food, pet foods, and snacks. Twenty-nine of Nestlé's brands have annual sales of over CHF1 billion (about US$1.1 billion), including Nespresso, Nescafé, Kit Kat, Smarties, Nesquik, Stouffer's, Vittel, and Maggi. Nestlé has 447 factories, operates in 189 countries, and employs around 339,000 people. It is one of the main shareholders of L'Oreal, the world's largest cosmetics company.

7. Is the product largely depending on Research and Development?

As a value investor we ignore that kind of company who is largely depend on R&D, but some exception is there like in Apple due to the iPhone product, warren buffet has bought the company, other than other businesses he doesn't have any R&D like in financial sector or in non-Durable such as Nestle, Johnson & Johnson.

There was many information technology company was started and when the tech bubble happened all company got bankrupted, this is one of the main issues and risk to buy such stock as compare as nestle sell coffee or baby powder etc, there is not much R&D, the product will be remaining same as now and always.

Consolidated Statement of Income McDonald's	
In millions, except per share data	Years ended December 31, 2019
REVENUES	
Sales by Company-operated restaurants	$ 9,420.8
Revenues from franchised restaurants	11,655.7
Total revenues	21,076.5
OPERATING COSTS AND EXPENSES	
Company-operated restaurant expenses	
Food & paper	2,980.3
Payroll & employee benefits	2,704.4
Occupancy & other operating expenses	2,075.9
Franchised restaurants-occupancy expenses	2,200.6
Selling, general & administrative expenses	2,229.4
Other operating (income) expense, net	(183.9)
Total operating costs and expenses	12,006.7

In the income statement of McDonald's there is nothing call R&D, they don't have to do any kind of expenses to update the product, that is one of the problems in the technology sector, if technology company like Apple, Google have poor R&D they will be vanished.

Apple Inc.

CONSOLIDATED STATEMENTS OF OPERATIONS
(In millions, except number of shares which are reflected in thousands and per share amounts)

	Years ended		
	September 29, 2018	September 30, 2017	September 24, 2016
Net sales	$ 265,595	$ 229,234	$ 215,639
Cost of sales	163,756	141,048	131,376
Gross margin	101,839	88,186	84,263
Operating expenses:			
Research and development	14,236	11,581	10,045
Selling, general and administrative	16,705	15,261	14,194
Total operating expenses	30,941	26,842	24,239

In the Apple Income Statement, they have shared the expenses in the R&D expenses, around 5.36% from the revenue they do the expenses, to update the product, the total amount expenses are around $14 Billion in a fiscal year 2018.

8. Does the company have superior product compare with competitor's product?

Product differentiation is a marketing strategy that strives to distinguish a company's products or services from the competition. Successful product differentiation involves identifying and communicating the unique qualities of a company's offerings while highlighting the distinct differences between those offerings and others on the market. Product differentiation goes hand-in-hand with developing a strong value proposition to make a product or service attractive to a target market or audience.

Product differentiation is intended to prod the consumer into choosing one brand over another in a crowded field of competitors. It identifies the qualities that set one product apart from other similar products and uses those differences to drive consumer choice. Differentiation marketing can also involve focusing on a niche market. For example, a small company might find it challenging to compete with a much larger competitor in the same industry

Let see the example of Apple vs. Samsung in Smartphone segment, both are into same manufacturing and selling of phone, but Apple iPhone is expensive compare with Samsung with the entire budget, but still customer like to buy Apple.

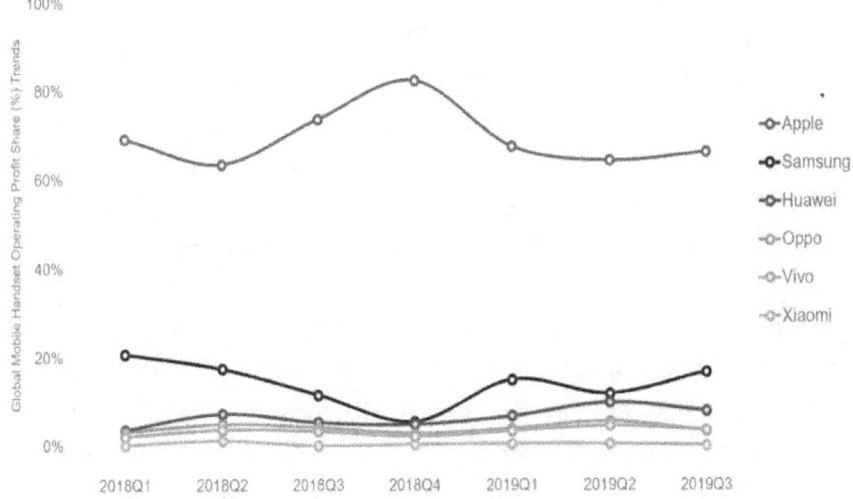

All smart phone manufacture mobile phone but Apple is only company who is making money in the industry.

Profit from Mobile Handset

- Apple 60%-80%
- Samsung 15% - 18%
- Others below 10%

With this example we can easily understand that apple have a superior product compare with their competitors' product.

9. Can company increase the price of product?

Pricing power generally refers to the ability to raise your price without reducing demand in your products. Basically, the more pricing power you have, the easier it is to raise prices. When you ask yourself, "How much pricing power do I have," it is the same as asking, "How much can I raise the price of my products before customers get upset?"

Providers in competitive industries tend to move in trends as well. Therefore, a single company's decision to raise prices may simply mean that pricing in the industry as a whole has increased. Often, more competition tends to restrict upward pricing in an industry. However, advanced technology or increases in product benefits can cause a single provider or the industry to go through price hike evolution. In essence, customers get more from the advances so companies charge more.

The biggest mistake many businesses make is to believe that price alone drives sales. Your ability to sell is what drives sales and that means hiring the right sales people and adopting the right sales strategy. "The first thing you have to understand is the selling price is a function of your ability to sell and nothing else," says Lawrence L. Steinmetz, co-author of *How to Sell at Margins Higher Than Your Competitors : Winning Every Sale at Full Price, Rate, or Fee* (Wiley 2005) and a business consultant in Boulder, Colo. for 40 years. "What's the difference between an $8,000 Rolex and a $40 Seiko watch? The Seiko is a better time piece. It's far more accurate". The difference is your ability to sell."

There are other reasons to go into business. Understand what you want out of your business when pricing your products. Aside from maximizing profits, it may be important for you to maximize market share with your product -- that may help you decrease your costs or it may result in what economists call "network effects," i.e., the value of your product increases as more people use it. (A great example of a product having network effect is Microsoft's Windows operating system. When more people began to use Windows over rival products, more software developers made applications to run on that platform.)

You may also want your product to be known for its quality, rather than just being the cheapest on the market. If so, you may want to price your product higher to reflect the quality. During a downturn, you may have other business priorities, such as sheer survival, so you may want to price your products to recoup enough to keep your company in business.

Apple enjoy the pricing power such as:

- **Generate Brand Awareness**
- **Create an Experience**
- **Build Trust**
- **Continuous improvement**
- **Foster Brand Loyalty**

Generate Brand Awareness

According to a *GraphicSprings* study, Apple's brand awareness tops all other global tech companies. Their ability to keep their branding simple, aesthetically pleasing, and also marketing in an exciting and informative way hugely contributes to their branding success.

Create an Experience

Obviously, Apple is very effective at nurturing this type of connection. One of the biggest reasons people love Apple is because they feel like their lives will be substantially improved by their products. Their products are powerful yet inclusive. They make our lives easier while making us feel like part of a group that is sleek, stylish and elite.

Build Trust

This is a huge component of Apple's business philosophy. There are device support phone numbers and tech support personnel at every store to help when people are having trouble with their devices. They are patient when releasing new products to guarantee quality and consistency. Consumers trust their standard of excellence, which demonstrates how their branding influences perception.

Continuous improvement

A big contributor to Apple's success is that they know that one successful product does not ensure brand power. In order to gain a competitive reputation, a company has to provide enough evidence that their name *guarantees* quality. This means products should evolve and continuously improve. Companies who do not continue to grow and adapt will always be left behind.

Foster Brand Loyalty

Apple's business model works in such a way that the more people spend on their products, the more valuable their investments become. Apple products work best with other Apple products. Whether it's pairing different devices, connecting with Bluetooth, or even just iMessaging/Facetiming with other Apple users, they have fostered a sense of community and status that comes with owning their products. Before people can even consider switching to a new provider, they have to consider all they would be giving up. The brand loyalty that they have instilled in their customers has aided them in becoming the industry leaders that they are today.

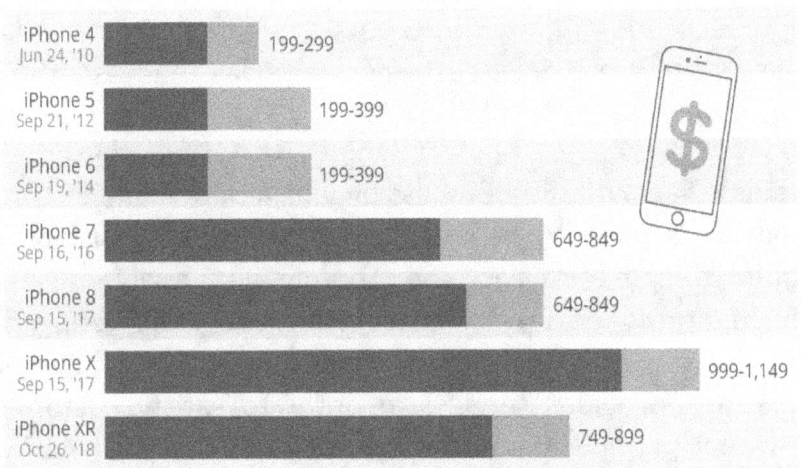

13

Customer Analysis

A customer is an individual or business that purchases another company's goods or services. Customers are important because they drive revenues; without them, businesses have nothing to offer. Most public-facing businesses compete with other companies to attract customers, either by aggressively advertising their products or by lowering prices to expand their customer bases.

Businesses often honor the adage "the customer is always right" because happy customers are more likely to award repeat business to companies who meet or exceed their needs. As a result, many companies closely monitor their customer relationships to solicit feedback on methods to improve product lines. Customers are categorized in many ways. Most commonly, customers are classified as external or internal.

Customer analytics is a process by which data from customer behavior is used to help make key business decisions via market segmentation and predictive analytics. This information is used by businesses for direct marketing, site selection, and customer relationship management. Marketing provides services in order to satisfy customers. With that in mind, the productive system is considered from its beginning at the production level, to the end of the cycle at the consumer. Customer analytics plays an important role in the prediction of customer behavior.

1. Customer is an individual or a business organization?

While doing the customer analysis, the first question we need to ask is the customer is an individual or an organization, to underhand this, we need to go through the annual report of the company, we wish to invest.

Individual

People buy for themselves or for the family.

Organization

Buy for the other business or associations.

Both individuals and organizations need to purchase items to accomplish their daily tasks. There is a large difference, however, in how and why an organization purchases goods and services versus how an individual shop. Understanding these differences is important if you want to tap into both an organizational and a consumer market.

Apple Inc

The Company's customers are primarily in the consumer, small and mid-sized business, education, enterprise and government markets. The Company sells its products and resells third-party products in most of its major markets directly to consumers and small and mid-sized businesses through its retail and online stores and its direct sales force. The Company also employs a variety of indirect distribution channels, such as third-party cellular network carriers, wholesalers, retailers and value-added resellers. During 2016, the Company's net sales through its direct and indirect distribution channels accounted for 25% and 75%, respectively, of total net sales.

JOHNSON & JOHNSON

Distributed to wholesalers, hospitals and retailers, and used principally in the professional fields by physicians, nurses, hospitals, eye care professionals and clinics.

Manpower Group

Governments, office, call centre and industrial services Company, IT company.

Axfood

Health-conscious consumers, residential Customer, Online and Large Convenience Store Chain.

2. Does business depends on multiple customers or largely single customer?

This question is based on the risk analysis, if the company largely depend on the single customer, in that case the risk of losing the single customer always will be high compare to the multiple customers, let see some example

Procter & Gamble

Customers: mass merchandisers, grocery stores, membership club stores, drug stores, department stores, distributors, baby stores, specialty beauty stores, e-commerce, high-frequency stores and pharmacies. We utilize our superior marketing and online presence. Wal-Mart Stores, Inc. and its affiliates represent approximately 15% of our total revenue in 2016, 2015 and 2014. No other customer represents more than 10% of our net sales. Our top ten customers account for approximately 35% of our total sales in 2016, 2015 and 2014.

Infosys

Customer

Financial services (FS) 27.1%

Manufacturing (MFG) 11.0%

Energy & utilities, Communication and Services (ECS) 22.5%

Retail, Consumer packaged goods and Logistics (RCL) 16.4%

Life Sciences, Healthcare and Insurance (HILIFE) 12.3%

Hi-Tech 7.5%

All other Segments 3.2%

DaVita

Customer

Medicare and Medicare-assigned plans 55 %

Medicaid and Medicaid-assigned plans 5 %

Other government-based programs 4 %

Total government-based programs 64 %

Commercial (including hospital dialysis services) 36 %

Total dialysis and related lab services revenues 100 %

It is better not to depend on single customer, when you look for a company, make sure look into this area.

3. Does each product segment have different customer?

Many companies sell different product in different industry, we need to analyse each and every segment, when company sell different product, then the customer will also differ as per the product segment.

NESTLE

SEGMENT	PRODUCT
Powdered and liquid beverages	Nescafé, Nespresso, Coffee-Mate, Nestea
Pet care	Purina, Dog Chow, Gourmet
Confectionery	Nestle Chocolates, Kit Kat, Crunch
Prepared dishes and cooking aids	Maggi, Buitoni, DiGiorno, Hot Pockets, Lean Cuisine
Nutrition and healthcare	Cerelac, Gerber
Milk products & ice cream	Nesquick, Ovaltine, Milo, Häagen-Dazs, Dreyer's, Edy's
Water	Perrier, Poland Spring, Pure Life, San Pellegrino

Nestle are in different product with different segment of customer from beverage to milk product and pet care.

APPLE

Segment	Brands
Computer	Mac
Software	iTunes, Software and Services
Consumer Electronic	iPhone
Music	iPod
Pay	other Product

Apple is in Smartphone to service segment and each segment have different customer.

4. Is customer willing to pay the higher price?

There are two ways to think before answer this question such as:

- Can company increase the price?
- Is customer still pay for the high price?

In the business analysis we have already understand about the increase in price by the company, but what if customer is ready to pay? that is the question we need to answer, we will look for the answer in two prospect such as

- When the company increase in price what is the number of Unit Company sold?
- Three things can happen; first sale will increase, stable or shrink.

As you are aware of Apple Inc. increase the price of iPhone every year, so we need to check the unit they have sold in that year to determine, even when price increase, customer willing to buy in high price.

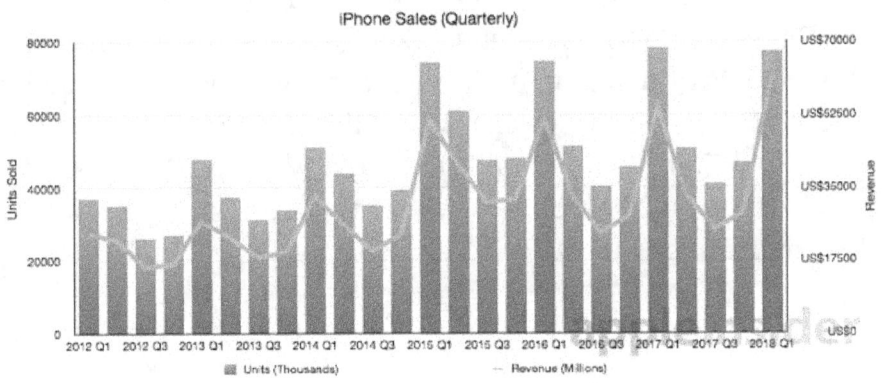

While apple was increasing the price and sale was also increasing, as a value investor, you need to look close to area, where price play an important role, those company don't have barrier to entry and are durable competitive advantage, cannot performance like apple. Smartphone industry is very price sensitive.

This is one of the reasons why warren buffet hold apple stock, price play everything in a company, if company don't be able to increase price wondering that sale will be effect, it states that there is no monopoly in the business, don't invest in such companies, you can never make money.

Fixed price of Coca-Cola from 1886 to 1959

Between 1886 and 1959, the price of a 6.5-oz glass or bottle of Coca-Cola was set at five cents, or one nickel, and remained fixed with very little local fluctuation. The Coca-Cola Company was able to maintain this price for several reasons, including bottling contracts the company signed in 1899, advertising, vending machine technology, and a relatively low rate of inflation. The fact that the price of the drink was able to remain the same for over seventy years is especially significant considering the events that occurred during that period, including the founding of Pepsi, World War I, Prohibition, changing taxes, a caffeine and caramel shortage, World War II, and the company's desire to raise its prices. Much of the research on this subject comes from "The Real Thing": Nominal Price Rigidity of the Nickel Coke, 1886–1959, a 2004 paper by economists Daniel Levy and Andrew Young.

5. Does customer base getting strong?

The customer base is the group of customers who repeatedly purchase the goods or services of a business. These customers are a main source of revenue for a company. The customer base may be considered the business's target market, where customer behaviors are well understood through market research or past experience. Relying on a customer base can make growth and innovation difficult.

Companies with a customer base consisting mainly of large companies may increase their customer base by pursuing small and mid-size companies.

As companies grow their customer base, and gain experience satisfying them, their customers grow accustomed to that business accomplishing a certain task for them. The company or product's brand name may even correlate with the task the customer uses it for. Xerox, Kleenex, and Band-Aid are some extreme cases of brand-names being used as the generic name of the product itself. In fact, as long as customers are continually satisfied with their purchases, the act of going to that company's brand to accomplish a specific task becomes habitual.

Repeat buyers and users are also useful for further reasons, as they are the source of "word of mouth" advertising. Studies have shown that customer satisfaction with a brand leads to more purchases, from both the same and new customers. A satisfied customer expresses their enjoyment in the product, or even shows a friend the product and has them try it out, and a dissatisfied customer may speak against a product or not mention it at all. Of course, the core consumer is the main spreader of the company's brand name, and the more they use and like what they consume, the more those that surround them will gain interest and then potentially become customers themselves.

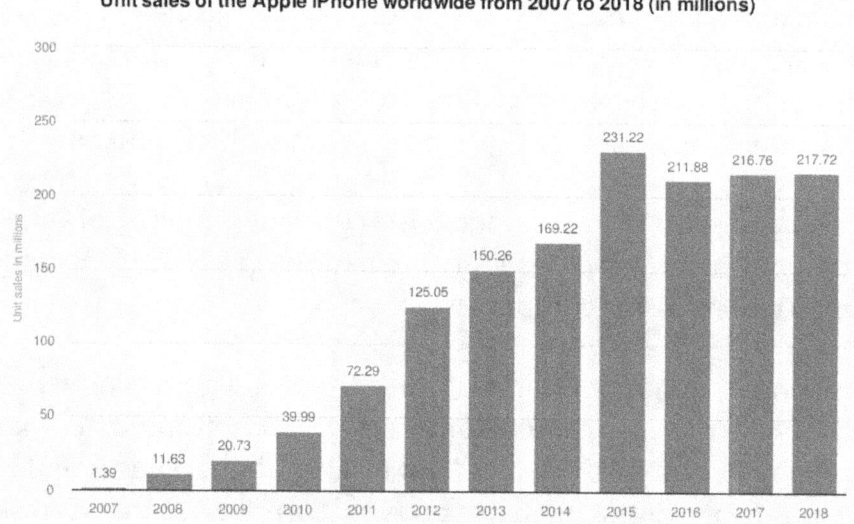

Number of unit state that the number of users purchase the iPhone, in this way, we can able to understand, are the customer base increasing or decreasing.

As in Apple in fiscal year 2007 was 1.39 million customers and in 2018 it is 217.72 million, there is a good increase in sale of iPhone and customer base.

Avenue Super Mart Ltd listen in India, it is primarily engaged in the business of organized retail and operates supermarkets under the brand name of D-Mart.

From 6.7 Crore total bill cut in 2014-2015 to 17.2 crore in 2018-2019, the increase in the bill cut state that the increase in customer base.

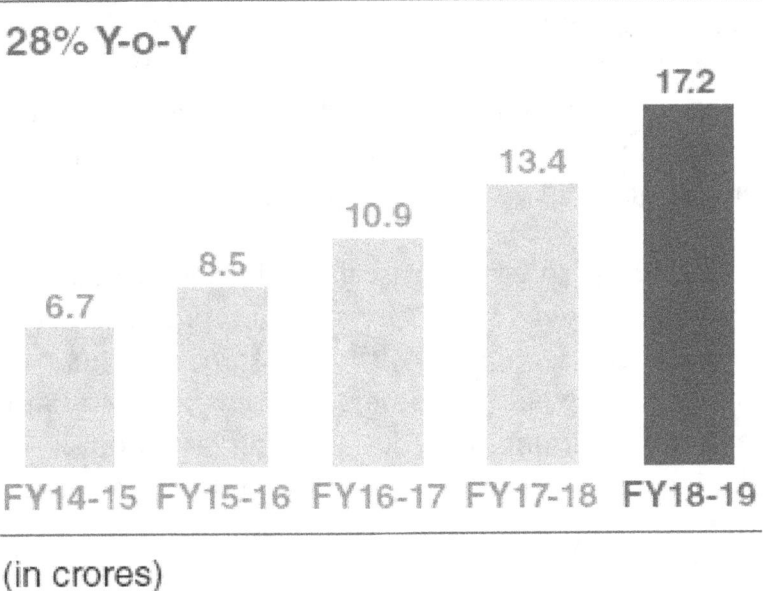

A value investor needs to look in this direction to understand the customer base and then invest.

6. Does customer base is sustainable?

Sustainable growth is among the biggest challenges any business, today company needed to create long-term value for the customer. In order to achieve sustainable success, companies must repeatedly re-examine their sense of purpose and make sure the organization serves it well.

Company wants to create a scalable business; you have to understand how crucial it is to build brand equity and emotional connections with customers. It's those attachments that link customers to your products and will keep them returning to you. Building a brand is about developing and sustaining those relationships over time.

As Emmet and Mark Murphy write in their book Leading on the Edge of Chaos, acquiring new customers can cost an organization around five times more than retaining current ones. In fact, a 2% increase in customer retention can have the same effect as decreasing a company's costs by 10%. To put it another way, reducing customer defection rates by just 5% could increase profitability by 25% to 130%, depending on the industry.

A company's needs change at each stage, its leaders need to keep evolving at the right pace. That requires introspection, self-awareness, and a keen sense of strategy—both in the short and long term.

I believe that an adaptive, flexible leadership style comes from being mindful. Our individual, interpersonal, and working lives are all interconnected. By being mindful, we understand those relationships and how best to utilize them to create, innovate, and lead.

And that allows us to arrange our lives and our organizations in a way that leads to long-term value creation. Indeed, the most sustainable way to create value is to continually invest in our capabilities, both as individuals *and* as organizations.

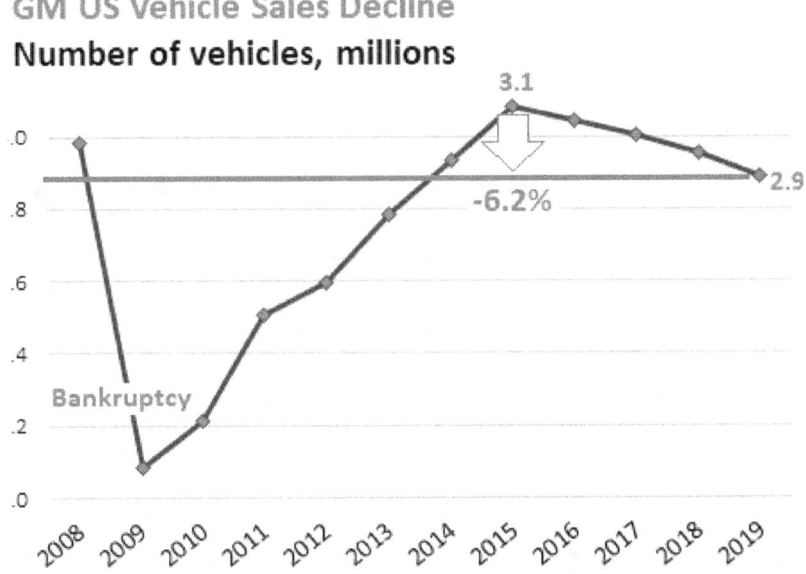

GM has no advantage in customer base, they sell car as per industry in 2015 the number is customer bought the car was 3.1 million and in 2019 it is 2.9 million and still its shows downward trend, as we compare with Amazon Prime in 2013 was 25 million and dec 2019 it was 112 million.

When we look at the company customer base in three ways such as:

- Increasing – Excellent
- Sustainable – Good
- Shrinking – Very Poor

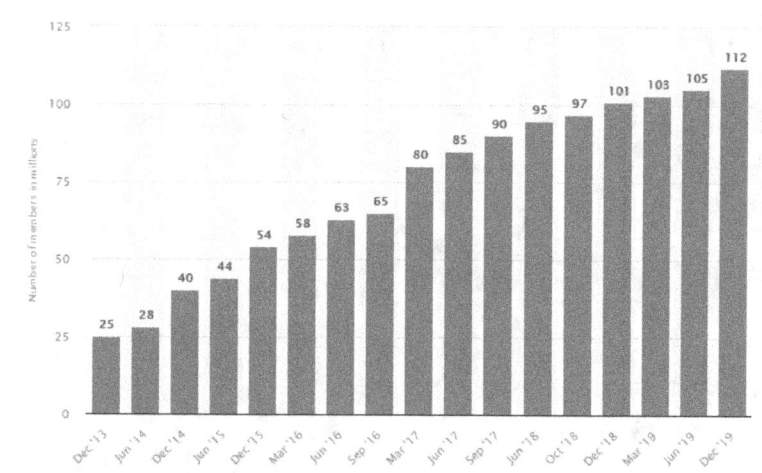

If you would have invested in GM in 2013 for paying $40 each stock, now it would be in 2020 $22 and if you would have invested in Amazon in 2013 for paying $300 and now it the current price is $ 2474.

This is kind of decision; you need to make while selecting the stock.

7. Does Company enjoy customer captivity?

Captive markets are markets where the potential consumers face a severely limited number of competitive suppliers; their only choices are to purchase what is available or to make no purchase at all. Captive markets result in higher prices and less diversity for consumers. [Citation needed] The term therefore applies to any market where there is a monopoly or oligopoly.

The customers who are "captured "by a product /vendor and are resistant to use another product/vendor primarily because of the following reasons:

The costs involved in switching to a competitor is high

This may be primarily because of the following reasons

- The customer has invested a lot of time in adapting to the product

- The customer's preferences and choices are not yet mastered by the competitors

- Traditionally the customers have been using it since a long time and they are reluctant in being accustomed to a different product altogether.

- The customer may not want to lose the advantages of the products such as offers, complementary products etc.

- The costs involved in searching for a competitor is high. This is the case especially when the customer searches for a new product/service.

- The product/vendor has become a habit for the customer.

The captive customer can be of great competitive advantage for any firm. The firms may encourage purchases by the captive customers through discounts, loyalty programs and various offers. They may also reinforce the competitive advantage by adding new features to the product. The firms may lose such competitive advantage in cases when the competitor's switching and searching costs are reduced.

Microsoft Corporation (NASDAQ: MSFT), one of the largest companies in the world, thoroughly understands how to build competitive advantage. Some call this advantage similar to a protective moat that keeps other firms from taking its market share. Economies of scale, the network effect, brand strength, intellectual property and regulation can all contribute to competitive moats. Without these factors in place, competition from comparable products and services eventually erode operating margins. This sustainability of *advantage* is hugely important for investors that follow the philosophies of Charlie Munger or Warren Buffett.

These competitive advantages illustrate how Microsoft operates globally with popular product suites such as Windows, Office and Azure. Network effect, economies of scale and strong brand all work in Microsoft's favor, but it operates in highly competitive markets that are changing at accelerating rates. Morningstar assigns Microsoft a wide economic moat based on the recent competitive success of Office and cloud products, but tumbling margins and profits approaching the opportunity cost of capital are troublesome signs that the moat may be unsustainable.

Warren Buffett helped develop and popularize the concept of an economic moat, defined as a sustainable competitive advantage that allows a company to generate an economic profit for the foreseeable future. Without a moat, margins will eventually erode until they become equal to return on invested capital (ROIC). Moats can be established by economies of scale, network effects, intellectual property, brand identity or legal exclusivity.

Buffett's strategy revolves around identifying companies with sustainable moats that generate cash flow, estimating the present value of future cash flows and purchasing stock when the price dips below the present value of those cash flows.

14

Supplier Analysis

A supplier is an entity that supplies goods and services to another organization. This entity is part of the supply chain of a business, which may provide the bulk of the value contained within its products. A supplier is usually a manufacturer or a distributor.

In a business we need to see who the supplier to the company is we would like to invest.

Many companies have supplier performance or supplier management programs. These programs, typically designed to measure, reward and penalize suppliers based on performance, often do more harm than good.

- suppliers and the supply chain
- demand and how it affects the market
- current prices, and factors that may affect the price
- market trends and technological developments
- present and future market behaviours that could affect price and availability
- competition within the market

1. Does Business depend on single supplier or multiple suppliers?

Value investor is interested in multiple suppliers, no single supplier. The problem company may face such as with single supplier

- Low bargaining power with the supplier.

- If there is only one source, it is more difficult for the buyer to ensure that they are keeping their company competitive.

- In periods of tight supply, the buyer may be at a disadvantage in being able to ask other suppliers to accept orders.

- Other suppliers may lose interest in trying to compete for the business if they see that a sole-source situation is likely to persist.

- Buyers may be facing a real risk if the single source has a catastrophic event, gets bought by a buyer's competitor, or has financial problems.

Advantage of Multiple suppliers

- Bargaining power with the company.

- Alternative sources of material in the case of stoppage by the supplier.

- Reduced probability of shortage of material.

- Increase competition between the suppliers that leads to better quality product.

- Enjoy the extension of credit from the supplier.

Bic

Company supplier includes plastics, metals, packaging, and inks from over 2000 supplier. Group, being a responsible Company means maintaining control over the entire value chain. To this end, the Purchasing departments analyse all risks: stock levels, diversification of suppliers and sourcing zones, risks associated with the country and the rarity of the resource.

2. Does supplier supply product in credit to the company?

To know this, we need to look at Accounts payable, from there we can able to understand company enjoy extension of credit against the goods or material.

Accounts payable (AP) is an account within the general ledger that represents a company's obligation to pay off a short-term debt to its creditors or suppliers. Another common usage of "AP" refers to the business department or division that is responsible for making payments owed by the company to suppliers and other creditors.

A company's total accounts payable (AP) balance at a specific point in time will appear on its balance sheet under the current liabilities section. Accounts payable are debts that must be paid off within a given period to avoid default. At the corporate level, AP refers to short-term debt payments due to suppliers. The payable is essentially a short-term IOU from one business to another business or entity. The other party would record the transaction as an increase to its accounts receivable in the same amount.

Accounts payable (AP) is an important figure in a company's balance sheet. If AP increases over a prior period, that means the company is buying more goods or services on credit, rather than paying cash. If a company's AP decreases, it means the company is paying on its prior period debts at a faster rate than it is purchasing new items on credit.

Accounts payable management is critical in managing a business's cash flow.

Let see some example

Balance Sheet — WAL MART STORES INC (WMT)

Standardized | As Reported
In millions, except per share items

	Jan-31-20 10-K
Assets	
Cash and equivalents	9,465.0
Accounts receivable, net	6,284.0
Inventories	44,435.0
Other current assets	1,622.0
Total current assets	61,806.0
Property, plant, and equipment, net	105,208.0
Goodwill	31,073.0
Other fixed assets	16,567.0
Total assets	236,495.0
Accounts payable	46,973.0
Accrued expenses	22,296.0
Short-term and curr portion of long-term debt [+]	5,937.0
Other current liabilities	2,584.0
Total current liabilities	77,790.0
Long-term debt	43,714.0
Other liabilities	12,961.0
Total liabilities	134,465.0

Walmart Accounts Receivable is $6 Billion it means that they received the cash early and make the payment to the supplier $46 Billion, after the product is sold to the customer, this state that company enjoy credit buy the supplier.

This is a good way to understand about financial cash cycle of the business and company enjoy competitive advantage.

15

Competitors Analysis

Any person or entity which is a rival against another. In business, a company in the same industry or a similar industry which offers a similar product or service. The presence of one or more competitors can reduce the prices of goods and services as the companies attempt to gain a larger market share. Competition also requires companies to become more efficient in order to reduce costs. Fast-food restaurants McDonald's and Burger King are competitors, as are Coca-Cola and Pepsi, and Wal-Mart and Target.

Competition in business is the contest or rivalry among the companies selling similar products and/or targeting the same target audience to get more sales, increase revenue, and gain more market share as compared to others.

An excellent example of direct competitors is Burger King and McDonald's business rivalry. Both of these companies –

- Operate in the same industry (fast-food)
- Offer similar products (burgers and related fast-food products)
- Satisfy the same need
- Use same channels of distribution (retail chains, takeaway, and home delivery)
- Target the same audience (working individuals)

A competitive analysis is a critical part of your company marketing plan. With this evaluation, you can establish what makes your product or service unique--and therefore what attributes you play up in order to attract your target market.

Evaluate your competitors by placing them in strategic groups according to how directly they compete for a share of the customer's dollar. For each competitor or strategic group, list their product or service, its profitability, growth pattern, marketing objectives and assumptions, current and past strategies, organizational and cost structure, strengths and weaknesses, and size (in sales) of the competitor's business.

1. Who are the major competitors?

Every business has major competitors that try to take the market share and make more profit out of that share.

Google (GOOG) is a technology company whose mission is to "organize the world's information and make it universally accessible and useful." Founded in 1998 and headquartered in Mountain View, Calif., the company has grown to become one of the most innovative companies in the modern technological age. Since Google was broken out into Google, Inc. and the parent company Alphabet, Inc., the company has only continued to grow, touching sectors from its traditional search engine to advertising, science, entertainment, and autonomous vehicles, just to name a few. Due to its cross-cutting products and services, Google's competitors vary.

In the online search arena, Google is nearly a monopoly with over 94% of the online search volume and market. This leaves little room for competitors trying to outsmart and outperform the search engine, which generates its revenue through ads. The second largest search engine and the main competitor to Google is Yahoo (AABA), which has a 2.32% market share as of October 2018.

Other companies considered to be Google's main competitors include technology giant Microsoft's search engine, Bing, as well as Internet pioneer and media company AOL. It should be noted that in other countries such as China, Google is banned from conducting business; there, the number one search engine is Baidu, which controls 76.05% of the market share.

Apple	Samsung Electronics	Sony	IBM	HP	Microsoft
Apple is a multinational corporation that designs, manufactures and markets mobile communication and media devices.	Samsung Electronics is a company engaged in the manufacture and distribution of electronic products.	Sony is a company that develops, designs, produces and sells electronic equipment, instruments, and devices for consumer, professional and industrial markets, as well as game hardware and software.	International Business Machines Corporation (IBM) is a company providing information technology products and services.	HP is a provider of products, technologies, software, solutions and services to individual consumers, small- and medium-sized businesses.	Microsoft is a technology company that develops and supports software, services, and devices.
1976	1938	1946	1911	1939	1975
Public	Public	Public	Public	Public	Public
Manufacturing & Industrial	Manufacturing & Industrial	Manufacturing & Industrial	Business Products & Services	Manufacturing & Industrial	Technology
Media & Entertainment	Technology	Media & Entertainment	Financial Services	Technology	application software
app development	appliances	appliances	Technology	cloud	artificial intelligence
consumer electronics	consumer electronics	conglomerates	cloud	cloud infrastructure(IaaS)	cloud
content provider	electronic components	consumer electronics	cloud infrastructure(IaaS)	consumer electronics	consumer software
electronics	electronics	distribution	cloud platforms(PaaS)	cybersecurity	developer tools
music	internet of things	electronics	cloud services(SaaS)	electronic components	enterprise software
wearables	semiconductors	platform	it consulting	imaging	games
		video	it services		internet of things
					social networks

2. What is the products wise competition?

Segment	Brands	Competitors
Computer	Mac	Lenova, HP, Toshiba, Acer, Dell
Software	iTunes, Software and Services	Oracle, Mcrosoft, Google
Consumer Electronic	iPhone	Samsung, Nokia, Amazon, Hauwai, Lenova, LG
Music	iPod	Xbox Music, Samsung
Pay	other Product	Google Wallet

Segment wise Apple main competitors list

For Apple Inc they have five segments and each segment they have major competition.

Many of Apple's primary competitors are primarily manufacturers of computers. Dell Technologies (DVMT) is a manufacturer of both desktop and mobile computing devices and one of Apple's primary competitors. The rivalry between these two companies goes back many years, with Dell even attempting to corner some of Apple's share of the mobile music player market with its Dell DJ, designed as an early competitor to the iPod. Dell has participated in numerous acquisitions and other partnerships in recent years, though it does not offer smart phones.

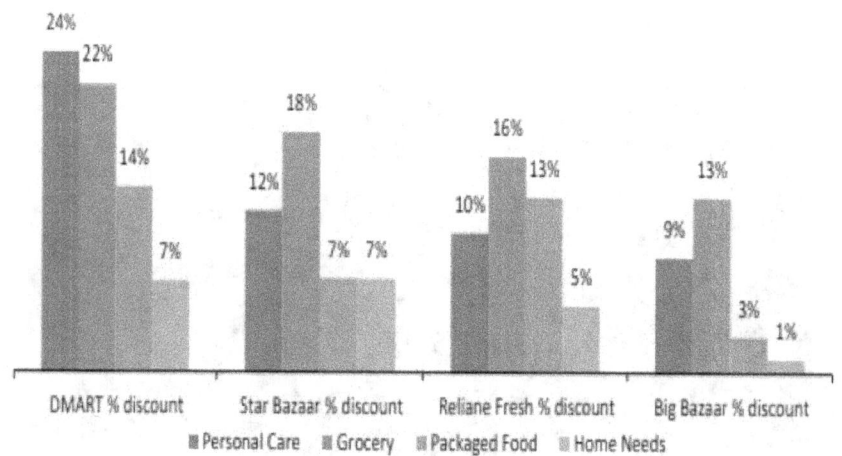

Avenue Super Mart Ltd

We need to check what is the product wise competition.

3. What is the product wise competitor's market share?

As of October 2019, Apple is second largest smartphone company in the world with 22.09% global market share. However, it faces a number of powerful competitors in its global smartphone markets. According to StatCounter (2019), the main competitors and their global market shares are as follows:

Samsung: 31.49%

Huawei: 10.02%

Xiaomi: 7.79%

Oppo: 4.1%

Others: 3.27%

Personal computer market is highly competitive and constantly changing due to technological innovations and the rapid changes in consumers' taste. As of 2018, Apple's market share in the global personal computer market is 6.9% which makes the company the 4th largest in the world. Its main competitors in this global market are Lenovo, HP Inc, Dell, Acer, and Asus.

Worldwide smartphone shipments and annual growth
Canalys Smartphone Market Pulse: Q4 2019

Vendor	Q4 2019 shipments (million)	Q4 2019 market share	Q4 2018 shipments (million)	Q4 2018 market share	Annual growth
Apple	78.4	21.3%	71.7	19.7%	+9%
Samsung	70.8	19.2%	69.9	19.2%	+1%
Huawei	56.0	15.2%	60.5	16.6%	-7%
Xiaomi	33.0	9.0%	26.8	7.3%	+23%
Oppo	30.3	8.2%	29.6	8.1%	+2%
Others	100.2	27.2%	105.6	29.0%	-5%
Total	368.7	100.0%	364.1	100.0%	+1%

ABBOTT INDIA

Market share

NAME OF THE BRAND	2014	2015
THYRONORM	47.50%	52.60%
DUPHASTON	20.30%	19.70%
DIGENE	18.10%	15.50%
UDILIV	23.90%	10.70%
VERTIN	30.00%	33.20%
DUPHALAC	13.70%	13.90%
CREMAFFIN	11.20%	11.80%
ZOLFRESH	16.80%	21.20%
CREMAFFIN PLUS	6.90%	7.60%
CREON	38.30%	37.40%
BRUFEN	97.80%	98.70%
PROTHIADEN		7.00%
HEPTRAL		8.00%
EPILEX		7.50%
NETONIN AST		14.00%
DUVADILAN		50.20%

Abbott India product wise market share, we need to check the product market share in the industry to understand the competition.

4. What is the gross margin and operating margin compare with the competitors?

It indicates how much EBIT is generated per dollar of sales. Naturally, because the operating profit margin accounts for administration and selling costs as well as materials and labor, it should be a much smaller figure than the gross margin.

When all the company are in the same industry, we need to analyse that the what are the profit margin they are operating.

Competitive Comparison Data — Apple

Company	Market Cap (M)	Gross Margin %
Apple Inc	$ 1,285,516.02	37.95
Samsung Electronics C...	$ 272,823.31	36.09
China Electronics Holdi...	$ 124,978.90	0.00
Sony Corp	$ 79,011.94	27.71
Midea Group Co Ltd	$ 53,254.87	28.99
Gree Electric Appliance...	$ 46,670.62	30.23
Xiaomi Corp	$ 31,588.12	13.05
Kyocera Corp	$ 19,565.82	28.12
Haier Smart Home Co ...	$ 18,423.09	28.98
Panasonic Corp	$ 18,018.00	28.82

Competitive Comparison Data Apple

Company	Market Cap (M)	Operating Margin %
Apple Inc	$ 1,285,516.02	24.71
Samsung Electronics ...	$ 272,823.31	12.05
China Electronics Hol...	$ 124,978.90	0.00
Sony Corp	$ 79,011.94	9.41
Midea Group Co Ltd	$ 53,254.87	9.38
Gree Electric Applianc...	$ 46,670.62	13.96
Xiaomi Corp	$ 31,588.12	-3.20
Kyocera Corp	$ 19,565.82	8.04
Haier Smart Home Co...	$ 18,423.09	6.04
Panasonic Corp	$ 18,018.00	4.58

Competitive Comparison Data Walmart Inc

Company	Market Cap (M)	Gross Margin %
Walmart Inc	$ 344,436.47	24.69
Costco Wholesale Corp	$ 133,798.73	12.96
Target Corp	$ 54,851.19	29.76
Dollar General Corp	$ 44,090.59	30.59
Wal - Mart de Mexico S...	$ 43,018.78	22.93
Avenue Supermarts Ltd	$ 20,003.73	31.97
Dollar Tree Inc	$ 18,900.19	29.82
Pan Pacific Internation...	$ 12,325.94	28.83
Dollarama Inc	$ 9,676.16	43.63
Lawson Inc	$ 5,206.30	71.99

Competitive Comparison Data — Walmart Inc

Company	Market Cap (M)	Operating Margin %
Walmart Inc	$ 344,436.47	3.93
Costco Wholesale Corp	$ 133,798.73	3.10
Target Corp	$ 54,851.19	5.96
Dollar General Corp	$ 44,090.59	8.30
Wal - Mart de Mexico ...	$ 43,018.78	8.37
Avenue Supermarts Ltd	$ 20,003.73	25.62
Dollar Tree Inc	$ 18,900.19	6.67
Pan Pacific Internatio...	$ 12,325.94	4.67
Dollarama Inc	$ 9,676.16	22.65
Lawson Inc	$ 5,206.30	8.99

By doing this analysis, you can able to judge the level of competition that reflect in their Gross Margin and Operating Margin.

16
Industry Analysis

An industry is a sector that produces goods or related services within an economy. The major source of revenue of a group or company is an indicator of what industry it should be classified in. When a large corporate group has multiple sources of revenue generation, it is considered to be working in different industries. The manufacturing industry became a key sector of production and labour in European and North American countries during the Industrial Revolution, upsetting previous mercantile and feudal economies. This came through many successive rapid advances in technology, such as the development of steam power and the production of steel and coal.

An industry is a group of companies that are related based on their primary business activities. In modern economies, there are dozens of industry classifications, which are typically grouped into larger categories called sectors.

Similar businesses are grouped into industries based on the primary product produced or sold; creating industry groups that can be used to isolate businesses from those who participate in different activities. Investors and economists often study industries to better understand the factors and limitations of corporate profit growth. Companies operating in the same industry can also be compared to each other to evaluate the relative attractiveness of a company within that industry.

An industry analysis is a business function completed by business owners and other individuals to assess the current business environment. This analysis helps businesses understand various economic pieces of the marketplace and how these various pieces may be used to gain a competitive advantage. Although business owners may conduct an industry analysis according to their specific needs, a few basic standards exist for conducting this important business function.

Industry analysis is a market assessment tool used by businesses and analysts to understand the competitive dynamics of an industry. It helps them get a sense of what is happening in an industry, i.e., demand-supply statistics, degree of competition within the industry, state of competition of the industry with other emerging industries, future prospects of the industry taking into account technological changes, credit system within the industry, and the influence of external factors on the industry.

Industry analysis, for an entrepreneur or a company, is a method that helps it to understand its position relative to other participants in the industry. It helps them to identify both the opportunities and threats coming their way and gives them a strong idea of the present and future scenario of the industry. The key to surviving in this ever-changing business environment is to understand the differences between yourself and your competitors in the industry and using it to your full advantage.

1. In which industry company operate in?

We need to check which all industry company operates in, some companies operate in different industry, so it's important to analyse.

Manpower Group

- **Industry:** Employment Service Industries, workforce solutions and services.

Axfood

- **Industry**: Retail food industry; Online Retail Industry, Food Distribution and Logistics

Procter & Gamble

- **Industry**: branded consumer packaged goods

DaVita

- **Industry:** healthcare industry

Infosys

- **Industry**: IT services, IT consulting

JOHNSON & JOHNSON

- **Industry**: Health Care/Life Sciences

Apple

- **Industry:** Technology industry - Computer hardware, Computer software, Consumer electronics, Digital distribution.

Amazon.com, Inc.

- **Industry:**

  - Cloud Computing
  - E-commerce
  - Artificial intelligence
  - Consumer electronics
  - Digital distribution
  - Grocery stores

Microsoft

- **Industry:**

  - Software development
  - Computer hardware
  - Consumer electronics
  - Social networking service
  - Cloud computing
  - Video games
  - Internet
  - Corporate venture capital

2. Does this Industry & Sector is within your circle of competence?

When you analyse the industry, first try to understand the industry, how it operates and which type of industry it is.

Circle of competence is the subject area which matches a person's skills or expertise. The mental model was developed by Warren Buffett and Charlie Munger to describe limiting one's financial investments in areas where an individual may have limited understanding or experience, concentrating in areas where one has the greatest familiarity, and to emphasize the importance of aligning a subjective assessment of one own's competence with actual competence. Buffett summarized the concept in the motto, "Know your circle of competence, and stick within it. The size of that circle is not very important; knowing its boundaries, however, is vital."

In his 1996 letter to Berkshire Hathaway, Buffett further expanded:

What an investor needs are the ability to correctly evaluate selected businesses. Note that word 'selected': You don't have to be an expert on every company, or even many. You only have to be able to evaluate companies within your circle of competence

"I'm no genius. I'm smart in spots-but I stay around those spots." – Tom Watson Sr., Founder of IBM

I have no understanding whatsoever

I have some high-level understanding

I have a pretty good understanding

I really understand this business and industry

"Everybody's got a different circle of competence. The important thing is not how big the circle is. The important thing is staying inside the circle."

— Warren Buffett

Circle of Competence applies outside of investing.

Buffett describes the circle of competence of one of his business managers, a Russian immigrant with poor English who built the largest furniture store in Nebraska:

I couldn't have given her $200 million worth of Berkshire Hathaway stock when I bought the business because she doesn't understand stock. She understands cash. She understands furniture. She understands real estate. She doesn't understand stocks, so she doesn't have anything to do with them. If you deal with Mrs. B in what I would call her circle of competence... She is going to buy 5,000 end tables this afternoon (if the price is right). She is going to buy 20 different carpets in odd lots, and everything else like that [snaps fingers] because she understands carpet. She wouldn't buy 100 shares of General Motors if it was at 50 cents a share.

It did not hurt Mrs. B to have such a narrow area of competence. In fact, one could argue the opposite. Her rigid devotion to that area allowed her to focus. Only with that focus could she have overcome her handicaps to achieve such extreme success.

So, here's my question: At the end of the day, what do you do? Do you go home and buy some Microsoft stock?

Gates: "You've got to have a computer."

Buffett: "Why?"

Gates: "You can keep track of your stock portfolio."

Buffett: "I only own one stock [Berkshire Hathaway]."

Gates: "Well, you can do your taxes."

Buffett: "I don't have any income. Berkshire doesn't pay a dividend."

Gates: "It's going to change everything."

Buffett: "Will it change whether people chew gum?"

Gates: "Probably not."

Buffett: "Well, then I'll stick to chewing gum, and you stick to computers."

As you might guess, following that meeting, Buffett did not buy a PC, and he didn't buy any Microsoft stock either. In fact, to this day he has never purchased a single share (though he did later buy a computer).

3. What is the Revenue of company compare with the competitors in the same industry?

We need to compare the revenue between two or more company in the same industry, try to find out who is having more revenue in the industry.

What has the trend in Total Revenues been like, for the two companies since 2011?

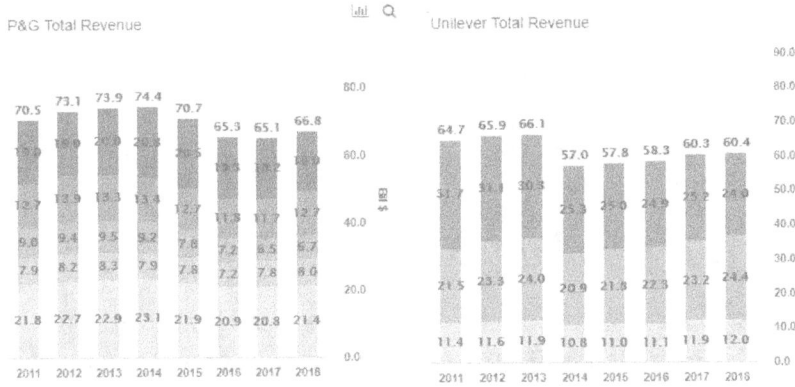

- Unilever and P&G both have seen an overall drop in revenue from 2011-2018, with a 1% average annual drop in revenue for Unilever and around 0.75% for P&G.

- This has been due to a lot of internal reshuffling, with Unilever scaling down on its Food & Refreshment business and instead focusing more on Personal Care, which is evident from the change in revenue share for these 2 segments.

- Similarly, P&G has been scaling back on grooming products, while increasing focus equally on all other segments of revenue.

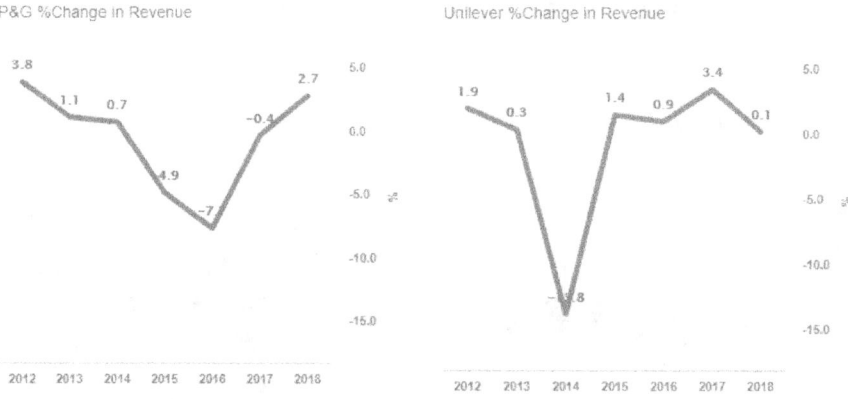

- Overall change in revenue for both companies has been broadly similar, with both experiencing drops in revenue between 2013 and 2016. (NOTE: P&G announces Q4 results in June, while Unilever does so in December).

- This drop was on account of a demand slowdown in emerging markets.

- However, things have gotten better, and both companies have stabilized since.

4. Trends in industry free entrance to competitors or restricted entry in the industry?

When we will do analysis, we need to understand, about the barrier to the entry.

- Free Entry
- Restricted Entry

Free Entry

In economics, free entry is a condition in which firms can freely enter the market for an economic good by establishing production and beginning to sell the product. The assumption of free entry implies that if there are firms earning excessively high profits in a given industry, new firms that also seek a high profit are likely to start to produce or change into a production of the same good to join the market. In such a case there are no barriers preventing a start-up firm from competing. Where an opportunity of a profit arises, we assume that there will also be firms entering the market for the certain good and compete for it. In most markets this condition is present only in the long run.

The assumption of free entry doesn't mean that a firm is simply able to set up a shop without any costs incurred. It is clear that the new entrant needs to gain the capital that they need for operating in the industry. Therefore, even with a free entry to a market the entrant still has to face the same cost structure as does an already existing firm.

Free entry is part of the perfect competition assumption that there are an unlimited number of buyers and sellers in a market. In conditions in which there is not a natural monopoly caused by unlimited economies of scale, free entry prevents any existing firm from maintaining a monopoly, which would restrict output and charge a higher price than a multi-firm market would.

Low barriers to entry

The airline industry is highly competitive and capital-intensive. Because of its capital-intensive nature, fixed costs and barriers to exit are high. Competition in the airline industry is intense as barriers to entry are low due to liberalization of market access, a result of globalization.

Restricted Entry

Barriers to entry enable market control by limiting the number of competitors and thus the availability of close substitutes. Barriers that limit entry into the supply side of market mean that buyers have fewer buying alternatives, which give the sellers greater market control. Barriers that limit entry into the demand side of market means that seller have fewer seller options which give the buyers greater market control.

Large-Scale Infrastructure Ensures Speedy Delivery And Makes Barriers To Entry High For Other E-Commerce Players: Amazon's huge network of delivery, sortation, and fulfilment centres brings the company even closer to the customer, and makes same-day delivery much easier to implement.

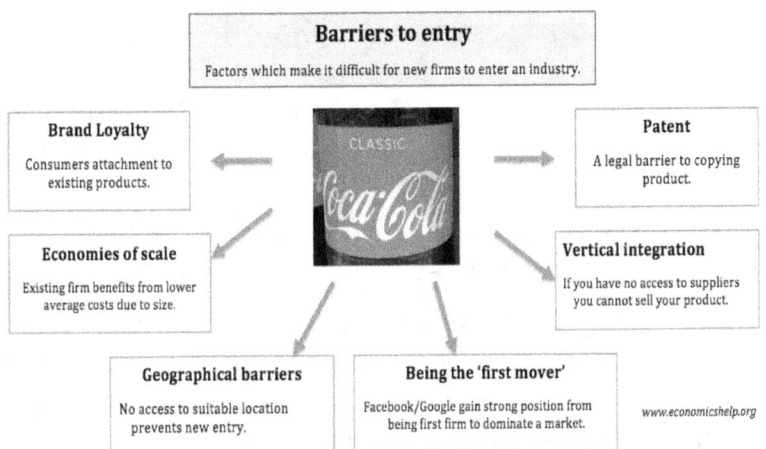

Economies of Scale. This means as firms produce more their average costs fall. Therefore, it is difficult for new, small firms to enter the market and be competitive. For example, a market like tap water is a natural monopoly. There is no point for a new firm to create the national infrastructure of a rival system of water pipes.

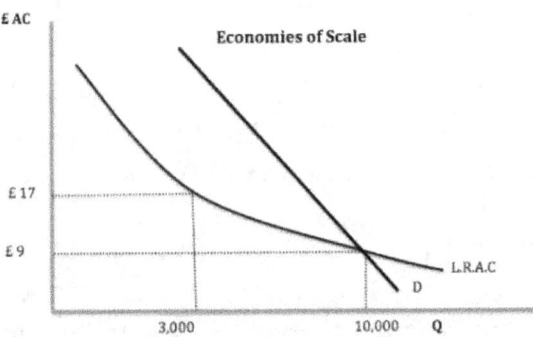

Current industry demand is 10,000. At this Q, average costs are just £9.

If a new firm enters at Q of 3,000, then average costs will be higher at £17.

5. What is the business market share in the industry?

Market share is the percentage of a market (defined in terms of either units or revenue) accounted for by a specific entity.

"Marketers need to be able to translate and incorporate sales targets into market share because this will demonstrate whether forecasts are to be attained by growing with the market or by capturing share from competitors. The latter will almost always be more difficult to achieve. Market share is closely monitored for signs of change in the competitive landscape, and it frequently drives strategic or tactical action." Additionally, market share is a key metric in understanding performance relative to the growth of the market as measurement of internal sales growth (or decline) only may be a result of similar growth or declines in the industry being measured.

Increasing market share is one of the most important objectives of business. The main advantage of using market share as a measure of business performance is that it is less dependent upon macro environmental variables such as the state of the economy or changes in tax policy.

Market share is the percent of total sales in an industry generated by a particular company. Market share is calculated by taking the company's sales over the period and dividing it by the total sales of the industry over the same period. This metric is used to give a general idea of the size of a company in relation to its market and its competitors.

Amazon totally dominates US ecommerce

US ecommerce market share:

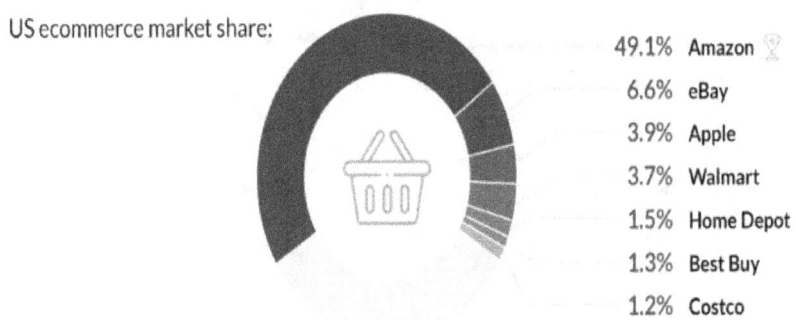

49.1% Amazon
6.6% eBay
3.9% Apple
3.7% Walmart
1.5% Home Depot
1.3% Best Buy
1.2% Costco

Amazon Leads $100 Billion Cloud Market

Worldwide market share of leading cloud infrastructure service providers in Q4 2019*

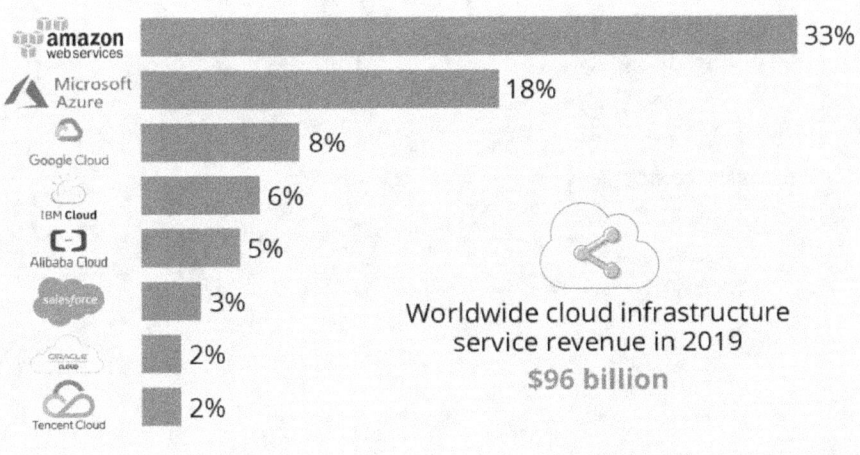

amazon web services — 33%
Microsoft Azure — 18%
Google Cloud — 8%
IBM Cloud — 6%
Alibaba Cloud — 5%
salesforce — 3%
ORACLE cloud — 2%
Tencent Cloud — 2%

Worldwide cloud infrastructure service revenue in 2019
$96 billion

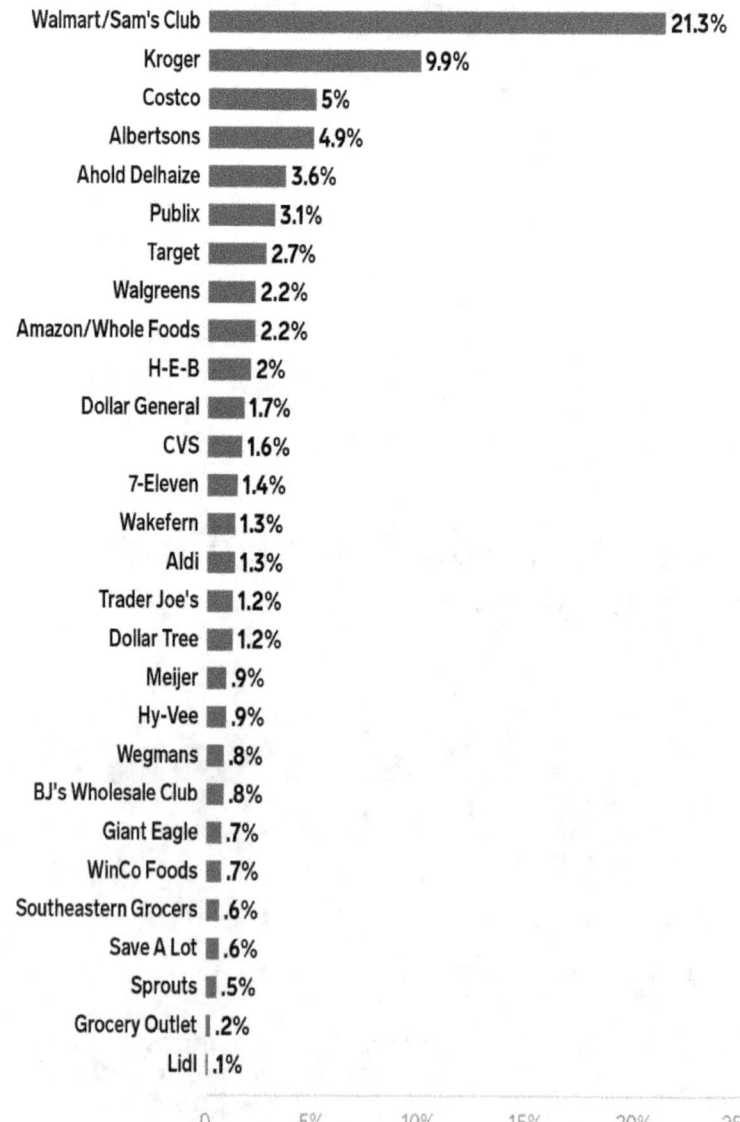

6. The industry are growing or declining?

- **Growing Industries**
- **Declining Industries**

Growing industries

A growth industry is that sector of an economy which experiences a higher-than-average growth rate as compared to other sectors. Growth industries are often new or pioneer industries that did not exist in the past. Their growth is a result of demand for new products or services offered by companies in the field. An example of a growth industry is the technology sector, whose products have become runaway hits with consumers and led to multibillion-dollar valuations for tech companies in the stock market.

Tesla, Inc. (TSLA), which has among the highest valuations of car companies, is an example of a company that benefits from changing regulations and its technology chops. Investors have flocked to the company due to its promise of a greener future as well as its cars, which incorporates state-of-the-art technology.

U.S. ECOMMERCE VS. TOTAL RETAIL* SALES
In $billions, 2017-2019

Online spending represented 16.0% of total retail sales for the year, according to a Digital Commerce 360 analysis of Commerce Department retail data. Amazon accounted for more than a third of all ecommerce in the United States.

Declining Industries

A declining industry is an industry where growth is either negative or is not growing at the broader rate of economic growth. There are many reasons for a declining industry: consumer demand may be steadily evaporating; the depletion of a natural resource may be occurring or there may be the emergent substitutes because of technological innovation.

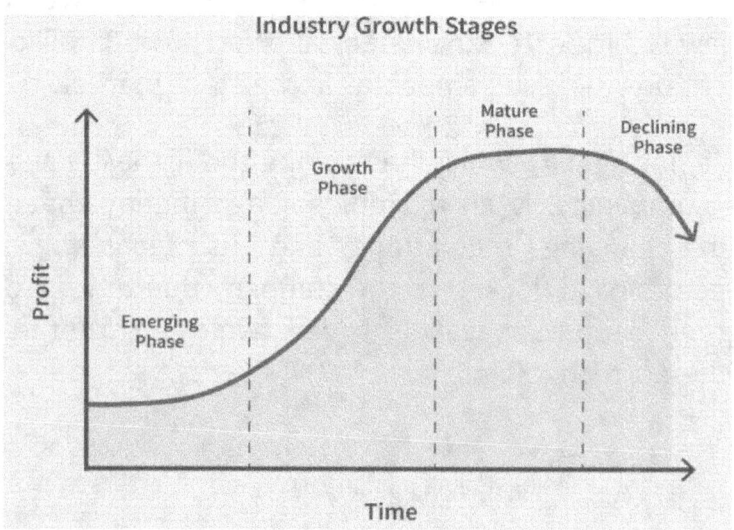

However, sometimes an industry does not grow when the rest of the economy grows. This can be the result of many factors, from changing consumer preferences, technological innovation that makes the industry or its products obsolete, or the emergence of substitutes. When the growth rate of an industry stagnates or starts to shrink, for any of these reasons, it is said to be in decline.

Even though Kodak and Fujifilm produced cameras, their core business was centered on film and post-processing sales. According to Forbes, Kodak "gladly gave away cameras in exchange for getting people hooked on paying to have their photos developed — yielding Kodak a nice annuity in the form of 80% of the market for the chemicals and paper used to develop and print those photos."

Trends in total world demand for color film and changes in revenue composition

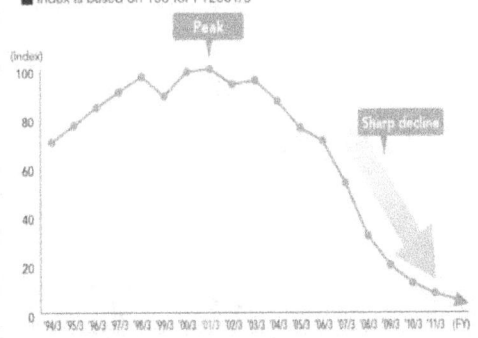

Source: Fujifilm Integrated Report 2017

	2000	2010
Kodak Sales	$14 billion	$7.2 billion (- 48%)

7. While declining industry, the market share of business increase?

Shrinking industry sales make the decline phase volatile. The extent to which escalating competitive pressures erode profitability during decline, however, depends on how readily industry participants pull out and how fiercely the companies that remain try to contain their shrinking sales, but this is not applicable for all the company, let see the example of apple.

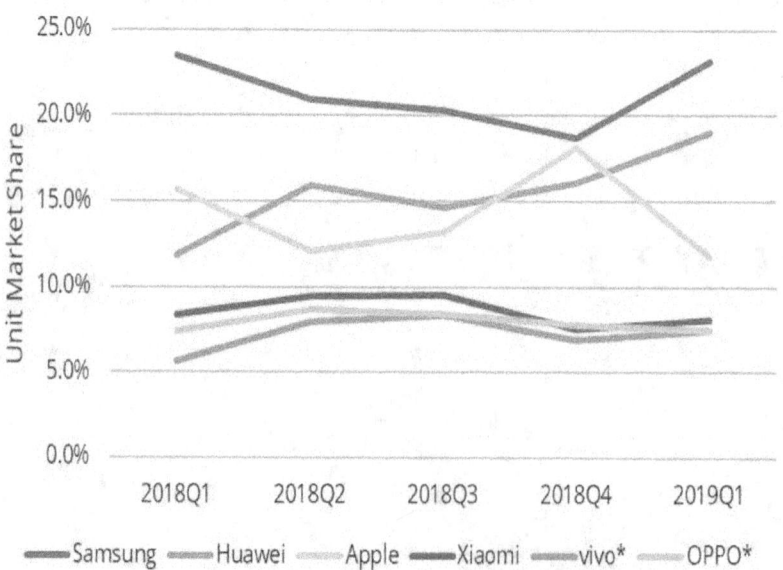

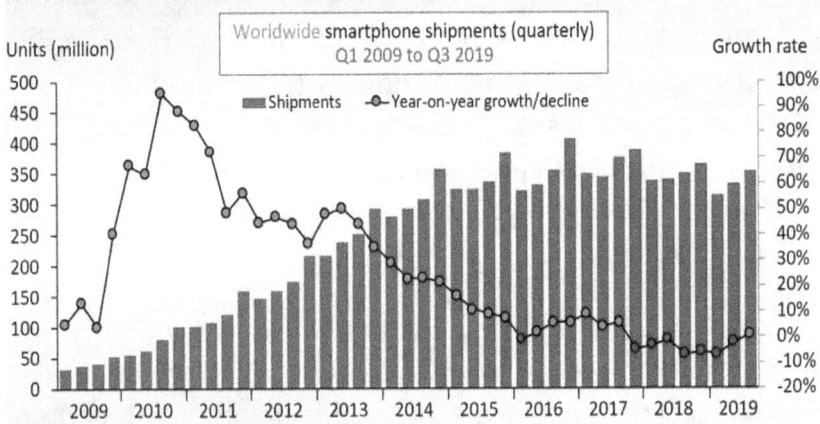

Apple market share in 2018 Q2 was 12% and Global year-on-year growth /decline was (-1%) and in 2018 Q4 was 17% and Global market was decline (-3%).

While market was in decline trend and Apple market share was increasing. This kind of understands you need to need to understand, what will happen when there is a decline in the market.

When the market decline, those company having economic moat will increase its market share.

8. Does the industry changing to value migration?

Value migration as a flow of economic and shareholder value away from obsolete business models to new, more effective designs that are better able to satisfy customers' most important priorities. Value migration occurs when there is a disconnect between customer priorities and existing business designs.

In marketing, value migration is the shifting of value-creating forces. Value migrates from outmoded business models to business designs that are better able to satisfy customers' priorities. Marketing strategy is the art of creating value for the customer. This can only be done by offering a product or service that corresponds to customer needs. In a fast-changing business environment, the factors that determine value are constantly changing.

- Traditional Banking to Digital Banking.

- Traditional Retail to ecommerce online retail Like Amazon.

- Personal Transport to Service Transport like Uber.

- Traditional Restaurant to Online food ordering like Uber Eat.

Slywotzky defines Marketing Strategy as the art of creating value for the customer. The caveat here he says of creating value for the customer, can only be done by offering a product or service that corresponds to customer needs. Slywotzky made a statement that was true in 1996 and has been proven even more so in 2012. "In a fast-changing business environment, the factors that determine value are constantly changing."

In the Slywotzky model there are three types and three stages of Value:

Three Types of Value

• Value flows between industries. Example: from airlines to entertainment.

• Value flows between companies. Example: from Corel WordPerfect to Microsoft.

• Value flows between business designs within a company. Example: from IBM mainframe computers to IBM PC's with system integration.

- Value migration could be cross-regions as well.
- Country-level migration is a very important concept.
- Value of manufacturing migration has happened to different countries over the decade.
- IT industry a prime example of value migration created in India.
- India seems set to be a prime contender of value inflow over the next 15 years.

Raamdeo Agrawal
Chairman, Motilal Oswal AMC

17

Geographical Analysis

Geographic organisation is an organisation structure where company hierarchy is divided on the basis of geographic location in which company operates which is headed by a centralised head office. This kind of organisational structure serves distinct needs of various different groups within and outside the country. Geographic organisation helps to understand local customer preferences which change according to geographic locations. Also, following geographical organisation structure can solve the logistic issues faced by the organisation as dedicated teams are allotted as per geographical divisions within the organisation.

When businesses expand to more than one location, they'll face opportunities and challenges. Two or more locations might be similar in operation, such as two or more restaurants or retail stores in a chain, or serve different functions, such as a production facility and an administrative office. Whichever is the case, you'll need to look the similarities and differences to effectively run both locations. Look to create strong managers and take advantage of economies of scale when running a business with multiple locations.

1. Which all country company operate?

We need to read annual report to get this information because revenue is coming from different sales location.

Sales by geographic areas Nestle	Differences 2019/2018 (in %)		in CHF millions
	in CHF	in local currency	
By principal markets			2019
United States	+4.4%	+3.0%	28 831
Greater China Region	−1.3%	+1.5%	6 913
France	−3.0%	+0.7%	4 423
Brazil	−1.0%	+5.1%	3 647
Mexico	+4.3%	+2.7%	2 934
United Kingdom	−0.5%	+2.2%	2 917
Philippines	+6.7%	+3.2%	2 643
Germany	−4.4%	−0.7%	2 632
Canada	+5.7%	+6.6%	2 182
Japan	+1.9%	−1.0%	1 816
Russia	+6.8%	+8.0%	1 703
Italy	−8.0%	−4.5%	1 674
India	+9.0%	+10.6%	1 667
Spain	−2.6%	+1.1%	1 512
Australia	−5.4%	−0.2%	1 468
Switzerland	−6.2%	−6.2%	1 164
Rest of the world	−0.1%	(a)	24 442
Total	+1.2%	(a)	92 568

JOHNSON & JOHNSON

(Dollars in Millions)

United States
Europe
Western Hemisphere excluding U.S.
Asia-Pacific, Africa
Segments total
General corporate
Other non long-lived assets
Worldwide total

Apple Inc

Americas:
Europe:
Greater China:
Japan:
Rest of Asia Pacific:

2. What is the product wise geography sale?

We need to look at the sale of a company by product, which geographical location they sell, which all product they sell. Company might have different product for different country

Did you know? Coca-Cola sells soup in a can! Bistrone is a nourishing meal on the go, available in two flavors in Japan.

So, we need to know what company sell in which country.

Coca-Cola Japan has a line of hot canned soups it calls Go:Good, which comes in three varieties. The first, corn potage (basically corn chowder) has been a vending machine mainstay for years, and is something a lot of other companies offer too. Minestrone is a little rarer, but again, Coca-Cola isn't the only canned drink maker with a tomato soup. What they, are, though, is the only one to offer hot shrimp bisque in a can.

	JOHNSON & JOHNSON	Sales to Customers	
(Dollars in Millions)		2019	2018
CONSUMER			
Baby Care			
U.S.		$ 362	422
International		1,313	1,436
Worldwide		1,675	1,858
Beauty			
U.S.		2,392	2,403
International		2,201	1,979
Worldwide		4,593	4,382
Oral Care			
U.S.		621	637
International		906	918
Worldwide		1,528	1,555
OTC			
U.S.		2,010	1,850
International		2,434	2,484
Worldwide		4,444	4,334

Zone EMENA

In millions of CHF **Nestle**

	2018*
Western	11 791
Eastern and Central	3 570
Middle East and North Africa	3 571
Powdered and Liquid Beverages	5 154
Milk products and Ice cream	1 067
Prepared dishes and cooking aids	3 923
Confectionery	3 293
PetCare	3 466
Nutrition and Health Science	2 029
Total sales	**18 932**
Underlying trading operating profit	3 545
Trading operating profit	3 206
Capital additions	1 422

3. What is the market share in each geographical location?

There are various types of market share. Market shares can be value or volume. Value market share is based on the total share of a company out of total segment sales. Volumes refer to the actual numbers of units that a company sells out of total units sold in the market. The value-volume market share equation is not usually linear: a unit may have high value and low numbers, which means that value market share, may be high, but volumes share may be low. In industries like FMCG, where the products are low value, high volume and there are lots of freebies, comparing value market share is the norm.

When company operate in different country, every country has a specific market and where company sell their product, market share state that company enjoy the maximum potion of the market.

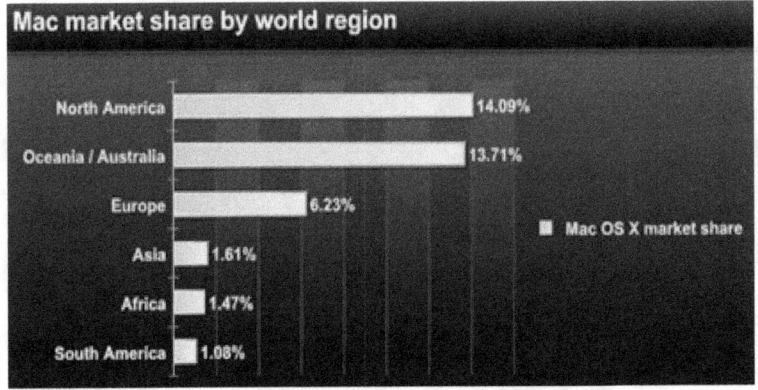

The top 10 nations for the iPhone as a percentage of total smart phones sold are:

1. **Japan - 53.8%**
2. **USA - 47.4%**
3. **Australia - 44.9%**
4. **Great Britain - 42.5%**
5. **South Korea - 33%**
6. **Germany - 21.4%**
7. **France - 20.8 %**
8. **China - 18.1 %**
9. **Italy - 17%**
10. **Spain - 9.7%**

4. What is the Revenue breakup each geographical location?

We need to check the annual report to know the details, Geographic segmentation is when a business divides its market on the basis of geography. There are several ways that a market can be geographically segmented. You can divide your market by geographical areas, such as by city, county, state, region, (like the West Coast), country, or international region, (like Asia). You can also divide the market into rural, suburban, and urban market segments. And, you can segment a market by climate or total population in each area.

Many enterprises provide groups of products and services or operate in geographical areas that are subject to differing rates of profitability, opportunities for growth, future prospects, and risks. Information about different types of products and services of an enterprise and its operations in different geographical areas - often called segment information - is relevant to assessing the risks and returns of a diversified or multi-locational enterprise but may not be determinable from the aggregated data. Therefore, reporting of segment information is widely regarded as necessary for meeting the needs of users of financial statements.

Since people in different locations are bound to display different characteristics and have a variety of wants and needs, geographic location is an integral factor in determining market positioning and product sales.

Apple Revenue by Country

		2018	2017	2016
Americas:				
Net	sales	1,12,093	96,600	86,613
Operating	income	34,864	30,684	28,172
Operaing Margin		31%	32%	33%
Europe:				
Net	sales	62,420	54,938	49,952
Operating	income	19,955	16,514	15,348
Operaing Margin		32%	30%	31%
Greater China:				
Net	sales	51,942	44,764	48,492
Operating	income	19,742	17,032	18,835
Operaing Margin		38%	38%	39%
Japan:				
Net	sales	21,733	17,733	16,928
Operating	income	9,500	8,097	7,165
Operaing Margin		44%	46%	42%
Rest Asia Pacific:				
Net	sales	17,407	15,199	13,654
Operating	income	6,181	5,304	4,781
Operaing Margin		36%	35%	35%

5. What is revenue growth as per each geographical location?

When we check the overall growth in the revenue or degrowth, we should find the reason behind the growth as well as degrowth, as see in case of Apple Inc, they have major decline in China Market in year 2016 and 2019.

Apple Inc

In millions, except per share items	Sep-28-19	Sep-29-18	Sep-30-17	Sep-24-16	Sep-26-15	Sep-27-14	Sep-28-13	Sep-29-12
	10-K	10-K	10-K	10-K	10-K	10-K	10-K	10-K
Revenues:								
Other countries	1,14,230	1,15,592	1,00,131	91,480	93,268	83,248	78,767	72,762
Revenue growth	-1.2%	15.4%	9.5%	-1.9%	12.0%	5.7%	8.3%	
U.S.	1,02,266	98,061	84,339	75,667	81,732	68,909	66,197	60,949
Revenue growth	4.3%	16.3%	11.5%	-7.4%	18.6%	4.1%	8.6%	
China	43,678	51,942	44,764	48,492	58,715	30,638	25,946	22,797
Revenue growth	-15.9%	16.0%	-7.7%	-17.4%	91.6%	18.1%	13.8%	
Total revenues [+]	2,60,174	2,65,595	2,29,234	2,15,639	2,33,715	1,82,795	1,70,910	1,56,508
Revenue growth [+]	-2.0%	15.9%	6.3%	-7.7%	27.9%	7.0%	9.2%	

This is a good understanding where the growth is coming from.

18

Management Analysis

Management (or managing) is the administration of an organization, whether it is a business, a not-for-profit organization, or government body. Management includes the activities of setting the strategy of an organization and coordinating the efforts of its employees (or of volunteers) to accomplish its objectives through the application of available resources, such as financial, natural, technological, and human resources. The term "management" may also refer to those people who manage an organization - individually: managers

Management is a distinct process consisting of planning, organising and acquitting the performance by the people and their resources.

> "The fundamental task of management is to make people capable of joint performance through common goals, common values, the right structure, and the training and development they need to perform and to respond to change."
> — *Peter Drucker*

Management by objectives (MBO):

This is considered to be one of the most important contributions made by Drucker to the field of management. Management by objectives (MBO) is a management approach where equilibrium is required to be achieved between the objectives of employees and the objectives of an organisation. There are certain conditions that must be met to make MBO management a success. Take a look at these conditions here:

- The objectives are set after discussions between the managers and employees;

- The set objectives are quantitative and qualitative in nature;

- Daily feedback must be given to the employees with regards to their performance;

- Employees with high performance must be rewarded;

- The guiding principle should be growth and development.

The main characteristics of management are as follows:

(i) It is Goal-Oriented:

The important goal of all management activities to achieve the objectives of a business concern. The objectives of the business may be economic, social and humane.

(ii) It is a Process:

When it is used in the sense of a process, it refers to what management does. In other words, it refers to the process of managing, planning, organising, staffing, guiding, directing supervising and controlling.

(iii) It is a Group Activity:

For the success of a business, it is necessary that all human and physical resources are co-ordinated to achieve the maximum levels of productivity. We all know that the combined productivity of various resources will always be higher than the total productivity of each resource.

(iv) Management is Universal:

It is required in all types of organisations, e.g., family, club, university, government, army, business. The basic principles of management are applicable in business as well as in other organisations. However, these principles are flexible and they can be modified to suit different situations.

(v) It is an Art and Science:

It consists of both the elements of science and art. The science of management gives a body of principles or laws for guidance in the solution of specific management problems and objective evaluation of results. The management as an art consists of this use of skill and effort for producing desirable results or situations in specific cases.

(vi) It is a Factor of Production:

Not only the land, labour and capital are of effective use for the production of goods and services but the managerial skills are also used effectively for this purpose.

(vii) Management is Dynamic:

Management denotes is an ever-changing environment, it involves adoption of an organisation to changes in its environment, and modifying the environment for the benefit of the organisation. Therefore, management is a constantly growing process.

(viii) Management is a Profession:

Management is considered to be a profession as it possesses all the attributes of profession as:

(i) A systematic corpus of knowledge,

(ii) A period of apprenticeship, and

(iii) A code of conduct.

(ix) Management is an Important Organ of Society:

Management has become an important organ of society. Management of large-scale undertakings influence the economic, social, moral, religious, political and institutional behaviour of the members of the society.

1. Does the Compensation of CEO is below 1% of net revenue?

Value investor always look for a competence CEO and the Compensation what company paid , the good number is below 1 % of net revenue, Warren Buffett take $100,000, he work as a business owner , we need to avoid those CEO , who like   partying, high society or upper class, it's always been proved that those kind of CEO never perform.

It's hard to read the business news without coming across reports about the salaries, bonuses, and stock option packages awarded to chief executives of publicly traded companies. Making sense of the numbers to assess how companies are paying their top brass is not easy. Investors must ensure that executive compensation is working in their favor.

- Pay for performance is a compensation strategy to align executive compensation with the company's success.

- Base salaries for CEOs are often high but offer little incentive for hard work or skillful management.

- Bonuses that are linked to company performance will encourage CEOs to work harder and make better decisions for stockholders.

- Stock options can cause CEOs to focus on short-term performance or to manipulate numbers to meet targets.

- Executives act more like owners when they have a stake in the business in the form of stock ownership.

Berkshire Hathaway owns over 50 companies, which include Geico, Duracell, and Benjamin Moore, and is one of the most successful companies in the world. Buffett owns approximately 283,00 shares of it and with a stock price of $334,860 as of Feb. 4, 2020, that's quite the holdings.

Even though Buffett is the head of one of the largest companies, he earns a small annual salary, relatively speaking, of $100,000. This number is 1.6x the approximate median salary of Berkshire employees, which is $61,000. Since at least the early 90s, Buffett's salary has remained the same, but his other benefits have fluctuated with the stock market, particularly with the value of Berkshire Hathaway.

Buffett earned his substantial wealth through smart investing. Why would he take on such a small salary when compared to other CEOs of such large corporations? There can be a few explanations. Firstly, Buffett is known to be a modest man with a humble demeanor. Despite his vast wealth, he does not live lavishly. In fact, he has lived in the same house he bought in 1958 before his massive wealth was accumulated. And he plans on giving away 99% of his wealth to charities upon his death. By taking on a small salary, it provides him with the moral and social capital that underlines his modest living, which allows him the leeway to lecture corporate America on its greed and to reign in its voracious appetite for wealth generation. Buffett has spoken out against the unfair distribution of wealth in the United States and believes in a larger tax rate for the wealthy.

Facebook Inc CEO Mark Zuckerberg has drawn a base salary of $1 for the past three years.

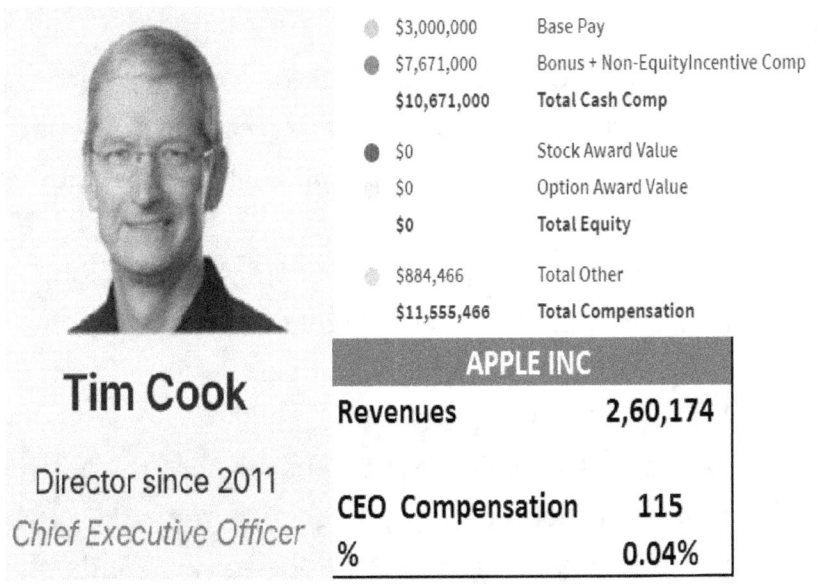

- Apple inch Revenue $260174 million
- Pay for the CEO Tim Cook is $115 Million for fiscal year 2019
- The % is .04% that is good.

Same way you can do for the other company.

2. Does **CEO Qualification or Experience** meet the requirement to be in management team?

There are three ways to understand this such as

- **Effective CEO**-Operate in a very highly competitive industry like automobiles, aviation, the job is to operate in very cost-effective way, and the operating cost should be very low, such as Tesla CEO Elon Reeve Musk

- **Portfolio CEO**- well established company, barrier to entry and CEO job is to allocate capital to generate good return, above cost of capital like Warren Buffett.

- **Excellent CEO** – In a growth company, his job is to grow company at 10 % annually such as Amazon CEO Jeffrey Preston Bezos.

    We have to evaluate CEO based on these three scenarios; each company need different CEO. Based on the company profile, it will be easy to understand which CEO is good.

    Apple CEO Tim Cook graduated from Auburn University with a bachelor's degree in industrial engineering and earned an MBA from Duke University's Fuqua School of Business. Following a 12-year career at IBM, Cook went on to executive roles at

Intelligent Electronics and Compaq, before joining Apple in 1998.

Elon Reeve Musk FRS born June 28, 1971 is an industrial designer, technology entrepreneur, and philanthropist. He is a citizen of South Africa, the United States (where he has lived most of his life and currently resides), and Canada. He is the founder, CEO and chief engineer/designer of SpaceX co-founder,CEO and product architect of Tesla, Inc.;founder of The Boring Company;co-founder of Neuralink; and co-founder and initial co-chairman of OpenAI. He was elected a Fellow of the Royal Society (FRS) in 2018. In December 2016, he was ranked 21st on the Forbes list of The World's Most Powerful People,and was ranked joint-first on the Forbes list of the Most Innovative Leaders of 2019. As of May 2020, he has a net worth of $39.4 billion and is listed by Forbes as the 23rd-richest person in the world.

Mark Elliot Zuckerberg born May 14, 1984 is an American internet entrepreneur and philanthropist. He is known for co-founding Facebook, Inc. and serves as its chairman, chief executive officer, and controlling shareholder. He also co-founded and is a board member of the solar sail spacecraft development project Breakthrough Starshot.

CEO vs OWNER	
One of the founding member	Founder of a business.
Chosen by the board of directors based upon their previous accomplishments and their ability to progress the company forward.	A successful business may have one founder.
Can be fired by a board vote.	Can not be fired by a board vote.
Several CEO-changes over the lifetime of the Company.	

When you look for an ethical management, make sure you deep dive into both aspects such as CEO and Founder. The right evaluation is very important.

3. Does CEO or Board of Director ever receive any award or best CEO ranking?

Check the past profile of the board; it is important for anyone studying management to know its history as it could help an individual understand how the today's organizations evolved. We can also learn about the mistakes that are made in the past and make the right decision now. History also tells us how different theories of management are developed.

Apple CEO Tim Cook to receive Irish award. Apple chief executive Tim Cook will receive an award in Dublin on January 20 in recognition of the iPhone maker's 40 years of investment here, Bloomberg reports. Taoiseach Leo Varadkar will present Cook with the accolade, according to IDA Ireland.

Microsoft CEO Satya Nadella was recognised as the Global Indian Business Icon at IBLA 2020.

Best CEOs In The World 2019: Most Influential Chief Executives

Rank	Name	Title	Country	Notes
1	C. Douglas McMillon	CEO	US	Walmart
2	Ben van Beurden	CEO	Netherlands	Royal Dutch Shell
3	Lakshmi Niwas Mittal	Chairman and CEO	Luxembourg	ArcelorMittal
4	Amin H. Nasser	CEO and President	Saudi Arabia	Saudi Aramco
5	Bob Dudley	Group chief executive	UK	BP
6	Darren Woods	CEO and Chairman	US	Exxon Mobil
7	Herbert Diess	CEO and Chairman of the Board	Germany	Volkswagen AG
8	Akio Toyoda	President Member of the Board of Directors	Japan	Toyota Motor
9	Timothy D. Cook	CEO	US	Apple
10	Warren E. Buffett	CEO	US	Berkshire Hathaway
11	Jeffrey P. Bezos	CEO	US	Amazon
12	David S.	CEO	US	UnitedHealth Group

4. Is management rational?

Rational management, which means making full use of the thinking ability of the people in an organization, is a continuing process. Rational Management aims at major change and therefore demands major commitment.

Rational organization theory is the idea that an organization, such as a business, is a tool for achieving a definable goal or set of goals. A rational organization uses a formal structure to define the role of each member of the organization. In a business where roles and goals are clearly defined, the process of management should be rational and predictable.

Good jockeys will do well on good horses but not on broken down nags. -warren (Pat win the race)

Bad Business (Mediocre)

- Better have great Manager (Airline, Automobile),

Great Business

- Genius not needed to run.

In investing Warren Buffett look for a great business, he doesn't simply invest look at the management. "I think back to August 30, 1983 – my birthday – when I went to see Mrs. B (Rose Blumkin), carrying a 1 1/4-page purchase proposal for NFM that I had drafted. (It's reproduced on pages 114 - 115.) Mrs. B accepted my offer without changing a word, and we completed the deal without the involvement of investment bankers or lawyers (an experience that can only be described as heavenly). Though the company's financial statements were unaudited, I had no worries. Mrs. B simply told me what was what, and her word was good enough for me." -- 2013 Letter to Shareholders

Sales at our one-and-only location were $159 million, up 4% from 1989. Though again the fact can't be conclusively proved, we believe NFM does close to double the volume of any other home furnishings store in the country.

The NFM formula for success parallels that of Borsheim's. First, operating costs are rock-bottom - 15% in 1990 against about 40% for Levitz, the country's largest furniture retailer, and 25% for Circuit City Stores, the leading discount retailer of electronics and appliances. Second, NFM's low costs allow the business to price well below all competitors. Indeed, major chains, knowing what they will face, steer clear of Omaha. Third, the huge volume generated by our bargain prices allows us to carry the broadest selection of merchandise available anywhere.

Some idea of NFM's merchandising power can be gleaned from a recent report of consumer behavior in Des Moines, which showed that NFM was Number 3 in popularity among 20 furniture retailers serving that city. That may sound like no big deal until you consider that 19 of those retailers are located in Des Moines, whereas our store is 130 miles away. This leaves customers driving a distance equal to that between Washington and Philadelphia in order to shop with us, even though they have a multitude of alternatives next door. In effect, NFM, like Borsheim's, has dramatically expanded the territory it serves - not by the traditional method of opening new stores but rather by creating an irresistible magnet that employs price and selection to pull in the crowds." -- Buffett 1990 Letter To Shareholders.

Mrs. B was 89 at the time and worked until 103 – definitely my kind of woman. Take a look at NFM's financial statements from 1946 on pages 116 - 117. Everything NFM now owns comes from (a) that $72,264 of net worth and $50 – no zeros omitted – of cash the company then possessed, and (b) the incredible talents of Mrs. B, her son, Louie, and his sons Ron and Irv.

The punch line to this story is that Mrs. B never spent a day in school. Moreover, she emigrated from Russia to America knowing not a word of English. But she loved her adopted country: At Mrs. B's request, the family always sang God Bless America at its gatherings.

Aspiring business managers should look hard at the plain, but rare, attributes that produced Mrs. B's incredible success. Students from 40 universities visit me every year, and I have them start the day with a visit to NFM. If they absorb Mrs. B's lessons, they need none from me." --- 2013 Letter to Shareholders.

5. Is management capable enough to generate enough return on retain earning above the cost of capital?

Net profit generated by the company are the 'owner's money'. Who are the owners of a publicly traded company? It's the shareholders. How shareholder can get hold of the net profit? In form of dividends.

But companies often do not distribute 100% of their net profits as dividends to its shareholders. They retain a chunk of net profit. These are called retained earnings.

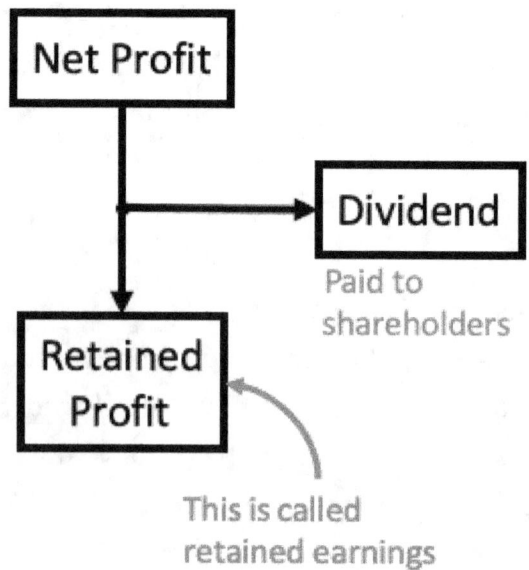

Return on retained earnings—the amount of money that is retained for future growth—reveals a lot about a company's efficiency and growth potential. A high RORE indicates that it should reinvest in the business. A low RORE suggests that it should distribute profits to shareholders by paying out dividends if it cannot work out how to make an adequate return by growing the business.

As a company progresses through its industry life cycle, RORE will tend to fall. In this sense, RORE is related to the retention ratio, also known as the "plowback ratio," which measures what percentage of earnings is retained. Both measures are most useful when comparing firms in the same industry or sector.

There are a few different ways to arrive at the return on retained earnings. The simplest way to calculate it is by using published information on earnings per share (EPS) over a period of your choosing:

- Return on retained earnings = (most recent EPS - first period EPS) / (cumulative EPS for the period - cumulative dividends paid for the period)

- The income money can be distributed (fully or partially) among the business owners (shareholders) in the form of dividends.

- It can be invested to expand the existing business operations, like increasing the production capacity of the existing products or hiring more sales representatives.

- It can be invested to launch a new product/variant, like a refrigerator maker foraying into producing air conditioners, or a chocolate cookie manufacturer launching orange- or pineapple-flavored variants.

- The money can be utilized for any possible merger, acquisition, or partnership that leads to improved business prospects.

- It can also be used for share buybacks.

- The earnings can be used to repay any outstanding loan (debt) the business may have.

Apple retained earnings (accumulated deficit) from 2006 to 2019. Retained earnings (accumulated deficit) can be defined as profits reinvested in the corporation after dividends have been paid out.

- Apple retained earnings (accumulated deficit) for the quarter ending December 31, 2019 were $43.977B, a **45.38% decline** year-over-year.
- Apple retained earnings (accumulated deficit) for 2019 were $45.898B, a **34.8% decline** from 2018.
- Apple retained earnings (accumulated deficit) for 2018 were $70.4B, a **28.4% decline** from 2017.
- Apple retained earnings (accumulated deficit) for 2017 were $98.33B, a **2.04% increase** from 2016.

Look for the growth in ROE of Apple Inc, to know the company investment and the return.

ROE %

Apple Annual Data

Sep15	Sep16	Sep17	Sep18	Sep19
46.25	36.90	36.87	49.36	55.92

Apple Quarterly Data

Dec18	Mar19	Jun19	Sep19	Dec19
70.97	41.34	39.72	58.57	98.82

Apple Annual Data

WACC %

Sep16	Sep17	Sep18	Sep19
9.99	9.74	9.88	7.67

In its report for the third quarter of 2019, Berkshire Hathaway (BRK-A, BRK-B) reported better-than-expected earnings and an all-time record cash pile of $128 billion.

Once again, the question will be asked: Why doesn't Berkshire-Hathaway pay a dividend to its shareholders?

The short answer is that company founder and CEO Warren Buffett believes that money can be better spent in other ways.

6. Is board of directors and CEO and chairman owns company shares and are one of the shareholders?

Another factor that has an impact on the effectiveness of a board of directors is compensation. Adequately compensating board members for their work is one way to ensure that they will make every effort to promote and protect investor interests. The members of a board of directors are paid in cash and/or stock. Likewise, management and employees also need to be aligned with investors, and this can be achieved through the compensation that both groups receive. This may include making both parties owners (investors) in the company.

When management and employees are also shareholders, they will be motivated to protect shareholder interests as their own. This helps to protect a company from mismanagement and weak employee productivity. Also, a bonus targeting system can be used in which employees and managers receive bonuses when certain goals are met. Such strategies help to align the interests of employees and management with those of investors.

If these groups are not aligned with the interests of investors, major problems can arise and destroy shareholder value. Although the average shareholder does not have control over the board of directors or the day-to-day operations of the company, the ultimate responsibility for the protection of shareholder value lies with each individual investor. The investor is ultimately responsible for reviewing corporate policy and governance as well as for the compensation of managers. Investors who feel that a company does not show an adequate level of commitment to shareholders can always sell their investment.

In any business, a chief executive officer is pilot of the ship, the individual who makes the final strategic decisions about products, markets, budgets and personnel. On the CEO's shoulders weighs the responsibility of setting out goals and establishing a culture that inspires employees. Traditional corporate structure begins with a CEO at the top of the chart -- but majority shareholder may be another individual, investor group or corporate parent

Tim Cook, Chief Executive Officer
Tim Cook is the current chief executive officer (CEO) of Apple and the second-largest individual shareholder with 878,425 shares as of Aug. 24, 2018. Prior to being named CEO, Cook served as Apple's chief operating officer, responsible for the company's international sales and operations. Before joining Apple in 1998, Cook worked for computer distributor Compaq as the company's Vice President for Corporate Materials.

Security Ownership of Directors and Executive Officers

Name	Title of Class of Stock	Shares Beneficially Owned (1)	Percentage of Outstanding Stock of Respective Class (1)	Percentage of Aggregate Voting Power of Class A and Class B (1)	Percentage of Aggregate Economic Interest of Class A and Class B (1)
Warren E. Buffett	Class A	259,382	37.1	31.0 (2)	16.0
	Class B	9,533	*		
Gregory E. Abel	Class A	5 (3)	*	*	*
	Class B	2,363 (3)	*		
Howard G. Buffett	Class A	869 (4)	0.1		

Zuckerberg is Facebook's largest shareholder by far. As mentioned, he co-founded Facebook and has been the company's long-time chairman and CEO. At the age of 35, Zuckerberg is also ranked seventh on the Forbes World's Billionaires List with a net worth of $54.7 billion. He currently holds over 4 million shares of Facebook, comprising a market value of around $82.2 billion.

Zuckerberg's holdings also give him a disproportionate share of voting rights. He controls 57.9% of the total voting shares, giving him effective control of the company

FACEBOOK

Name of Beneficial Owner	Shares Beneficially Owned				% of Total Voting Power (1)
	Class A		Class B		
	Shares	%	Shares	%	
Named Executive Officers, Directors, and Nominees:					
Mark Zuckerberg (2)	4,284,831	*	363,588,585	81.8	53.1
Shares subject to voting proxy (3)	—	—	32,595,276	7.3	4.8
Total (2)(3)	4,284,831	*	396,183,861	89.1	57.9

Biographical Information

Jeffrey P. Bezos
Founder, Chairman, and CEO of Amazon

Background

Mr. Bezos has been Chairman of the Board since founding the Company in 1994 and Chief Executive Officer since May 1996. Mr. Bezos served as President from founding until June 1999 and again from October 2000 to the present.

Qualifications and Skills

Mr. Bezos' individual qualifications and skills as a director include his customer-focused point of view, his willingness to encourage invention, his long-term perspective, and his on-going contributions as founder and CEO.

AMAZON

Name and Address of Beneficial Owner	Amount and Nature of Beneficial Ownership	Percent of Class
Jeffrey P. Bezos 410 Terry Avenue North, Seattle, WA 98109	75,049,750[1]	15.1%

7. Does the past management done any fraud?

Accounting scandals are business scandals which arise from intentional manipulation of financial statements with the disclosure of financial misdeeds by trusted executives of corporations or governments. Such misdeeds typically involve complex methods for misusing or misdirecting funds, overstating revenues, understating expenses, overstating the value of corporate assets, or underreporting the existence of liabilities this can be done either manually, or by the means of deep learning, it involves an employee, account, or corporation itself and is misleading to investors and shareholders.

Misappropriation of assets — often called defalcation or employee fraud — occurs when an employee steals a company's asset, whether those assets are of monetary or physical nature. Typically, assets stolen are cash, or cash equivalents, and company data or intellectual property. However, misappropriation of assets also includes taking inventory out of a facility or using company assets for personal purpose without authorization. Company assets include everything from office supplies and inventory to intellectual property.

Lehman Brothers United States 15 Sep 2008 Banking

Lehman Brothers' financial strategy in from 2003 was to invest heavily in mortgage debt, in markets which were being deregulated from consumer protection by the US government. Losses mounted, and Lehman Brothers was forced to file for Chapter 11 bankruptcy after the US government refused to extend a loan. The collapse triggered a global financial market meltdown. Barclays, Nomura and Bain Capital purchased the assets which were not indebted.

AIG United States 16 Sep 2008 Insurance

Out of $441 billion worth of securities originally rated AAA, as the US sub-prime mortgage crisis unfolded, AIG found it held $57.8 billion of these products. It was forced to take a 24-month credit facility from the US Federal Reserve Board.

SATYAM SCANDAL (2009)

Company: Indian IT services and back-office accounting firm.

What happened: Falsely boosted revenue by $1.5 billion.

Main player: Founder/Chairman Ramalinga Raju.

How he did it: Falsified revenues, margins and cash balances to the tune of 50 billion rupees.

How he got caught: Admitted the fraud in a letter to the company's board of directors.

Penalties: Raju and his brother charged with breach of trust, conspiracy, cheating and falsification of records

FREDDIE MAC (2003)

Company: Federally backed mortgage-financing giant.

What happened: $5 billion in earnings were misstated.

Main players: President/COO David Glenn, Chairman/CEO Leland Brendsel, ex-CFO Vaughn Clarke, former senior VPs Robert Dean and Nazir Dossani.

How they did it: Intentionally misstated and understated earnings on the books.

How they got caught: An SEC investigation.

Penalties: $125 million in fines and the firing of Glenn, Clarke and Brendsel.

WASTE MANAGEMENT SCANDAL (1998)

Company: Houston-based publicly traded waste management company

What happened: Reported $1.7 billion in fake earnings.

Main players: Founder/CEO/Chairman Dean L. Buntrock and other top executives; Arthur Andersen Company (auditors)

How they did it: The Company allegedly falsely increased the depreciation time length for their property, plant and equipment on the balance sheets.

How they got caught: A new CEO and management team went through the books.

Penalties: Settled a shareholder class-action suit for $457 million. SEC fined Arthur Andersen $7 million.

8. Does the management buy back the shares?

A buyback, also known as a share repurchase, is when a company buys its own outstanding shares to reduce the number of shares available on the open market. Companies buy back shares for a number of reasons, such as to increase the value of remaining shares available by reducing the supply or to prevent other shareholders from taking a controlling stake.

A buyback allows companies to invest in themselves. Reducing the number of shares outstanding on the market increases the proportion of shares owned by investors. A company may feel its shares are undervalued and do a buyback to provide investors with a return. And because the company is bullish on its current operations, a buyback also boosts the proportion of earnings that a share is allocated. This will raise the stock price if the same price-to-earnings (P/E) ratio is maintained.

The share repurchase reduces the number of existing shares, making each worth a greater percentage of the corporation. The stock's earnings per share (EPS) thus increases while the price-to-earnings ratio (P/E) decreases or the stock price increases. A share repurchase demonstrates to investors that the business has sufficient cash set aside for emergencies and a low probability of economic troubles.

Shareholder's demand returns on their investments in the form of dividends which is a cost of equity—so the business is essentially paying for the privilege of accessing funds it isn't using. Buying back some or all of the outstanding shares can be a simple way to pay off investors and reduce the overall cost of capital. For this reason, Walt Disney (DIS) reduced its number of outstanding shares in the market by buying back 73.8 million shares, collectively valued at $7.5 billion, back in 2016.

Apple Share Buyback Determined to ask, "what would Steve do?" it appears that Apple got their answer, and it's a good one if you subscribe to the Warren Buffett ways of managing your stock. Along with the announcement of the dividend, Apple instituted a $10 billion share buyback that will start in October and last for three years, according to the March 19 announcement. By decreasing the amount of shares outstanding, the value of those shares rises, but the investor takes on no tax burden. Warren Buffett's company, Berkshire Hathaway, even went so far as to announce the maximum price they would pay for each share in their buyback program, providing an instant boost in value.

1) At times companies have excess cash which they are not using as they do not have enough opportunities for expansion. This cash can be used for buying back stocks as idle capital is no going to help in bringing any income and by doing sso, they can use cash in an efficient manner.

2) When a company buys back its stocks it conveys a positive message to its shareholders and further enhances their confidence by making them believe that management is sure that in future they will perform well and their stocks price is most likely to rise.

3) Buyback of shares reduces the chances of takeover of company by some other company as promoter stake increases.

9. Does the management pledge the stock?

A pledged asset is a valuable possession that is transferred to a lender to secure a debt or loan. A pledged asset is collateral held by a lender in return for lending funds. Pledged assets can reduce the down payment that is typically required for a loan as well as reduces the interest rate charged. Pledged assets can include cash, stocks, bonds, and other equity or securities.

Share pledge can be troublesome for companies at times, as promoters are required to maintain the value of the collateral all the time by providing additional shares to lenders when their value erodes. In case promoters fail to make up for the difference, lenders can sell the shares in the open market to recover the money. This can lead to a reduction in the promoters' shareholding in the company, further value erosion in the stock due to infusion of additional paper in the market, and even sudden change of guard in the company because of alteration in shareholding pattern.

Oracle Corp (ORCL.N) founder and chairman Larry Ellison leads the pack with about $11 billion of company stock pledged for personal loans. The arrangement, which accounts for 7 percent of Oracle's market cap, is reviewed every quarter by Oracle's governance and compensation committees to ensure Ellison has enough money to pay off the loans without selling the pledged shares. Ellison's latest disclosed total annual pay was $63.6 million, according to Oracle's proxy statement. Oracle declined to comment.

A Reuters analysis of thousands of U.S. corporate disclosures shows that most of stock pledging activity is concentrated at Oracle, Tesla Motors Inc (TSLA.O), Estee Lauder Companies Inc (EL.N), FedEx Corp (FDX.N), AutoZone Inc (AZO.N) and by T. Boone Pickens at Clean Energy Fuels Corp (CLNE.O).

Tesla chairman and CEO Elon Musk has pledged 7.4 million shares of company stock to secure personal loans worth about $1.6 billion, according to company disclosures. Goldman Sachs and Morgan Stanley have been named as lenders in the arrangements with Musk. Tesla did not return messages seeking comment.

This is because pledging of shares is a sign of poor cash flow, low-creditability high-debt Company and inability to meet the short-term requirements. (If the promoters have pledged a high percentage of shares, then it's always worthwhile to find out the reason.) A decreasing pledging of shares over time is a good sign for the investors. On the other hand, an increasing pledging of shares can be dangerous for both promoters and shareholders. Even quality companies can become a victim if the pledging of shares is not reduced over time.

10. How was the management performance in acquisitions?

An acquisition is when one company purchases most or all of another company's shares to gain control of that company. Purchasing more than 50% of a target firm's stock and other assets allows the acquirer to make decisions about the newly acquired assets without the approval of the company's shareholders. Acquisitions, which are very common in business, may occur with the target company's approval, or in spite of its disapproval. With approval, there is often a no-shop clause during the process.

Companies acquire other companies for various reasons. They may seek economies of scale, diversification, greater market share, increased synergy, cost reductions, or new niche offerings. Other reasons for acquisitions include those listed below.

An acquisition is defined as a corporate transaction where one company purchases a portion or all of another company's shares or assets. Acquisitions are typically made in order to take control of, and build on, the target company's strengths and capture synergies. There are several types of business combinations: acquisitions (both companies survive), mergers (one company survives), and amalgamations (neither company survives).

- Apple spent over $7.3B on its top 10 deals, over 40% of which went to its $3B acquisition of Beats Electronics.

- Many of Apple's top acquisitions have been aimed at building and improving its largest success to date, the iPhone. Four of its largest acquisitions focus on chip performance, including Intel's smartphone modem business, Dialog Semiconductor, Anobit Technologies, and PA Semi.

- Overall, these top deals reflect Apple's strategy evolution, from a focus on the Mac platform (NeXT Computer) in the late 1990s, to a focus on mobile (Intel, Dialog Semiconductor, Quattro Wireless), and most recently to a focus on services like Apple Music (Beats, Shazam).

- Other well-known features of the iPhone that have been impacted by Apple's top acquisitions include fingerprint-enabled payment solution Apple Pay, with AuthenTec, and facial recognition tech, with PrimeSense.

Apple Acquires AI Startup Voysis to Improve Siri Functionality. As Bloomberg reports, Apple acquired Voysis, an artificial intelligence startup that aims to improve Siri's performance when communicating with humans. Voysis provides a platform for digital voice assistants to better understand natural language.

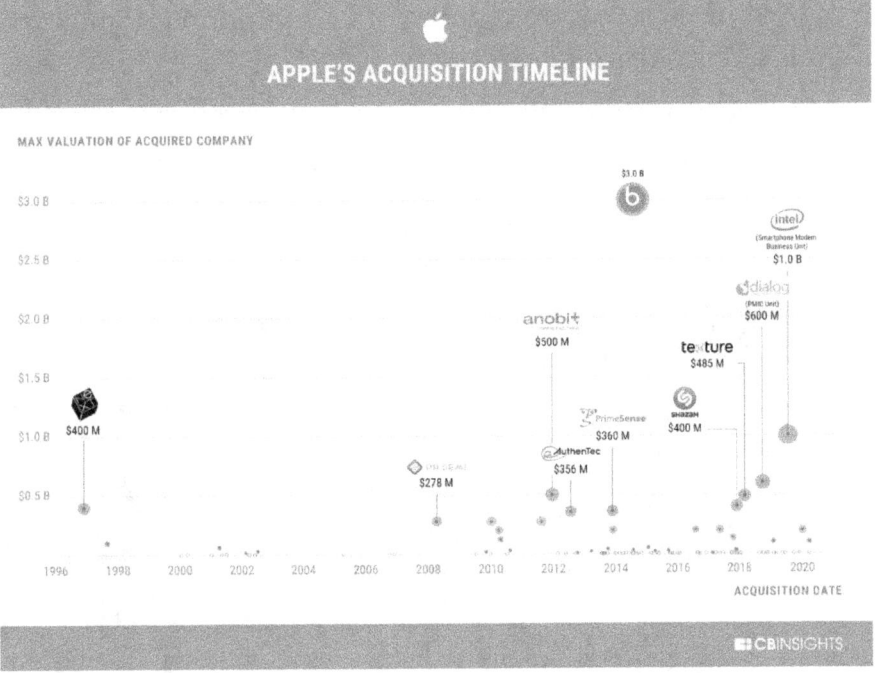

Amazon

Whole Foods Market

- Type of Business: Organic grocery store
- Acquisition price: $13.7 billion
- Date it was purchased: August 28, 2017 [2]

Whole Foods is a prominent grocery store chain with the distinction of being the only USDA-Certified Organic grocer in the United States. The company was founded in 1978 as SaferWay. At the time of its acquisition by Amazon, Whole Foods was an independent company with a market cap of almost $10 billion. It was ranked #176 in the 2017 Fortune 500 list.[3] Since then, Amazon has lowered prices on key food items and has integrated its Prime service into the Whole Foods customer experience.

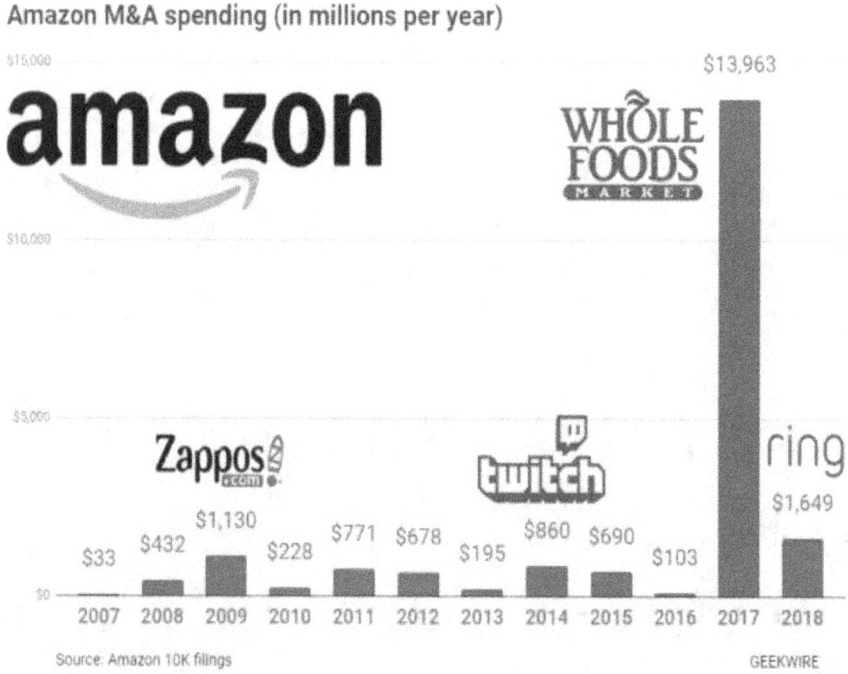

Amazon spent $1.65 billion on acquisitions in 2018, according to a new regulatory filing from the company. That makes it the second most acquisitive year in the company's history by dollar volume, behind only 2017, when the tech giant spent more than $13 billion to buy Whole Foods Market.

11. Is the management keep transparency with their shareholders?

We look for three things when we hire people. We look for intelligence, we look for initiative or energy, and we look for integrity. And if they don't have the latter, the first two will kill you, because if you're going to get someone without integrity, you want them lazy and dumb.
-Warren Buffett

The financial statements of some firms are designed to hide rather than reveal information. Investors should steer clear of companies that lack transparency in their business operations, financial statements or strategies. Companies with impossible to understand financials and complex business structures are riskier and less valuable investments.

The word "transparent" can be used to describe high-quality financial statements. The term has quickly become a part of mainstream business vocabulary. Dictionaries offer many definitions for the word, but those synonyms relevant to financial reporting are: "easily understood," "very clear," "frank" and "candid."

The reason is simple: less information means less certainty for investors. When financial statements are not transparent, investors can never be sure about a company's real fundamentals and true risk. For instance, a firm's growth prospects are related to how it invests. It's difficult, if not impossible, to evaluate a company's investment performance if its investments are funnelled through holding companies and are hidden from view. A lack of transparency may also obscure the company's debt level. If a company hides its debt, investors can't estimate their exposure to bankruptcy risk.

High-profile cases of financial shenanigans, such as those at Enron and Tyco, showed everyone that managers may employ fuzzy financials and complex business structures to hide unpleasant news. An overall lack of transparency can mean nasty surprises to come.

Good Management like Warren Buffett is very clear about the current environment in the company. PUBLISHED CNBC SAT, MAY 2 2020

- Berkshire Hathaway Chairman and billionaire value investor Warren Buffett said that the conglomerate has sold the entirety of its position in the U.S. airline industry.

- The prior stake, worth north of $4 billion dollars, included positions in United, American,

- "The world has changed for the airlines. And I don't know how it's changed and I hope it corrects itself in a reasonably prompt way," he said.

- Buffett said he admires the airlines, but that sometimes there are events like the coronavirus "on the lower levels of probabilities" that necessitate a quick change.

- He added: "When we sell something, very often it's going to be our entire stake: We don't trim positions."

"The world has changed for the airlines. And I don't know how it's changed and I hope it corrects itself in a reasonably prompt way," he said during Berkshire's annual shareholder meeting Saturday, which was virtual this year. "I don't know if Americans have now changed their habits or will change their habits because of the extended period."

But "I think there are certain industries, and unfortunately, I think that the airline industry, among others, that are really hurt by a forced shutdown by events that are far beyond our control," he added.

He explained: "When we sell something, very often it's going to be our entire stake: We don't trim positions. That's just not the way we approach it any more than if we buy 100% of a business. We're going to sell it down to 90% or 80%."

12. Is the management creating value to the shareholders?

Shareholder value is the financial worth owners of a business receive for owning shares in the company. An increase in shareholder value is created when a company earns a return on invested capital (ROIC) that is greater than its weighted average cost of capital (WACC). Put more simply, value is created for shareholders when the business performs better than they expect it to.

$$ROIC > WACC$$

Where;
ROIC = Return on Invested Capital
WACC = Weighted Average Cost of Capital

The truth is that when you think about creating shareholder value, you're really considering how to make more money. Any smart business owner has a long-term plan to increase the value of their company – and drive a successful business – with profits higher than its costs, which will automatically create shareholder value.

Company	Market Cap (M)	WACC %	ROIC %
Johnson & Johnson	$ 390,944.68	4.51	26.67
Roche Holding AG	$ 298,616.23	4.33	38.87
Pfizer Inc	$ 208,813.13	3.25	12.81
Merck & Co Inc	$ 196,123.49	2.58	23.90
Novartis AG	$ 195,805.16	4.56	10.15
Eli Lilly and Co	$ 147,029.82	1.63	33.67
Bristol-Myers Squibb Com...	$ 136,336.04	3.59	15.67
Amgen Inc	$ 135,761.39	3.86	39.59
AstraZeneca PLC	$ 134,552.71	2.89	5.16
Sanofi SA	$ 123,737.60	2.01	9.33

Company	Market Cap (M)	WACC %	ROIC %
Apple Inc	$ 1,264,820.00	6.98	48.13
Samsung Electronics Co Ltd	$ 271,493.59	8.07	11.52
China Electronics Holding...	$ 124,978.90	0.00	0.00
Sony Corp	$ 77,661.81	5.22	18.09
Midea Group Co Ltd	$ 53,253.36	6.27	22.94
Gree Electric Appliances I...	$ 46,669.30	8.44	0.00
Xiaomi Corp	$ 31,543.36	0.00	0.00
Kyocera Corp	$ 18,913.02	6.68	5.05
Haier Smart Home Co Ltd	$ 18,422.57	7.31	12.88
Panasonic Corp	$ 17,208.95	4.93	12.00

19

Franchise Value Analysis

One of the things that make certain businesses more successful than other businesses over long periods of time is the presence of franchise value. A company with franchise value can often sell more measurement units of its products and services, resulting in higher revenue, and generate more net income applicable to common than other businesses in the same sector or industry.

As long as the capital structure is intelligently managed, businesses with high franchise value can more easily survive periods such as the Great Depression of 1929-1933 or the Great Recession of 2007-2009. Though you may not be familiar with the concept, businesses with high franchise value have such distinctive characteristics.

In your own mind, you probably link bleach with Clorox, tissue with Kleenex, soda with Coca-Coca, Pepsi, or Dr. Pepper, soup with Campbell's, coffee with Starbucks or Dunkin Donuts, fast food with McDonald's, and chocolate with Hershey's. Apple, Google, and Tesla all have high franchise value as well.

The quickest way to determine if a business or brand has high franchise value is to ask yourself a series of questions.

1. Am I willing to pay more for the brand (e.g., Hershey's) as opposed to another, cheaper brand (e.g., the generic chocolate bar)?

2. If a store didn't have the brand in which I was interested, would I walk across the street to buy the product I wanted due to it being better or me having more trust in it?

3. If I started a business in direct competition with this product or service, what are my chances of success? Would I be able to make a dent in its market share or is the product so firmly entrenched it would be difficult to wrestle away even a small portion?

Strategic Analysis

Durable Competitive Advantage

1. Does business have durable competitive advantage?

2. Does business enjoy high market share?

3. Does business have above average margin compare with their competitors?

Barrier to entry

1. Does the business have barrier to entry?

2. Barrier to entry in a business is supply based or demand based?

Durable Competitive Advantage

1. Does business have durable competitive advantage?

Durable Competitive Advantage is a fundamental concept of value investing. Investors like Warren Buffett, Peter Lynch and many more have always advocated for the importance of durable competitive advantage as one of the most crucial factors that determines the long-term success, sustainability and longevity of a business.

Other competitive advantages exist when a company is the low-cost producer, such as Wal-Mart, possesses another attribute that turns potential competitors away.

Commodity-type businesses rarely have sustainable competitive advantages. Ultimately, they're resolved to share the market space with many competitors until the economic profit is zero or, in other words, the cost of capital is equal to the required rate of return that investors demand on their money.

Buffett revisited the challenges facing the industry in his 1991 letter titled "A change in media economics and some valuation math"

"In last year's report, I stated my opinion that the decline in the profitability of media companies reflected secular as well as cyclical factors. The events of 1991 have fortified that case: The economic strength of once-mighty media enterprises continues to erode as retailing patterns change and advertising and entertainment choices proliferate. In the business world, unfortunately, the rear-view mirror is always clearer than the windshield: A few years back no one linked to the media business — neither lenders, owners nor financial analysts — saw the economic deterioration that was in store for the industry. (But give me a few years and I'll probably convince myself that I did.)

The fact is that newspaper, television, and magazine properties have begun to resemble businesses more than franchises in their economic behavior. Let's take a quick look at the characteristics separating these two classes of enterprise, keeping in mind, however, that many operations fall in some middle ground and can best be described as weak franchises or strong businesses.

An economic franchise arises from a product or service that: (1) is needed or desired; (2) is thought by its customers to have no close substitute and; (3) is not subject to price regulation. The existence of all three conditions will be demonstrated by a company's ability to regularly price its product or service aggressively and thereby to earn high rates of return on capital.

Moreover, franchises can tolerate mis-management. Inept managers may diminish a franchise's profitability, but they cannot inflict mortal damage. In contrast, "a business" earns exceptional profits only if it is the low-cost operator or if supply of its product or service is tight. Tightness in supply usually does not last long. With superior management, a company may maintain its status as a low- cost operator for a much longer time, but even then unceasingly faces the possibility of competitive attack. And a business, unlike a franchise, can be killed by poor management.

Until recently, media properties possessed the three characteristics of a franchise and consequently could both price aggressively and be managed loosely. Now, however, consumers looking for information and entertainment (their primary interest being the latter) enjoy greatly broadened choices as to where to find them. Unfortunately, demand can't expand in response to this new supply: 500 million American eyeballs and a 24-hour day are all that's available. The result is that competition has intensified, markets have fragmented, and the media industry has lost some – though far from all – of its franchise strength"."

2. Do business enjoy high market share?

The term economic moat, popularized by Warren Buffett, refers to a business' ability to maintain competitive advantages over its competitors in order to protect its long-term profits and market share from competing firms. Just like a medieval castle, the moat serves to protect those inside the fortress and their riches from outsiders.

One of the basic tenets of modern economics, however, is that, given time, competition will erode any competitive advantages enjoyed by a firm. This effect occurs because once a firm establishes competitive advantages, its superior operations generate boosted profits for itself, thus providing a strong incentive for competing firms to duplicate the methods of the leading firm or find even better operating methods.

US Smartphone Shipments Market Share (%)	2018 Q4	2019 Q1	2019 Q2	2019 Q3	2019 Q4
Apple	47%	39%	41%	42%	49%
Samsung	22%	28%	21%	25%	20%
LG	12%	11%	13%	12%	9%
Lenovo#	6%	8%	8%	8%	8%
Others	13%	14%	17%	13%	14%

Apple has competitive Advantage with the market share 49%

Q3 2019 Highlights

- Smartphone volumes fell 2% YoY, from continued weakness of high-end premium Android devices. Mid-tier devices increased in sales but could not offset the premium decline.

- Apple increased YoY with the help of the new iPhone 11 series. The iPhone 11 quickly became the flagship device of choice for budget conscious Apple fans. Apple continues to make headways with its services expansion, launching Apple TV+.

- Samsung declines another quarter. The S10 series continues to see weakness in the premium line-up. The Note 10 shows promise and the Note 10 Plus 5G could become a strong 5G seller as carriers are experimenting with different monthly pricing configurations and financing options.

- Among the "Others" Google Pixel grew 139% YoY as the Pixel 3a and 3a XL are overtaking sales of the Pixel 3. Google will look to the Pixel 4 in Q4 to help boost its premium device sales however early market response for the device seems lackluster.

3. Does business have above average Gross Profit Margin, Operating Margin and Net Profit Margin compare with their competitors?

We need to compare three margins to understand competitive advantages.

- Investors who know how to calculate and analyze a corporate profit margin gain insight into a company's current effectiveness in generating profits and its potential to generate future profits.

- The three-key profit-margin ratios investors should analyze when evaluating a company are gross profit margins, operating profit margins, and net profit margins.

- Companies with large profit margins frequently have a competitive advantage over other companies in their industry.

- Understanding a company's margin ratios can be a starting point for further analysis to decide if a company would be a good investment option.

Competitive Comparison Data

Company	Market Cap (M)	Gross Margin %
Apple Inc	$ 1,264,820.00	37.95
Samsung Electronics C...	$ 271,493.59	36.09
China Electronics Holdi...	$ 124,978.90	0.00
Sony Corp	$ 77,661.81	27.71
Midea Group Co Ltd	$ 53,253.36	28.99
Gree Electric Appliance...	$ 46,669.30	30.23
Xiaomi Corp	$ 31,543.36	13.05
Kyocera Corp	$ 18,913.02	28.12
Haier Smart Home Co ...	$ 18,422.57	29.48
Panasonic Corp	$ 17,208.95	28.82

Competitive Comparison Data

Company	Market Cap (M)	Operating Margin %
Apple Inc	$ 1,264,820.00	24.71
Samsung Electronics ...	$ 271,493.59	12.05
China Electronics Hol...	$ 124,978.90	0.00
Sony Corp	$ 77,661.81	9.41
Midea Group Co Ltd	$ 53,253.36	9.38
Gree Electric Applianc...	$ 46,669.30	13.96
Xiaomi Corp	$ 31,543.36	-3.20
Kyocera Corp	$ 18,913.02	8.04
Haier Smart Home Co...	$ 18,422.57	4.58
Panasonic Corp	$ 17,208.95	4.58

Competitive Comparison Data

Company	Market Cap (M)	Net Margin %
Apple Inc	$ 1,264,820.00	21.49
Samsung Electronics C...	$ 271,493.59	9.33
China Electronics Holdin...	$ 124,978.90	0.00
Sony Corp	$ 77,661.81	7.61
Midea Group Co Ltd	$ 53,253.36	8.60
Gree Electric Appliances...	$ 46,669.30	13.30
Xiaomi Corp	$ 31,543.36	7.22
Kyocera Corp	$ 18,913.02	7.79
Haier Smart Home Co Ltd	$ 18,422.57	3.65
Panasonic Corp	$ 17,208.95	3.76

Apple Inc have above average Gross Profit Margin, Operating Margin and Net Profit Margin compare with their competitors.

Barrier to entry

1. Does the business have barrier to entry?

Barriers to entry are the economic term describing the existence of high start-up costs or other obstacles that prevent new competitors from easily entering an industry or area of business. Barriers to entry benefit existing firms because they protect their revenues and profits.

Common barriers to entry include special tax benefits to existing firms, patents, strong brand identity or customer loyalty, and high customer switching costs. Others include the need for new firms to obtain proper licenses or regulatory clearance before operation.

Generally, firms favor barriers to entry when already comfortably ensconced in an industry to limit competition and claim a larger market share. Other barriers to entry occur naturally, often evolving over time as certain industry players establish dominance.

Supply Based
- *Patents*
- *Regulatory Licenses*
- *Cost advantage/Economic of Scale*

Demand Based
- *Network Switching Cost*
- *Habits*
- *Search*

2. Barrier to entry is supply based or demand based?

Supply Based

Companies that can deliver their goods or services at a low cost, typically due to economies of scale, have a distinct competitive advantage because they can undercut their rivals on price.

Wal-Mart (WMT) is a great example of a low-cost producer, and its low costs allow it to price its products the most attractively. As a dominant player in retailing, the company's size provides it with enormous scale efficiencies, or operating leverage, that it uses to keep costs low. Scale allows Wal-Mart to do its own purchasing more efficiently since it has roughly 5,000 large stores worldwide, and it gives the company tremendous bargaining power with its suppliers. Since the company positions itself as a low-cost retailer, it wants to ensure it gives the lowest prices to its customers. This can translate into tough bargaining terms for those firms that want to sell their products on Wal-Mart's shelves. As a result, Wal-Mart is able to offer prices that competitors have a difficult time matching--one reason why you don't see too many Kmarts around anymore.

Apple has what Warren Buffett calls a strong moat: competitive advantages that protect it from rivals and enable its large profits. Apple's intellectual property—specifically, its patents and—contributes to the depth of its moat. As a household name, Apple's brand name is a significant part of its moat.

Demand Based

Microsoft Corporation (NASDAQ: MSFT), one of the largest companies in the world, thoroughly understands how to build competitive advantage. Some call this advantage similar to a protective moat that keeps other firms from taking its market share. Economies of scale, the network effect, brand strength, intellectual property and regulation can all contribute to competitive moats. Without these factors in place, competition from comparable products and services eventually erode operating margins. This sustainability of *advantage* is hugely important for investors that follow the philosophies of Charlie Munger or Warren Buffett.

These competitive advantages illustrate how Microsoft operates globally with popular product suites such as Windows, Office and Azure. Network effect, economies of scale and strong brand all work in Microsoft's favor, but it operates in highly competitive markets that are changing at accelerating rates. Morningstar assigns Microsoft a wide economic moat based on the recent competitive success of Office and cloud products, but tumbling margins and profits approaching the opportunity cost of capital are troublesome signs that the moat may be unsustainable.

Facebook the website — was opened up to the general public in 2006. From then onward, anyone 13 years old or older could sign up for a Facebook member page.

A couple of months ago, on July 26, 2017, just eleven years later, the website had about 2 billion active members. The market valuation of Facebook's stock exceeded $500 billion (416 billion euros). Its 2016 revenues were $27.6 billion, of which an astounding $10.2 billion were net income.

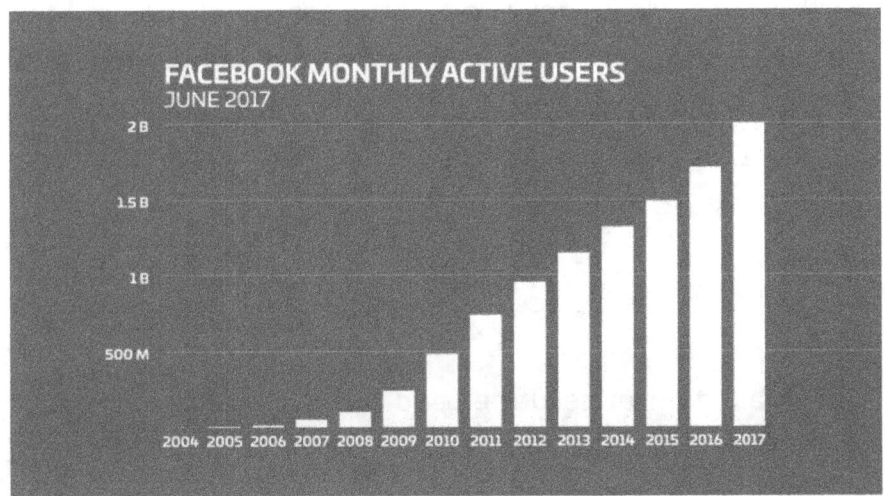

20

Quantitative Analysis

Qualitative analysis, of which Warren Buffett is a notable practitioner, is the foundation of a broad array of investment and financial devision-making methods. However, it is not the only way to determine whether an investment is worthwhile. Many investors also perform quantitative analysis of companies and investments, whereby things such as the company's cost of capital percentage change in sales over time, or trends in net income as a percentage of sales or other measures are considered.

In Buffett Partnership Letter October 9, 1967, Buffett said,

"The evaluation of securities and businesses for investment purposes has always involved a mixture of qualitative and quantitative factors. At the one extreme, the analyst exclusively oriented to qualitative factors would say, "Buy the right company (with the right prospects, inherent industry conditions, management, etc..) and the price will take care of itself." On the other hand, the quantitative spokesman would say, "Buy at the right price and the company (and stock) will take care of itself." As is so often the pleasant result in the securities world, money can be made with either approach. And, of course, any analyst combines the two to some extent – his classification in either school would depend on the relative weight he assigns to the various factors and not to his consideration of one group of factors to the exclusion of the other group.

Quantitative Analysis

- PORTFOLIO DIVERSIFICATION
- BUSINESS VALUATION
- BUSINESS RISK
  - STOCK RISK
  - MACROECONOMICS RISK

21

Portfolio Diversification

The definition of diversification is the act of, or the result of, achieving variety. In finance and investment planning, portfolio diversification is the risk management strategy of combining a variety of assets to reduce the overall risk of an investment portfolio.

"There is a close logical connection between the concept of a safety margin and the principle of diversification."

--Benjamin Graham

Diversification is a risk management strategy that mixes a wide variety of investments within a portfolio. A diversified portfolio contains a mix of distinct asset types and investment vehicles in an attempt at limiting exposure to any single asset or risk. The rationale behind this technique is that a portfolio constructed of different kinds of assets will, on average, yield higher long-term returns and lower the risk of any individual holding or security.

Studies and mathematical models have shown that maintaining a well-diversified portfolio of 25 to 30 stocks yields the most cost-effective level of risk reduction. The investing in more securities generates further diversification benefits, albeit at a drastically smaller rate.

Billionaire investor Warren Buffett famously stated that "diversification is protection against ignorance. It makes little sense if you know what you are doing." In Buffet's view, studying one or two industries in great depth, learning their ins and outs, and using that knowledge to profit on those industries is more lucrative than spreading a portfolio across a broad array of sectors so that gains from certain sectors offset losses from others.

Warren Buffett Portfolio

Stock Ticker	Stock Name	Amount Invested	Percentage of Total
AAPL	Apple	47783	36.8%
KO	Coca-Cola	18240	14.1%
BAC	Bank of America	15671	12.1%
AXP	American Express	13389	10.3%
WFC	Wells Fargo &	12493	9.6%
KHC	Kraft Heinz	9566	7.4%
MCO	Moodys	5973	4.6%
USB	U.S. Bancorp	3040	2.3%
BK	Bank of New	2189	1.7%
LUV	Southwest Airlines Co	1391	1.1%

Sector	Amount Invested	Percentage of Porfolio	Number of Stocks in the Sector
Technology	47783	36.8%	1
Financials	46782	36.1%	5
Consumer Staples	27806	21.4%	2
Services & Goods	5973	4.6%	1
Transports	1391	1.1%	1

1. Do you understand economy of the business?

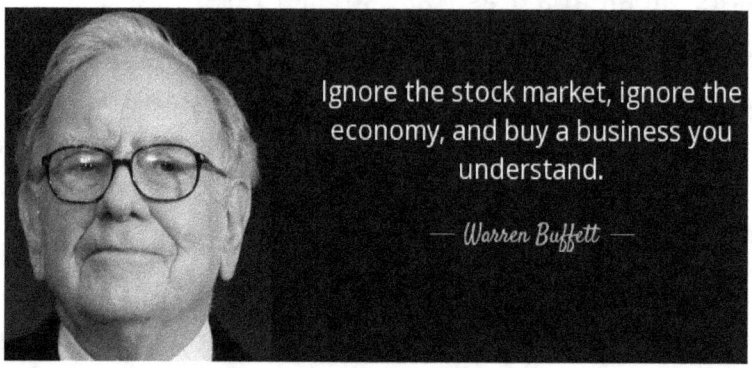

Knowing all the aspect about the company such as who are the customers, where company operated and what are the earning, financial ratios etc.

Business economics is a field of applied economics that studies the financial, organizational, market-related, and environmental issues faced by corporations. Economic theory and quantitative methods form the basis of assessments on factors affecting corporations such as business organization, management, expansion, and strategy. Studies might include how and why corporations expand, the impact of entrepreneurs, the interactions among corporations, and the role of governments in regulation.

The field of business economics addresses economic principles, strategies, standard business practices, the acquisition of necessary capital, profit generation, the efficiency of production, and overall management strategy. Business economics also includes the study of external economic factors and their influence on business decisions such as a change in industry regulation or a sudden price shift in raw materials.

Scope of Business Economics: As regards the scope of business economics, no uniformity of views exists among various authors. However, the following aspects are said to generally fall under business economics.

1. Demand Analysis and Forecasting

2. Cost and production Analysis.

3. Pricing Decisions, policies and practices.

4. Profit Management.

5. Capital Management.

Business economics helps in reaching a variety of business decisions in a complicated environment. Certain examples are :

(i) What products and services should be produced?

(ii) What input and production technique should be used?

(iii) How much output should be produced and at what prices it should be sold?

iv) What are the best sizes and locations of new plants?

(v) When should equipment be replaced?

(vi) How should the available capital be allocated?

Different aspects of business need attention of the chief executive. He may be called upon to choose a single option among the many that may be available to him. It would he in the interest of the business to reach an optimal decision- the one that promotes the goal of the business firm. A scientific formulation of the business problem and finding its optimals solution requires that the business firm is he equipped with a rational methodology and appropriate tools.

Understanding How the iPhone Makes Money

Investors and analysts cannot easily calculate how much profit Apple earns on each product. Apple, in the past, had reported unit sales for each product. However, the company has stopped that practice and instead, reports revenue by product. The table below contains the products and services revenues for the past three years. The data was pulled from the company's 10K report on September 28, 2019.

Apple reported $260 billion in revenue for the end of the company's 2019 fiscal year—highlighted in green in the table below.

The iPhone generated $142.3 billion in revenue in 2019, meaning the iPhone represented approximately 55% of the total revenue for the year.

Apple Inc. Revenue from Product Sales					
Net sales by category:	2019	% Change	2018	% Change	2017
iPhone	$ 142,381	-14%	$ 164,888	18%	$ 139,337
Mac	25,740	2%	25,198	-1%	25,569
iPad	21,280	16%	18,380	-2%	18,802
Wearables, Home and Accessories	24,482	41%	17,381	36%	12,826
Services	46,291	16%	39,748	22%	32,700
Total net sales	$ 260,174	-2%	$ 265,595	16%	$ 229,234

The iPhone revenue declined in 2019 by 14% versus 2018. However, revenue for 2017 was an 18% increase from the year prior.

2. Do you think the idea of excessive diversification is madness?

"The idea of excessive diversification is madness. Wide diversification, which necessarily includes investment in mediocre businesses, only guarantees ordinary results."
— Charlie Munger

We try to exert a Ted Williams kind of discipline. In his book The Science of Hitting, Ted explains that he carved the strike zone into 77 cells, each the size of a baseball. Swinging only at balls in his "best" cell, he knew, would allow him to bat .400; reaching for balls in his "worst" spot, the low outside corner of the strike zone, would reduce him to .230. In other words, waiting for the fat pitch would mean a trip to the Hall of Fame; swinging indiscriminately would mean a ticket to the minors.
— Warren Buffett

We say we are trying to buy into businesses with excellent economics, run by honest and able people at a decent price. We buy very few securities, so we look at it as "focused" investing.
— Warren Buffett

If you know how to value businesses, it's crazy to own 50 stocks or 40 stocks or 30 stocks, probably because there aren't that many wonderful businesses understandable to a single human being in all likelihood. To forego buying more

of some super-wonderful business and instead put your money into #30 or #35 on your list of attractiveness just strikes Charlie and me as madness.
— Warren Buffett

The average mutual fund that holds 150 names goes that far out on the spectrum more for business reasons than for performance reasons. This is a profession where managers focus a lot on the question: 'What mistake would it take to get me fired?' The answer usually centers around underperforming by a certain amount, so they develop a strategy to minimize the probability of that outcome.
— Bill Nygren

Diversification is like ice cream. It's good, but only in moderation. The common consensus is that a well-balanced portfolio with approximately 20 stocks diversifies away the maximum amount of market risk. Owning additional stocks takes away the potential of big gainers significantly impacting your bottom line, as is the case with large mutual funds investing in hundreds of stocks.

According to Warren Buffett, "wide diversification is only required when investors do not understand what they are doing." In other words, if you diversify too much, you might not lose much, but you won't gain much either.

3. Excess diversification is to reduce risk or reduce gain?

Risk
- *Systematic Risk*
- *Unsystematic Risk*

Systematic risk

Systematic risk refers to the risk inherent to the entire market or market segment. Systematic risk, also known as "undiversifiable risk," "volatility" or "market risk," affects the overall market, not just a particular stock or industry. This type of risk is both unpredictable and impossible to completely avoid. It cannot be mitigated through diversification, only through hedging or by using the correct asset allocation strategy.

Unsystematic risk

Unsystematic risk is unique to a specific company or industry. Also known as "nonsystematic risk," "specific risk," "diversifiable risk" or "residual risk," in the context of an investment portfolio, unsystematic risk can be reduced through diversification.

Systematic Risk vs. Unsystematic Risk

While systematic risk can be thought of as the probability of a loss that is associated with the entire market or a segment thereof, unsystematic risk refers to the probability of a loss within a specific industry or security.

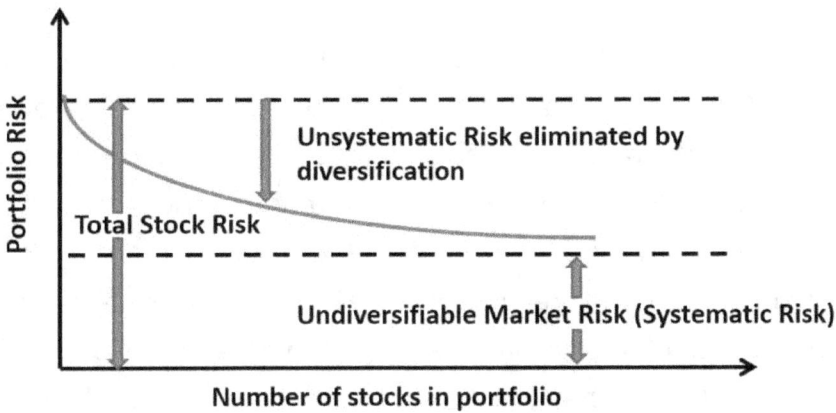

Key Point

- Just to reduce risk, it will be not good for excess diversification.
- Excess diversification can reduce your gain, it is better to invest in a company which you can understand.
- The average number of stocks to keep it 25 to 30.
- All the stock must have deep moat and competitive advantage.

22

Financial Analysis & Valuation

In financial markets, stock valuation is the method of calculating theoretical values of companies and their stocks. The main use of these methods is to predict future market prices, or more generally, potential market prices, and thus to profit from price movement – stocks that are judged undervalued (with respect to their theoretical value) are bought, while stocks that are judged overvalued are sold, in the expectation that undervalued stocks will overall rise in value, while overvalued stocks will generally decrease in value.

Every investor who wants to beat the market must master the skill of stock valuation. Essentially, stock valuation is a method of determining the intrinsic value (or theoretical value) of a stock. The importance of valuing stocks evolves from the fact that the intrinsic value of a stock is not attached to its current price. By knowing a stock's intrinsic value, an investor may determine whether the stock is over- or under-valued at its current market price.

Valuing stocks is an extremely complicated process that can be generally viewed as a combination of both art and science. Investors may be overwhelmed by the amount of available information that can be potentially used in valuing stocks (company's financials, newspapers, economic reports, stock reports, etc.).

Therefore, an investor needs to be able to filter the relevant information from the unnecessary noise. Additionally, an investor should know about major stock valuation methods and the scenarios in which such methods are applicable.

Value investing is based on the basic concept of buying and selling. If the actual value of any product is known then you can buy it at a discount and sell it at a higher value. This is how value investing for stocks works. The investor identifies the best value stock, then buys it at a discount and holds it till the time it reaches its actual value to derive huge returns.

In an ideal situation, the share price in the stock should be equal to its intrinsic value. In long run, the price of stock will be approximately equal to its value, but the same doesn't exist in the short run for various reasons. The reasons could be macroeconomic disturbances, or the cyclical nature of the sector the business belongs to. The value investors expect the market to eventually recognize the mispricing and correct it. This is why experienced investors participate in value investing by going for fundamentally strong stocks, trading at a low price. Thus, determining the intrinsic value is the primary benchmark to decide whether the stock is cheap to buy or it is overpriced to be sold. Without this reference point, it will be impossible to execute the "buy low, sell high" investment strategy.

1. Does the company have sustainable barrier to entry and Competitive Advantage, you can proceed with valuation and buy the stock?

"Different people understand different businesses. And the important thing is to know which ones you do understand and when you're operating within what I call your circle of competence."
— Warren Buffett, 1999 Berkshire Hathaway Annual Meeting

It states that you should fist check the all aspect of the qualitative analysis before you do your valuation, you should not value any company, if the company don't have barrier to entry, what we will franchise value.

Competitive advantage is the leverage a business has over its competitors. This can be gained by offering clients better and greater value. Advertising products or services with lower prices or higher quality piques the interest of consumers. Target markets recognize these unique products or services. This is the reason behind brand loyalty, or why customers prefer one particular product or service over another.

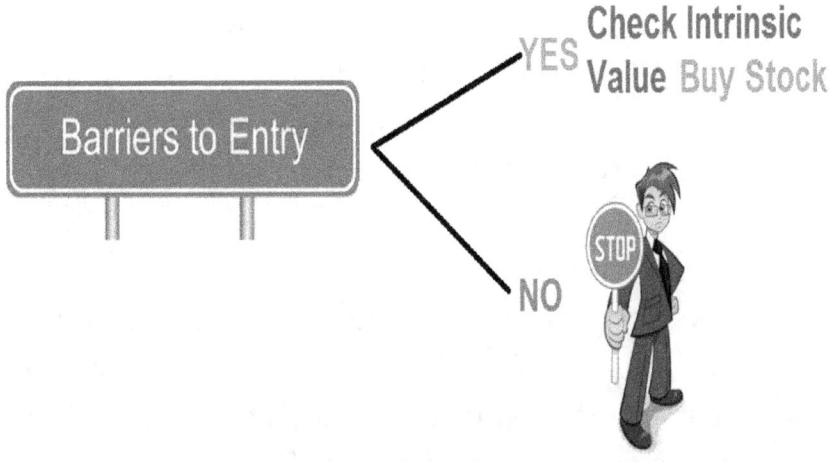

If company don't have barrier to entry, don't move to analysis the intrinsic value.

2. Are you buying a stock below the intrinsic value? And are you are getting growth for free?

Margin of safety is a principle of investing in which an investor only purchases securities when their market price is significantly below their intrinsic value. In other words, when the market price of a security is significantly below your estimation of its intrinsic value, the difference is the margin of safety. Because investors may set a margin of safety in accordance with their own risk preferences, buying securities when this difference is present allows an investment to be made with minimal downside risk.

"On the margin of safety, which means, don't try and drive a 9,800-pound truck over a bridge that says it's, you know, capacity: 10,000 pounds. But go down the road a little bit and find one that says, capacity: 15,000 pounds."
— Warren Buffett, 1996 Berkshire Hathaway Annual Meeting

Though Buffett believes the market is frequently wrong about the fair value of stocks, he doesn't believe himself to be infallible. If he estimates a company's fair value at $80 per share, and the company's stock sells for $77, he will refrain from buying despite the apparent undervaluation. That small discrepancy does not provide an adequate margin of safety, another concept borrowed from Ben Graham. No one can predict cash flows into the distant future with precision, not even for stable businesses with durable competitive advantages. Therefore, any estimate of fair value must include substantial room for error.

If you understood a business perfectly and the future of the business, you would need very little in the way of a margin of safety. So, the more vulnerable the business is, assuming you still want to invest in it, the larger the margin of safety you'd need. If you're driving a truck across a bridge that says it holds 10,000 pounds and you've got a 9,800 pound vehicle, if the bridge is 6 inches above the crevice it covers, you may feel okay; but if it's over the Grand Canyon, you may feel you want a little larger margin of safety.

–Warren Buffett.

Margin of Safety = (Intrinsic Value Per Share – Stock Price) / Intrinsic Value Per Share

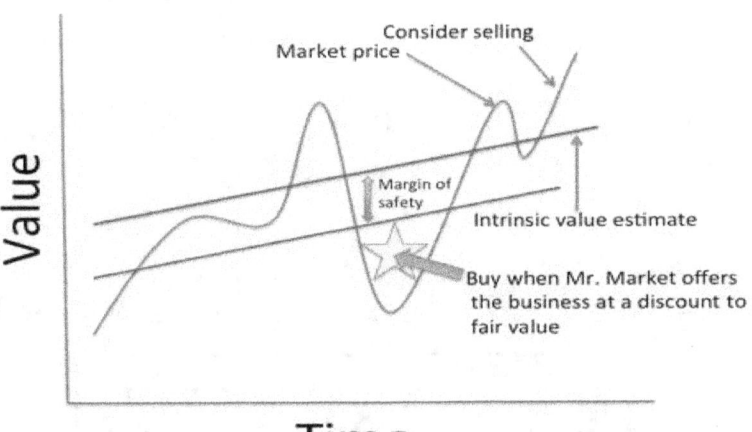

If you are buying the below the intrinsic value, and when price will increase, the return you will get is free because you have bought below the intrinsic value.

3. Growth in Gross profit margin or sustainable?

The gross profit margin ratio analysis is an indicator of a company's financial health. A higher gross profit margin indicates that a company can make a reasonable profit on sales, as long as it keeps overhead costs in control. Investors tend to pay more for a company with higher gross profit.

The gross profit margin ratio, also known as gross margin, is the ratio of gross margin expressed as a percentage of sales. Gross margin, alone, indicates how much profit a company makes after paying off its Cost of Goods Sold. It is a measure of the efficiency of a company using its raw materials and labor during the production process. The value of gross profit margin varies from company and industry. The higher the profit margin, the more efficient a company is. This can be assigned to single products or an entire company.

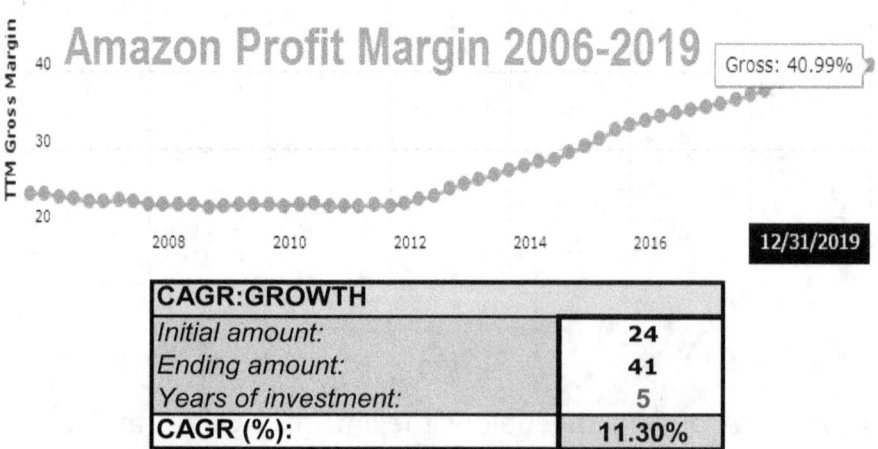

CAGR:GROWTH	
Initial amount:	24
Ending amount:	41
Years of investment:	5
CAGR (%):	11.30%

There is an upward trend, it is a good indicator.

4. Growth in operating profit margin or sustainable?

The higher the margin that a company has, the less financial risk it has – as compared to having a lower ratio, indicating a lower profit margin. Continued increases in profit margin. It measures the amount of net profit a company obtains per dollar of revenue gained. Over time shows that profitability is improving.

Operating margin is equal to operating income divided by revenue. Operating margin is a profitability ratio measuring revenue after covering operating and non-operating expenses of a business. Also referred to as return on sales, the operating income is the basis of how much of the generated sales is left when all operating expenses are paid off.

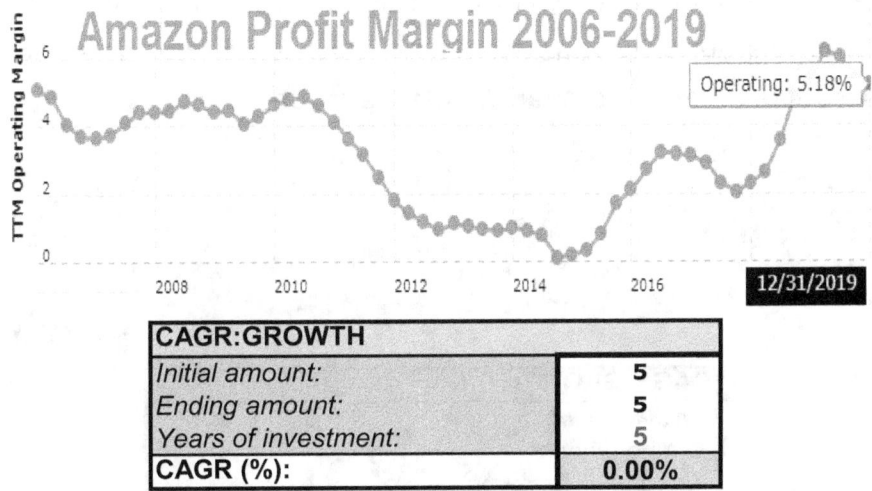

There is a sustainable trend, it is a good indicator.

5. Growth in net profit margin or sustainable?

When a company's net margin exceeds the average for its industry, it is said to have a competitive advantage, meaning it is more successful than other companies that have similar operations. While the average net margin for different industries varies widely, how businesses can gain a competitive advantage remains constant, whether they increase sales or reduce expenses.

Improving the net margin through increasing revenue is generally the most popular option. Businesses can increase sales income by raising the price of products or by selling more of them.

Net profit margin is the percentage of revenue remaining after all operating expenses, interest, taxes and preferred stock dividends (but not common stock dividends) have been deducted from a company's total revenue.

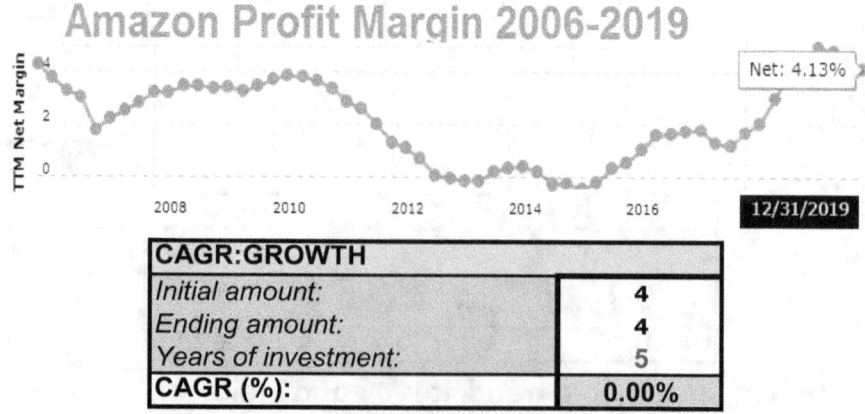

CAGR:GROWTH	
Initial amount:	4
Ending amount:	4
Years of investment:	5
CAGR (%):	0.00%

There is a sustainable trend, it is a good indicator.

6. Retune of equity Ratio (ROE) above the cost of capital (WACC)?

Return on equity (ROE) is a ratio that provides investors with insight into how efficiently a company (or more specifically, its management team) is handling the money that shareholders have contributed to it. In other words, it measures the profitability of a corporation in relation to stockholders' equity. The higher the ROE, the more efficient a company's management is at generating income and growth from its equity financing.

ROE is often used to compare a company to its competitors and the overall market. The formula is especially beneficial when comparing firms of the same industry since it tends to give accurate indications of which companies are operating with greater financial efficiency and for the evaluation of nearly any company with primarily tangible rather than intangible assets.

ROE is especially used for comparing the performance of companies in the same industry. As with return on capital, a ROE is a measure of management's ability to generate income from the equity available to it. ROEs of 15-20% are generally considered good. ROE is also a factor in stock valuation, in association with other financial ratios. While higher ROE ought intuitively to imply higher stock prices, in reality, predicting the stock value of a company based on its

ROE is dependent on too many other factors to be of use by itself.

WACC is the amount we will pay from financing the capital. This includes the portion of debt we are carrying. But ROE is a return based on equity.

The weighted average cost of capital (WACC) is the rate that a company is expected to pay on average to all its security holders to finance its assets. The WACC is commonly referred to as the firm's cost of capital. Importantly, it is dictated by the external market and not by management. The WACC represents the minimum return that a company must earn on an existing asset base to satisfy its creditors, owners, and other providers of capital, or they will invest elsewhere.

Competitive Comparison Data

Company	Market Cap (M)	WACC %
Apple Inc	$ 1,264,820.00	6.98
Samsung Electronics Co Ltd	$ 271,493.59	8.07
China Electronics Holding...	$ 124,978.90	0.00
Sony Corp	$ 77,661.81	5.22
Midea Group Co Ltd	$ 53,253.36	6.27
Gree Electric Appliances I...	$ 46,669.30	8.44
Xiaomi Corp	$ 31,543.36	0.00
Kyocera Corp	$ 18,913.02	6.68
Haier Smart Home Co Ltd	$ 18,422.57	7.31
Panasonic Corp	$ 17,208.95	4.93

7. Growth in Return of Equity?

Return on Equity (ROE) – a profitability ratio measuring the ability of a company to generate profits from the investments of the shareholders. The computation formula is flexible enough, and users, who want to measure the return on common equity only, may subtract the preferred stock from calculation. This would allow holders of the company's common stock to estimate the return generated by their shares. Calculating the ratio for different periods helps to understand the changes in profitability.

Growth in ROE state that company is increasing profit.

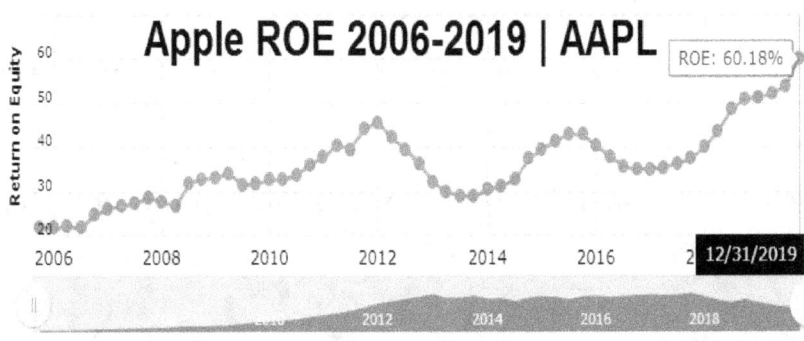

CAGR:GROWTH	
Initial amount:	9
Ending amount:	60
Years of investment:	15
CAGR (%):	13.48%

Apple Inc Growth in ROE is 13.48%

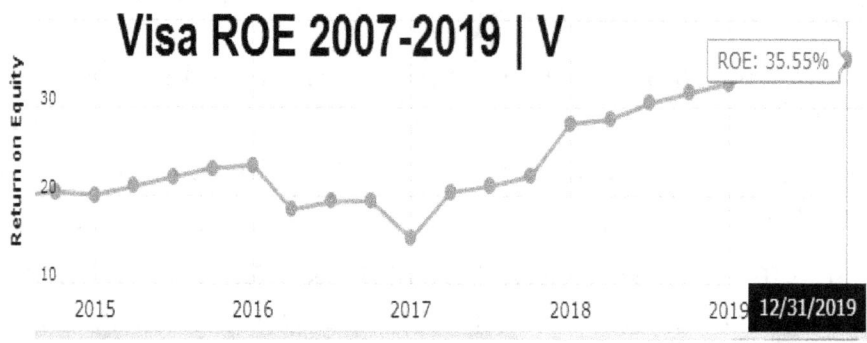

CAGR:GROWTH	
Initial amount:	20
Ending amount:	35
Years of investment:	5
CAGR (%):	11.84%

It is a good ratio to understanding, how company is creating value to the shareholders and about the profit and shares outstanding.

8. Does Earning Per Share growing in a company?

EPS growth (earnings per share growth) illustrates the growth of earnings per share over time. EPS growth rates help investors identify stocks that are increasing or decreasing in profitability.

Earnings per share measures the amount of money a company earns allocated on a per share basis. The earnings per share growth rate is a metric that tells you whether or not earnings per share have increased during the last year compared to the year before. EPS growth rate is thus a useful measure for investors because it reveals whether a company is becoming more profitable over time.

- Earnings per share (EPS) is a company's net profit divided by the number of common shares it has outstanding.

- EPS indicates how much money a company makes for each share of its stock and is a widely used metric for corporate profits.

- A higher EPS indicates more value because investors will pay more for a company with higher profits.

AAPL - EPS - Earnings per Share
Annual Values (US $)

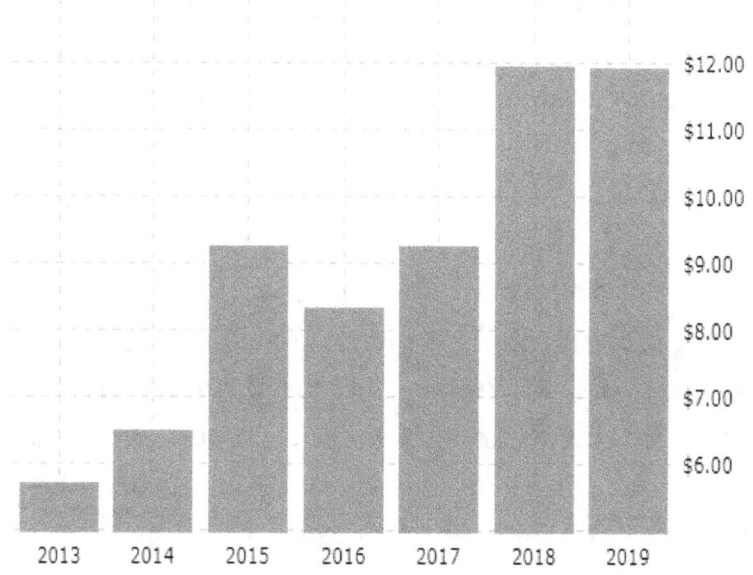

CAGR:GROWTH	
Initial amount:	5.7
Ending amount:	12
Years of investment:	7
CAGR (%):	11.13%

Apple Inc EPS growth is 11.13%

AMZN - EPS - Earnings per Share
Annual Values (US $)

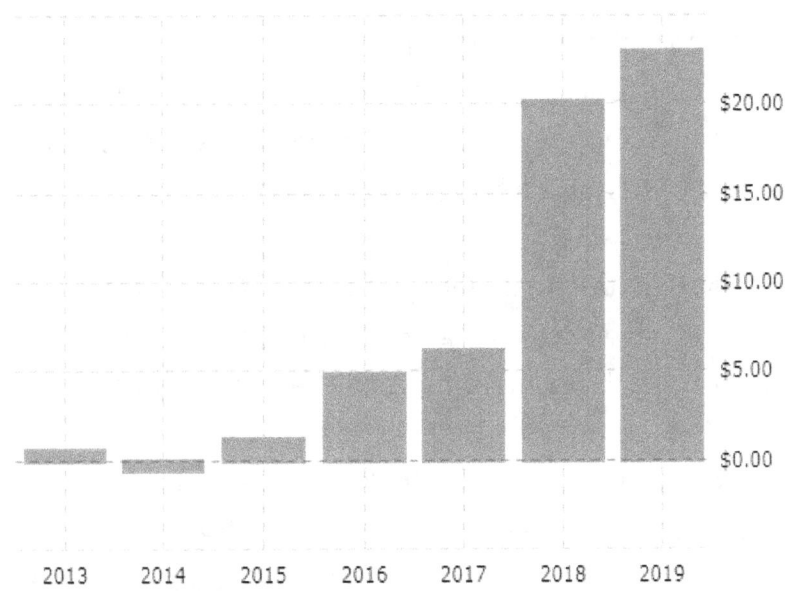

CAGR:GROWTH	
Initial amount:	0.6
Ending amount:	23
Years of investment:	7
CAGR (%):	68.77%

Amazon EPS growth is 68.77%

9. Does Book Value Per Share growing in a company?

Book value of equity per share (BVPS) is the ratio of equity available to common shareholders divided by the number of outstanding shares. This figure represents the minimum value of a company's equity, and measures the book value of a firm on a per-share basis.

The book value of equity per share (BVPS) metric can be used by investors to gauge whether a stock price is undervalued, by comparing it to the firm's market value per share. If a company's BVPS is higher than its market value per share—its current stock price—then the stock is considered undervalued. If the firm's BVPS increases, the stock should be perceived as more valuable, and the stock price should increase.

Book value growth tells an investor how quickly a company is building its asset base. A company may increase its book value by buying more assets or decreasing its liabilities. The book value growth rate helps to determine how strong the overall growth-orientation is for a stock.

Growth rate is how much a company's equity is growing over the year. The company is not a dead company and it is growing. The value of the business is in the growth rate.

AMZN - Book Value Per Share
Annual Values

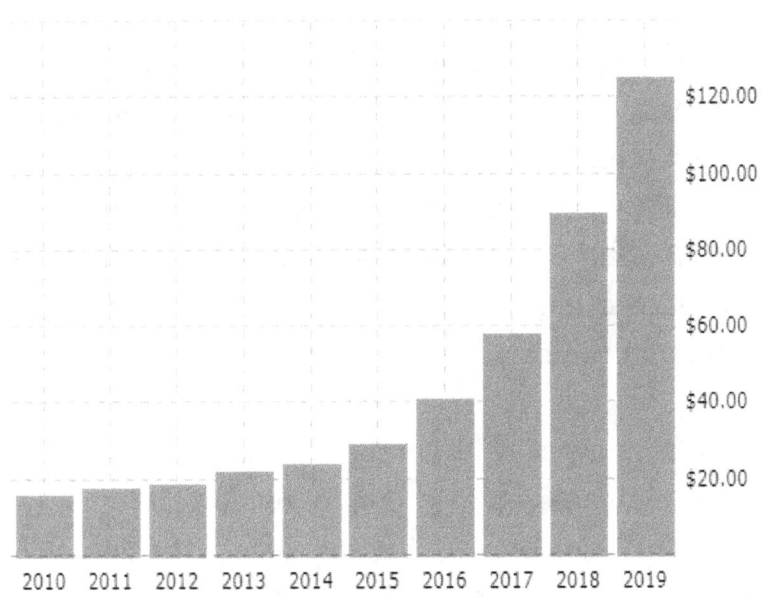

CAGR:GROWTH	
Initial amount:	7.7
Ending amount:	125
Years of investment:	10
CAGR (%):	32.17%

The Amazon BVPS grows to 125 from 7.2 with growth of 32.17% in 10 years.

10. Is the Return on capital employed (ROCE) is above 15%?

Return on capital employed (ROCE) is a financial ratio that measures a company's profitability and the efficiency with which its capital is used. In other words, the ratio measures how well a company is generating profits from its capital. The ROCE ratio is considered an important profitability ratio and is used often by investors when screening for suitable investment candidates.

Capital employed is the total amount of capital that a company has utilized in order to generate profits. It is the sum of shareholders' equity and debt liabilities. It can be simplified as total assets minus current liabilities. Instead of using capital employed at an arbitrary point in time, analysts and investors often calculate ROCE based on the average capital employed, which takes the average of opening and closing capital employed for the time period under analysis.

Instead of just looking at the revenue generated by each company, the capital employed by both companies should be compared. Although Procter & Gamble had more sales for the year and more assets, in terms of value, Colgate-Palmolive's ROCE of 43.51% is higher than P&G's 15.47% ROCE.

Apple Annual Data				
Sep15	Sep16	Sep17	Sep18	Sep19
39.76	30.79	28.60	35.00	42.43

Apple Inc ROCE

Amazon.com Annual Data				
Dec15	Dec16	Dec17	Dec18	Dec19
12.97	32.62	15.18	31.67	22.84

Amazon ROCE

Costco Wholesale Annual Data				
Aug15	Aug16	Aug17	Aug18	Aug19
23.23	20.67	22.42	26.40	29.01

Costco ROCE

Nike Annual Data				
May15	May16	May17	May18	May19
43.05	43.38	43.68	21.58	49.34

Nike ROCE

11. Growth in Free Cash Flow Per Share?

The simplest definition of free cash flow is the amount of leftover money in a company. Free cash flow is the amount of cash (operating cash flow) which remains in a business after all expenditures (debts, expenses, employees, fixed assets, plant, rent etc.) have been paid. Free cash flow represents a company's current cash value (not considering growth potential).

Free cash flow (FCF) represents the cash a company generates after accounting for cash outflows to support operations and maintain its capital assets. Unlike earnings or net income, free cash flow is a measure of profitability that excludes the non-cash expenses of the income statement and includes spending on equipment and assets as well as changes in working capital from the balance sheet.

The generic Free Cash Flow FCF Formula is equal to Cash from Operations minus Capital Expenditures. FCF represents the amount of cash generated by a business, after accounting for reinvestment in non-current capital assets by the company. This figure is also sometimes compared to Free Cash Flow to Equity or Free Cash Flow to the Firm (see a comparison of cash flow types).

If you don't have the cash flow statement handy to find Cash from Operations and Capital Expenditures, you can derive it from the Income statement and balance sheet.

AMZN - Free Cash Flow Per Share
Annual Values

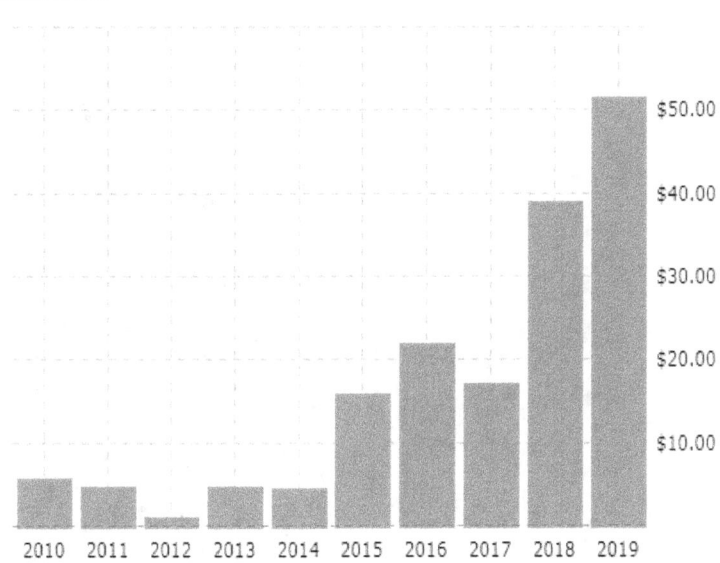

CAGR:GROWTH	
Initial amount:	5.5
Ending amount:	51
Years of investment:	10
CAGR (%):	25.00%

The Amazon grows to 51 from 5.5 with growth of 25 % in 10 years.

AAPL - Free Cash Flow Per Share
Annual Values

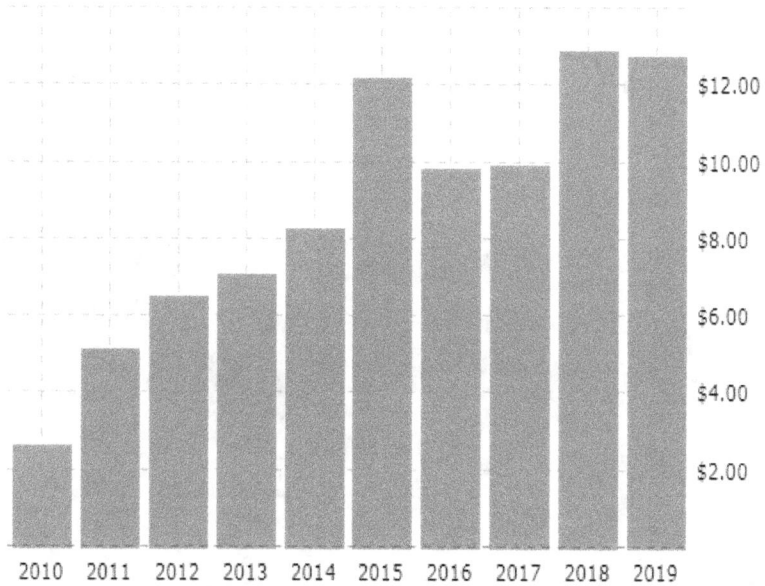

CAGR:GROWTH	
Initial amount:	2.5
Ending amount:	13
Years of investment:	10
CAGR (%):	17.56%

The Apple grows to 13 from 2.5 with growth of 17.56 % in 10 years.

12. Company Debt to Equity ratio is below .50?

The debt-to-equity (D/E) ratio is calculated by dividing a company's total liabilities by its shareholder equity. These numbers are available on the balance sheet of a company's financial statements.

The ratio is used to evaluate a company's financial leverage. The D/E ratio is an important metric used in corporate finance. It is a measure of the degree to which a company is financing its operations through debt versus wholly-owned funds. More specifically, it reflects the ability of shareholder equity to cover all outstanding debts in the event of a business downturn.

The debt-to-equity ratio (D/E) is a financial ratio indicating the relative proportion of shareholders' equity and debt used to finance a company's assets. Closely related to leveraging, the ratio is also known as risk, gearing or leverage. The two components are often taken from the firm's balance sheet or statement of financial position (so-called book value), but the ratio may also be calculated using market values for both, if the company's debt and equity are publicly traded, or using a combination of book value for debt and market value for equity financially.

The debt and equity components come from the right side of the firm's balance sheet. Debt is what the firm owes its creditors plus interest.☐ In the debt-to-equity ratio, only long-term debt is used in the equation. Long-term debt is debt that has a maturity of more than one year. Long-term debt includes mortgages, long-term leases, and other long-term loans.

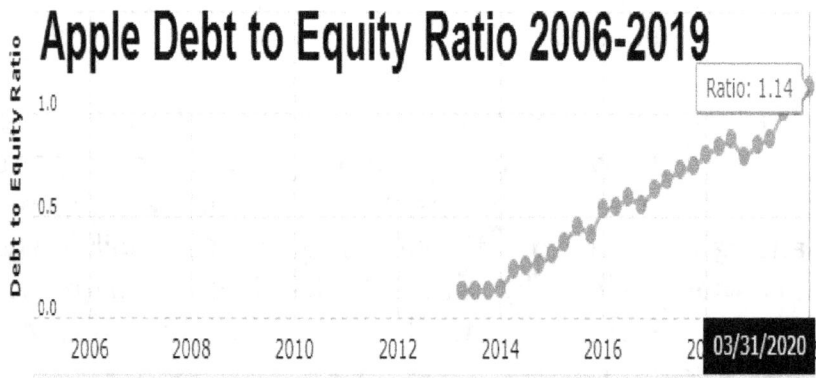

The cash is in different countries, so if the company access cash from any countries to united states, they are liable to pay taxes, that the reason Apple takes debts to pay dividend and buyback shares.

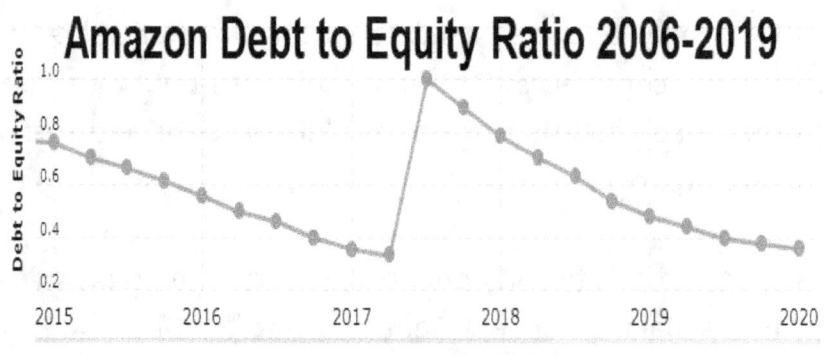

Amazon Ratio **0.38**

13. Enterprises Value to EBIDTA should be below 7?

Enterprise multiple, also known as the EV multiple, is a ratio used to determine the value of a company. The enterprise multiple looks at a firm in the way that a potential acquirer would by considering the company's debt. Stocks with an enterprise multiple of less than 7x based on the last 12 months (LTM) is generally considered a good value.

- Enterprise multiple, also known as the EV/EBITDA multiple, is a ratio used to determine the value of a company.

- It is computed by dividing enterprise value by EBITDA.

- Enterprise multiples can vary depending on the industry. It is reasonable to expect higher enterprise multiples in high-growth industries and lower multiples in industries with slow growth.

$$Enterprise\ Multiple = \frac{EV}{EBITDA}$$

The ratio of EV/EBITDA is used to compare the entire value of a business with the amount of EBITDA it earns on an annual basis. This ratio tells investors how many times EBITDA they have to pay, were they to acquire the entire business.

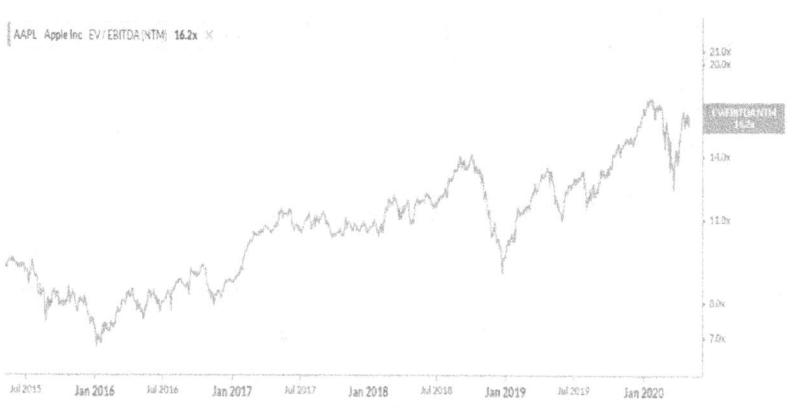

Apple Inc EV / EBITDA (ntm) for the quarter ending May 05, 2020 was 16.49 a 3.48% increase of 0.57 year over year.

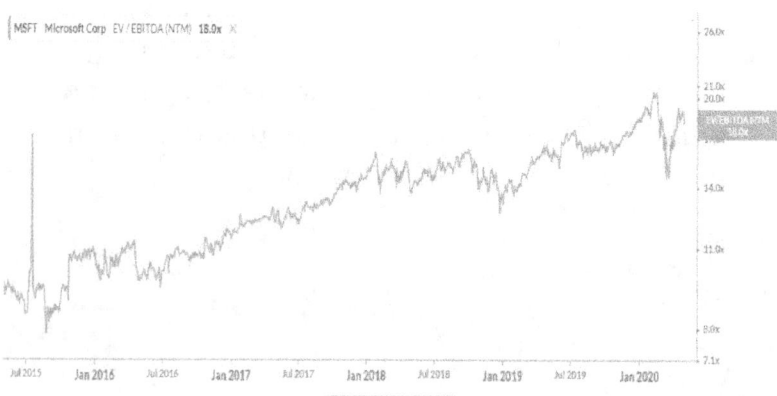

Microsoft Corp EV / EBITDA (ntm) for the quarter ending May 05, 2020 was 18.48 a -0.42% decrease of -0.08 year over year.

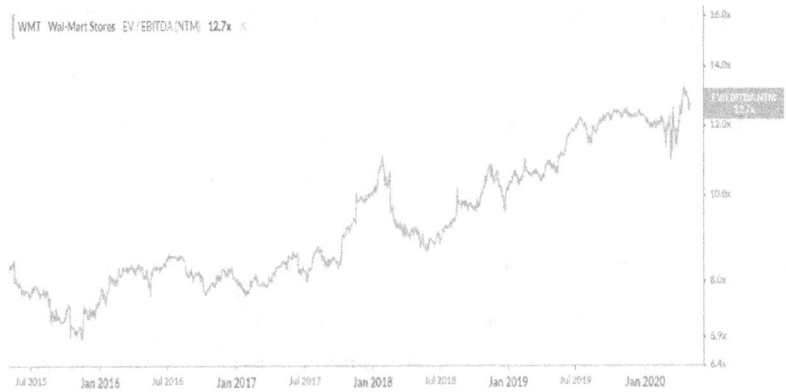

Wal-Mart Stores EV / EBITDA (ntm) for the quarter ending May 05, 2020 was 12.56 a -2.51% decrease of -0.32 year over year

Biogen Inc EV / EBITDA (ntm) for the quarter ending May 05, 2020 was 6.90 a -3.93% decrease of -0.27 year over year.

14. Company Price to free cash flow is below 8?

Price to free cash flow is an equity valuation metric used to compare a company's per-share market price to its per-share amount of free cash flow (FCF). This metric is very similar to the valuation metric of price to cash flow but is considered a more exact measure, owing to the fact that it uses free cash flow, which subtracts capital expenditures (CAPEX) from a company's total operating cash flow, thereby reflecting the actual cash flow available to fund non-asset-related growth. Companies use this metric when they need to expand their asset bases either in order to grow their businesses or simply to maintain acceptable levels of free cash flow.

$$\text{Price to FCF} = \frac{\text{Market Capitalization}}{\text{Free Cash Flow}}$$

- The price-to-cash flow ratio is a multiple that compares a company's market value to its operating cash flow or its stock price per share to operating cash flow per share.

- The price-to-cash flow multiple works well for companies that have large non-cash expenses such as depreciation.

- A low multiple implies that a stock may be undervalued.

Apple Inc., current P/FCFE calculation, comparison to benchmarks

No. shares of common stock outstanding	4,334,335,000
Selected Financial Data (US$)	
Free cash flow to equity (FCFE) (in millions)	51,077
FCFE per share	11.78
Current share price (P)	289.07
Valuation Ratio	
P/FCFE	24.53

23

Risk

An investor may experience losses due to factors affecting the overall performance of financial markets. Stock market bubbles and crashes are good examples of heightened market risk. The risk of investments declining in value because of economic developments or other events that affect the entire market.

As per the value investor approach, we will understand the risk in two ways: -

- **Stock Risk**
- **Macroeconomics Risk**

While you cannot totally avoid risks, you can take steps to manage them. Make sure you know what you are buying and whether it is reasonably priced. It is important to consider whether a listed company can achieve sustainable profits to support its stock price growth in the long run. Be careful when trading a stock affected by rumours or speculation. Should the rumour not be correct a correction in stock price is likely.

Stock Risk

1. Does business have enough margin of safety?

In chapter 20 of "The Intelligent Investor," Benjamin Graham discusses the margin of safety for two kinds of securities:

Common Stocks. For common stocks, Graham distinguishes three cases.

2.1. Under depression conditions, an investor may consider a stock has a margin of safety when it is selling for less than the corresponding amount of debt that could be safely issued against its property and earning power.

2.2. Under normal conditions (neither under depression nor mania conditions) The Margin of Safety is determined by an expected earning power considerably above the current rate of bonds. Graham offers the following example: A company has an earning power of 9 percent on the price (i.e., This is the reciprocal of the famous ratio), the bond rate is 4 percent. Thus, the stock buyer will have a 5% premium accruing in his favor.

2.3. When applied to the field of undervalued or bargain securities (value investing) The margin of safety is defined as favorable difference between value and price .

Notwithstanding that Benjamin Graham suggests the margin of safety as the difference between Value and Price, later on the chapter, he advises the purchase of a secondary company stock when the price is two thirds or less of its value. It is this definition of margin of safety, in relative terms, that personally I find more congruent to work with in the case of undervalued stocks.

It's also important to realize that some companies are riskier and harder to predict than others. In general, the riskier a company is, the larger the margin of safety should be.

The Margin of safety is very important because the valuation cannot be totally perfect; it is the assumption to predict the value of the stock, so that, if there is a gap in value of the stock, we must have enough margin of safety to minimize our risk in investing.

2. What we don't know, what is happing in the company like corporate governance or fraud?

Accounting scandals are business scandals which arise from intentional manipulation of financial statements with the disclosure of financial misdeeds by trusted executives of corporations or governments. Such misdeeds typically involve complex methods for misusing or misdirecting funds, overstating revenues, understating expenses, overstating the value of corporate assets, or underreporting the existence of liabilities (this can be done either manually, or by the means of deep learning). It involves an employee, account, or corporation itself and is misleading to investors and shareholders

We will never know what is behind the annual report, we read the annual report to understand the company business ecosystem, but still, there is some information, the company may not disclose, this is where they do frauds. Let see some examples.

Financial statement manipulation is an ongoing problem in corporate America. Although the Securities and Exchange Commission (SEC) has taken many steps to mitigate this type of corporate malfeasance, the structure of management incentives, the enormous latitude afforded by the Generally Accepted Accounting Principles (GAAP) and the ever-present conflict of interest between the independent auditor and the corporate client continues to provide the perfect environment for such activity. Due to these factors, investors who purchase individual stocks or bonds must be aware of the issues, warning signs and the tools that are at their disposal in order to mitigate the adverse implications of these problems.

There are two general approaches to manipulating financial statements. The first is to exaggerate current period earnings on the income statement by artificially inflating revenue and gains, or by deflating current period expenses. This approach makes the financial condition of the company look better than it actually is in order to meet established expectations.

The second approach requires the exact opposite tactic, which is to minimize current period earnings on the income statement by deflating revenue or by inflating current period expense.

Financial Shenanigans (2002) by Howard Schilit outlines seven primary ways in which corporate management manipulates the financial statements of a company.

1. **Recording Revenue Prematurely or of Questionable Quality**

    1. Recording revenue prior to completing all services.
    2. Recording revenue prior to product shipment.
    3. Recording revenue for products that are not required to be purchased.
    4. Recording revenue prior to completing sales.
2. **Recording Fictitious Revenue**

1. Recording revenue for sales that did not take place.
2. Recording investment income as revenue.
3. Recording proceeds received through a loan as revenue.

3. Increasing Income with One-Time Gains

1. Increasing profits by selling assets and recording the proceeds as revenue.
2. Increasing profits by classifying investment income or gains as revenue.

4. Shifting Current Expenses to an Earlier or Later Period

1. Amortizing costs too slowly.
2. Changing accounting standards to foster manipulation.
3. Capitalizing normal operating costs in order to reduce expenses by moving them from the income statement to the balance sheet.

5. Failing to Record or Improperly Reducing Liabilities

1. Failing to record expenses and liabilities when future services remain.
2. Changing accounting assumptions to foster manipulation.

6. **Shifting Current Revenue to a Later Period**

    1. Creating a rainy-day reserve as a revenue source to bolster future performance.
    2. Holding back revenue.

7. **Shifting Future Expenses to the Current Period as a Special Charge**

    1. Accelerating expenses into the current period.
    2. Changing accounting standards to foster manipulation, particularly through provisions for depreciation, amortization, and depletion.

Your annual report is more than a legal requirement. It's an opportunity to be transparent about your financial health and make a

bold statement about your brand. It's also an opportunity to engage with many different audiences.

The Wells Fargo account fraud scandal is an ongoing controversy brought about by the creation of millions of fraudulent savings and checking accounts on behalf of Wells Fargo clients without their consent. News of the fraud became widely known in late 2016 after various regulatory bodies, including the Consumer Financial Protection Bureau (CFPB), fined the company a combined US$185 million as a result of the illegal activity. The company has faced and faces additional civil and criminal suits reaching an estimated $2.7 billion by the end of 2018.

Wells Fargo clients began to notice the fraud after being charged unanticipated fees and receiving unexpected credit or debit cards or lines of credit. Initial reports blamed individual Wells Fargo branch workers and managers for the problem, as well as sales incentives associated with selling multiple "solutions" or financial products. This blame was later shifted to a top-down pressure from higher-level management to open as many accounts as possible through cross-selling.

The bank took relatively few risks in the years leading up to the financial crisis of 2007–2008, which led to an image of stability on Wall Street and in the financial world. The bank's stable reputation was tarnished by the widespread fraud, the subsequent coverage, and the revelation of other fraudulent practices employed by the company. The controversy resulted in the resignation of CEO John Stumpf, an investigation into the bank led by U.S. Senator Elizabeth Warren, a number of settlements between Wells Fargo and various parties, and pledges from new management to reform the bank.

3. Does the operating margin is decreasing and inventory is increasing and the status of cash flow in a business?

A simple but especially concerning driver of declining operating profit is slumping revenue. Even if you maintain the same costs of doing business, lower revenue means that you have less profit. Declining revenue can result from either a loss of customers or markdowns on prices. Neither factor is positive. Significant customer attrition can signal underlying problems in the customer experience with products or services. If you have excess inventory or if demand wanes at regular price points, you may have to mark down goods to create transactions.

The company operates in a highly competitive sector like automobiles and aviation, is on the risk of change in the business cycle and that can affect the operating margin, change in supply and demand, change in the customer preference, and change in the price, one of the major factors.

You need to first gather the data that affects the product(s) you sell. This includes more than just the current cost of the raw material and the current sales prices. You should consider some of the following (Keep in mind that this isn't a complete list.):

• Historically, how often has the commodity price changed?

• What additional capital assets company will need to purchase to keep operating in business?

• What selling price will the market accept?

• What margins do company need to stay competitive?

• What types of margins are realistic?

- What are my fixed overhead costs, and what is the likelihood they will vary from year to year?

The main purpose of carrying inventory is to provide customers with an expected level of product availability. In other words, you need the right products in stock at the right time.

If the operating margin is decreasing and inventory, it indicates that company is not in a good position, we need to avoid those companies, if there is decrease in the sale, that will affect in increasing in inventory and cash flow will be restricted.

4. Business is taking more leverage?

Basically, the higher the amount of debt a company uses as leverage, the higher - and the riskier - is its financial leverage position. Also, the more leveraged debt a company absorbs, the higher the interest rate burden, which represents a financial risk to companies and their shareholders.

Leveraged investing is a technique that seeks higher investment profits by using borrowed money. These profits come from the difference between the investment returns on the borrowed capital and the cost of the associated interest. Leveraged investing exposes an investor to higher risk.

"My partner Charlie says there is only three ways a smart person can go broke: liquor, ladies and leverage," he said. "Now the truth is — the first two he just added because they started with L — it's leverage."

-Warren Buffett

Buffett has said that borrowing is to some extent like Russian Roulette:

"At rare and unpredictable intervals...credit vanishes and debt becomes financially fatal. A Russian-roulette equation-- usually win, occasionally die--may make financial sense for someone who gets a piece of a company's upside but does not share in its downside".

A business is said to be overleveraged when it is carrying too much debt when compared to its operating cash flows and equity. An overleveraged company has difficulty in paying its interest and principal payments and is often unable to pay its operating expenses because of excessive costs due to its debt burden, which often leads to a downward financial spiral. This results in the company having to borrow more to stay in operation, and the problem gets worse. This spiral usually ends when a company restructures its debt or files for bankruptcy protection.

- A company is said to be overleveraged when it has too much debt, impeding its ability to make principal and interest payments and to cover operating expenses

- Being overleveraged typically leads to a downward financial spiral resulting in the need to borrow more.

- Companies typically restructure their debt or file for bankruptcy to resolve their overleveraged situation.

- Leverage can be measured using the debt-to-equity ratio or the debt-to-total assets ratio.

- Disadvantages of being overleveraged include constrained growth, loss of assets, limitations on further borrowing, and the inability to attract new investors.

5. Can you invest in this business for a long-term horizon?

An Investment Time Horizon, or just Time Horizon, is the period of time one expects to hold an investment until they need the money back. Time horizons are largely dictated by investment goals and strategies.

Investments in equity front are advisable to be made with a long-term horizon. This is because a long-term horizon allows investors to ride the risk of volatility.

Deciding the right time horizon is very crucial and helps in choosing the right investment option. For instance, investing in equity markets with an investment horizon of just two years will not benefit the investor as they are exposed to the risk of volatility and the only way to combat this is staying invested for as long as possible.

The basic principle of value investor applicable for long term horizon

- Value investing is a long-term strategy which focuses upon a thorough analysis to identify and then purchase those stocks where the market price is below the stock's intrinsic value.
- The main idea is to buy a stock for less than it is truly worth according to the firm's financial statements in the expectation that over time this intrinsic value will be recognized by the market.

Macroeconomics Risk

Macroeconomics is a branch of economics that studies how an overall economy—the market systems that operate on a large scale—behaves. Macroeconomics studies economy-wide phenomena such as inflation, price levels, rate of economic growth, national income, gross domestic product (GDP), and changes in unemployment.

Some of the key questions addressed by macroeconomics include: What causes unemployment? What causes inflation? What creates or stimulates economic growth? Macroeconomics attempts to measure how well an economy is performing, to understand what forces drive it, and to project how performance can improve.

Macroeconomics deals with the performance, structure, and behavior of the entire economy, in contrast to microeconomics, which is more focused on the choices made by individual actors in the economy ((like people, households, industries, etc.).

Macroeconomics analyzes all aggregate indicators and the microeconomic factors that influence the economy. Government and corporations use macroeconomic models to help in formulating of economic policies and strategies.

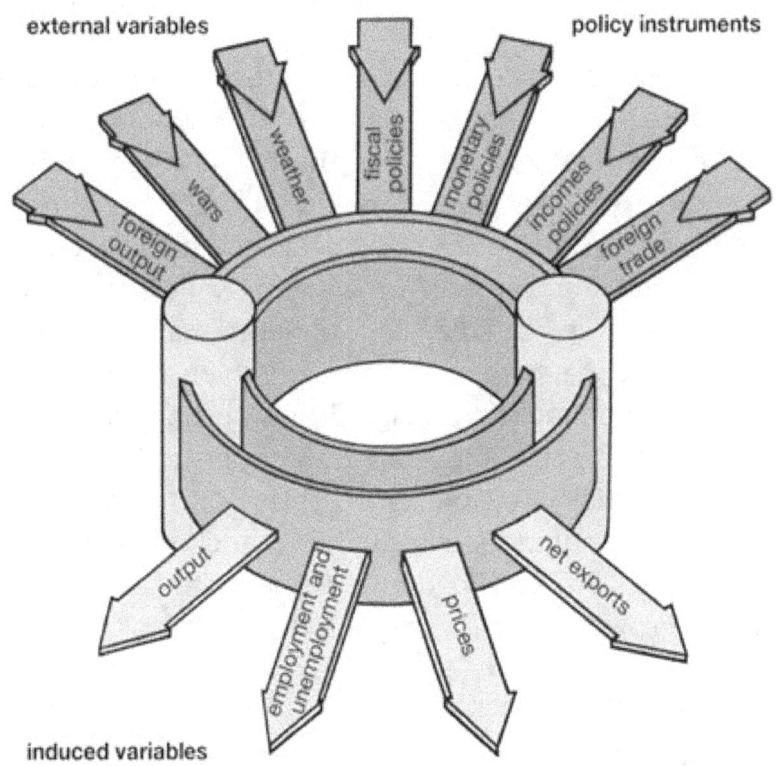

Most investments are "long the economy," meaning that they fair better when the economy (global or domestic) is growing and they perform poorly when the economy is in recession. Macroeconomic (aka "economic") risk simply refers to the risk of a slowing economy that could result in generally poor investment performance due to reduced aggregate demand, profit margins, earnings growth, etc.

1. How the business will perform in the Recession?

In economics, a recession is a business cycle contraction when there is a general decline in economic activity. Recessions generally occur when there is a widespread drop in spending (an adverse demand shock). This may be triggered by various events, such as a financial crisis, an external trade shock, an adverse supply shock, the bursting of an economic bubble, or a large-scale natural or anthropogenic disaster (e.g. a pandemic). In the United States, it is defined as "a significant decline in economic activity spread across the market, lasting more than a few months, normally visible in real GDP, real income, employment, industrial production, and wholesale-retail sales". In the United Kingdom, it is defined as a negative economic growth for two consecutive quarters.

A recession is a macroeconomic term that refers to a significant decline in general economic activity in a designated region. It had been typically recognized as two consecutive quarters of economic decline, as reflected by GDP in conjunction with monthly indicators such as a rise in unemployment. However, the National Bureau of Economic Research (NBER), which officially declares recessions, says the two consecutive quarters of decline in real GDP are not how it is defined anymore. The NBER defines a recession as a significant decline in economic activity spread across the economy, lasting more than a few months, normally visible in real GDP, real income, employment, industrial production, and wholesale-retail sales.

- Not all businesses and industries feel the same pain during economic downturns.

- Some businesses even benefit as consumers cut back on substitute products and other competing options.

- Many of the businesses that do well during recessions either provide goods and services that increase in demand directly due to recession conditions, offer cheaper alternatives to luxuries or big-ticket purchases, or for which demand is relatively inflexible to changes in income.

Essential Industries Perform in Recession

Healthcare, food, consumer staples, and basic transportation are examples of relatively inelastic industries that can perform well in recessions. They may also benefit from being considered essential industries during the public health emergency.

2. How the business will perform in the Inflation?

Inflation is the tax on everyone, and if it's too high, it can destroy value and create recessions. Although we believe inflation is under our control, the cure of higher interest rates may, at some point, be as bad as the problem. With the massive government borrowing to fund the stimulus packages, it is only a matter of time before inflation returns.

☐Investors have historically retreated to hard assets, such as real estate and precious metals, especially gold, in times of inflation, because they're likely to withstand the change. Inflation hurts investors on fixed incomes the most since it erodes the value of their income stream. Stocks are the best protection against inflation since companies can adjust prices to the rate of inflation. A global recession may mean stocks will struggle for a protracted amount of time before the economy is strong enough to bear higher prices.

It is not a perfect solution, but that is why even retired investors should maintain some of their assets in stocks.

Investors, the Federal Reserve, and businesses continuously monitor and worry about the level of inflation. ☐Inflation—the rise in the price of goods and services—reduces the purchasing power each unit of currency can buy. Rising inflation has an insidious effect: input prices are higher, consumers can purchase fewer goods, revenues, and profits decline, and the economy slows for a time until a measure of economic equilibrium is reached.

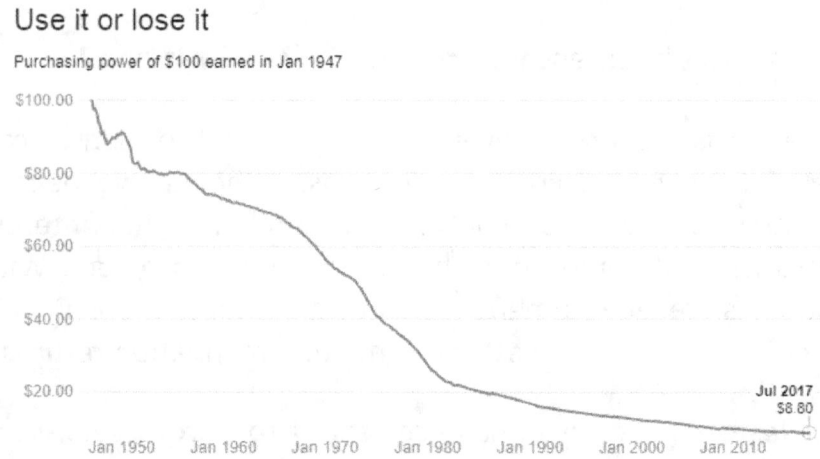

Try to beat inflation by investing in stocks, funds, or other instruments that return more than the average amount of annual inflation, or the average inflation of the lifetime of the investment.

Only those company can increase the price is essential consumer type companies.

24

Value Investor Discipline Approach

Do you know the major difference between a successful and unsuccessful investor? Successful investors are disciplined! Their investment decisions are not driven by greed, fear, and emotions. They know how to react when the market turns volatile. Well, investment discipline isn't easy. Despite knowing all the factors that can lead to losses, many investors react emotionally to market moods. Most times, investors don't even follow the long-term investment plans. So, if you haven't built a disciplined plan yet, here is your opportunity to start working towards it!

One of the biggest mistake's investors make is changing their investment strategy at unexpected times. Don't second-guess yourself; this may lead to high losses. In fact, to be a successful investor you need to follow some strategies consistently, and one of the most important ones is to have a long-term view!

Many investors tend to buy high and sell low because of their short-term views; however, wealth creation requires a long-term view.

If you are going to pull out of your investments within less than 5 years, then you are not giving sufficient time for your money to grow.

Alternatively, if you invest for a time frame of 10 years, which is a long-term, you give your investments the time to perform well. In long-run, you can avoid the negative effects of short-term market volatility. You may choose to invest in high-risk investment options for the long term. Many people think that risky investment options like stocks and equities can be a place to earn quick money. This belief is totally wrong. Expecting quick gains from such options may lead to quick losses.

A study conducted by J.P. Morgan Asset Management using data of the S&P 500's largest moves between 31, Dec 1993 and 31, Dec 2013 showed that staying invested for all 20 years would have given a return of 483% for investors of the broad-based index.

It stated that missing 10 biggest moves up in these time spans would have cut your return to just 191%. Even the 30 best days in a 20-year period, would have given you returns less than 20%. So, the whole point here shows that staying invested in a disciplined way reduces your risk of missing out on the big gains.

Value investing is a strange mix of common sense and contrarian thinking. While most investors can agree that a detailed examination of a company is important, the idea of sitting out a bull market goes against the grain. It's undeniable that funds held constantly in the market have outperformed cash held outside the market that is waiting for a downturn to end. This is a fact, but a deceiving one. The data is derived from following the performance of market measures like the S&P 500 Index over a number of years. This is where passive investing and value investing get confused.

"I would feel somewhat better qualified to speak on self-discipline if I weighed about 20 pounds less, but — (laughter) — for the moment we'll ignore that." Warren Buffett, BRK 2003

"Only when you combine sound intellect with emotional discipline do you get rational behaviour" Warren Buffett

"In making investments, I have always believed that you must act with discipline whenever you see something you truly like." Li Lu

"Value investing requires deep reservoirs of patience and discipline" Seth Klarman

"The most important thing in investments is not having a high IQ, thank God. I mean, the important thing is realism and discipline. And you don't need to be extraordinarily bright to do well in investments, if you are realistic and disciplined." Warren Buffett

1. Avoid market is it in high multiple?

Companies have high multiples because markets expect high earnings growth. However, the way the growth rate comes into the mathematical formula implies growth forever. ... That is why value investors tend to avoid high-multiple firms. It is very difficult to make money when you buy overvalued firms.

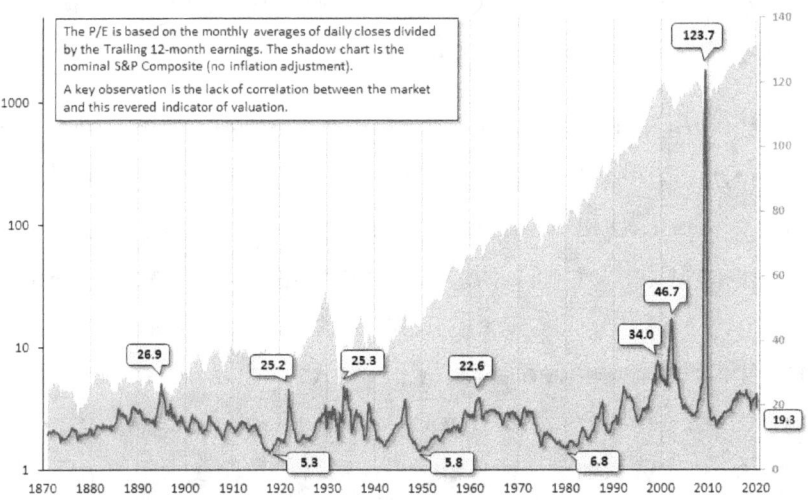

Current S&P 500 PE Ratio: 20.30 -0.59 (-2.81%)
4:00 PM EDT, Fri May 1

Mean: 15.78
Median: 14.82
Min: 5.31   (Dec 1917)
Max: 123.73   (May 2009)

2. Have you checked margin of safety?

There is no substitute for the margin of safety, to be a good value investor, you need to keep the margin of safety, and your purpose is to make money, to keep control of your portfolio risk. If you don't keep a margin of safety, there are high possibilities that your portfolio is at risk.

To understand the margin of safety with respect to stocks, we need to understand the tipping point. The tipping point is the point at which the margin of safety is the highest and makes the most business sense to buy the stock.

A stock's intrinsic value is based on a variety of factors. There are financial factors such as growth in sales, growth in profits, operating margins, P/E ratio, and dividend yield. However, it is not just about quantitative factors. There are qualitative factors as well such as the management quality, entry barriers created by the product, corporate governance standards, and brand reputation. The final valuation is arrived at by combining the impact of these financial and non-financial factors. This is what gives you the intrinsic value of a stock.

It is not just enough to know if the stock underpriced or overpriced. You need to know the extent to which the stock overpriced or underpriced. It is this gap between the market price and the intrinsic value that is known as the margin of safety.

3. Are you holding enough cash?

A common-sense strategy may be to allocate no less than 5% of your portfolio to cash, and many prudent professionals may prefer to keep between 10% and 20% on hand at a minimum. Evidence indicates that the maximum risk/return trade-off occurs somewhere around this level of cash allocation.

For most people, the absolute minimum level of cash to keep on hand is an emergency fund that would cover typical expenses for least six months. Emergency funds allow you to get through unexpected disasters or surprises without having to sell off your assets. Being forced to sell assets at an inopportune time could trigger excess taxes and suboptimal returns—potentially at a time when you're already struggling financially.

That's just what happened in 2008. Buffett's large cash balance not only insulated Berkshire from the broader market turmoil, but it also gave the group optionality to take advantage of others' weaknesses. Buffett explained this principle in a meeting with the University of Maryland students in November 2013:

"BRK always has $20 billion or more in cash. It sounds crazy, never need anything like it, but some day in the next 100 years when the world stops again, we will be ready. There will be some incident, it could be tomorrow. At that time, you need cash. Cash at that time is like oxygen.

When you don't need it, you don't notice it. When you do need it, it's the only thing you need. We operate from a level of liquidity that no one else does. We don't want to operate on bank lines.

Something like that will happen maybe a couple of times in your lifetime. Two things when it happens again – don't let it ruin you, and if you have money/guts, you'll have an opportunity to buy things at prices that don't make sense. Fear spreads fast, it is contagious. It doesn't have anything to do with IQ. Confidence only comes back one at a time, not en masse. There are periods when fear paralyzes the investment world. You don't want to owe money at that time, and if you have money, then you want to buy at those times. Be greedy when others are fearful and fearful when others are greedy."

- Warren Buffett has kept a strangely low profile as the coronavirus outbreak continues to shake markets.

- The billionaire boss of Berkshire Hathaway, armed with a $128 billion cash pile, could capitalize on the recent sell-off to bolster his portfolio or throw a lifeline to companies as he did during the financial crisis.

- We asked investing enthusiasts on Reddit to speculate on what Buffett is up to, and their suggestions included biding his time, boosting his Apple and Amazon stakes, investing in Google, and striking bailout deals.

4. Are you being conservative, prudent, is a virtue, not a defect?

When you don't find a good company, don't worry, wait for the right time, don't be aggressive, that is your enemy, you have to be very conservative investors have risk tolerances ranging from low to moderate. As such, a conservative investment portfolio will have a large amount of low-risk, high-quality stocks. Although a conservative investing strategy may protect against inflation, it may not earn significant returns over time when compared to more aggressive strategies.

Be prudent, a prudent investment refers to the recognized use of financial assets that are suitable for an investor's goals and objectives. A prudent investment considers the risk/return profile and the time horizon of an investor.

These are the characteristic of the value investor, if you will be like this, it doesn't mean you are defeated. Buying and selling daily are not a winner strategy, till today this kind of trading has not made anyone billionaires, to be a value investor, you need to be like this to make enormous wealth.

5. Why is this opportunity available only to me?

As a value investor, you should be asking this questing, why you think about this opportunity available only for you.

"The stock investor is neither right nor wrong because others agreed or disagreed with him; he is right because his facts and analysis are right."

– Benjamin Graham

Investing with the crowd or based on current euphoria is as wise as bungee jumping with fishing line. This is similar to investing using your emotions and not actual numbers. If you don't believe me then consider this: if most people in your social circle started eating rocks for dinner, would you follow suit? I didn't think so. Why should investing be any different?

You see this opportunity because you have done your research and you know the facts and now you see the investment as an opportunity, before you put single penny, first do your checklist and understand as much about the company in three prospect such as :

- Learn about the Past
- What is the present scenario?
- What is the future look like?

This is how value investor thinks before investing and take benefit of the opportunity.

6. What is the other side of transition coming from?

It state that what other side of the transition know, that I don't know, why other side of the transition want to see the stock, what information is available in the market for the other side.

A market theory that evolved from a 1960's Ph.D. dissertation by Eugene Fama, the efficient market hypothesis states that at any given time and in a liquid market, security prices fully reflect all available information. The EMH exists in various degrees: weak, semi-strong and strong, which addresses the inclusion of non-public information in market prices. This theory contends that since markets are efficient and current prices reflect all information, attempts to outperform the market are essentially a game of chance rather than one of skill.

We value investor don't agree with the EMH , we believe market never value the company with the information available, it is just a swing, every company has an intrinsic value, we need to find that value to invest.

7. Why others for selling and where I am buying Mr. Market offers?

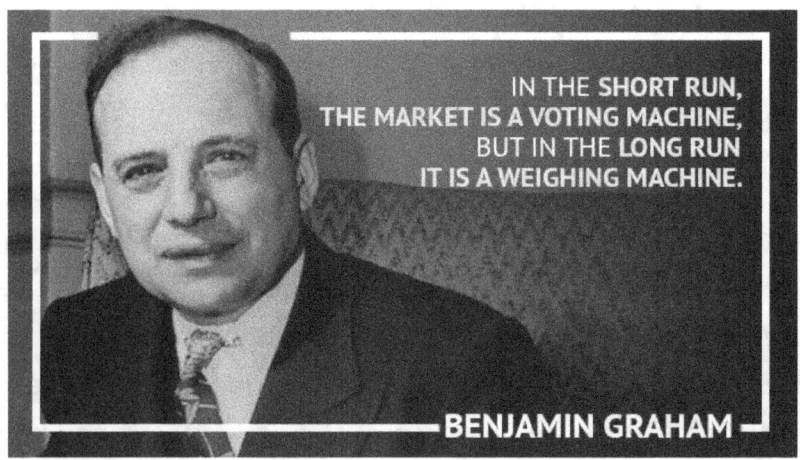

The value of your interest should be determined by rationally appraising the business's prospects, and you can happily sell when Mr. Market quotes you a ridiculously high price and buy when he quotes you an absurdly low price. The best part of your association with Mr. Market is that he does not care how many times you take advantage of him. No matter how many times you saddle him with losses or rob him of gains, he will arrive the next day ready to do business with you again.

"Mr. Market" by Warren Buffett

Whenever Charlie and I buy common stocks for Berkshires's insurance companies (leaving aside arbitrage purchases, discussed in the next essay), we approach the transaction as if we were buying into a private business. We look at the economic prospects of the business, the people in charge of running it, and the price we must pay. We do not have in mind any time or price for sale. Indeed, we are willing to hold a stock indefinitely so long as we expect the business to increase in intrinsic value at a satisfactory rate. When investing, we view ourselves as business analysts, and not even as security analysts.

Our approach makes an active trading market useful since it periodically presents us with mouth-watering opportunities. But by no means is it essential: a prolonged suspension for trading in the securities we hold would not bother us anymore that does the lack of daily quotations on World Book or Fechheimer. Eventually, our economic fate will be determined by the economic fate of the business we own, whether our ownership is partial or total.

Ben Graham, my friend and teacher, long ago described the mental attitude toward market fluctuations that I believe to be the most conducive to investment success. He said that you should imagine market quotations as coming from a remarkably accommodating fellow named Mr. Market who is your partner in a private business. Without fail, Mr. Market appears daily and names a price at which he will either buy your interest or sell you his.

Even though the business that the tow of you own may have economic characteristics that are stable, Mr. Market's quotations will be anything but. For, sad to say, the poor fellow has incurable emotional problems. At times he feels euphoric and we can see only the favorable factors affecting the business. When in that mood, he names a very high buy-sell price because he fears that you will snap up his interest and rob him of imminent gains. At other times he is depressed and can see nothing but trouble ahead for both the business and the world. On these occasions he will name a very low price, since he is terrified that you will unload your interest on him.

Mr. Market has another endearing characteristic: He doesn't mind being ignored. If his quotation is uninteresting to you today, he will back with a new one tomorrow. Transactions are strictly at your option. Under these conditions, the more manic-depressive his behavior, the better for you. (This means NOW, 2015 — Cokie's words.)

But, like Cinderella at the ball, you must heed one warning or everything will turn into pumpkins and mice: Mr. Market is there to serve you, not to guide you. It is his pocketbook, not his wisdom, that you will find useful. If he shows up some day in a particularly foolish mood, you are free to either ignore him or to take advantage of him, but it will be disastrous if you fall under his influence. Indeed, if you aren't certain that you understand and can value your business far better than Mr. Market you don't belong in the game. As they say in poker, "If you've been in the game 30 minutes and you don't know who the patsy is, you're the patsy." (Ahem, don't be the patsy, contact Alphavest to help negotiate Mr. Market's moods for you.)

Ben's Mr. Market allegory may seem out-of-date in today's investment world, in which most professionals and academicians talk of efficient markets, dynamic hedgings and betas. Their interest in such matters is understandable, since techniques shrouded in mystery clearly have value to the purveyor of investment advice. After all, what witch doctor has ever achieved fame and fortune by simply advising "Take two aspirins"?

The value of market esoterica to the consumer of investment advice is a different story. In my opinion, investment success will not be produced by arcane formulae, computer programs or signals flashed by the price behavior of stocks and markets. Rather an investor will succeed by coupling good business judgment with an ability to insulate his thoughts and behavior from the super-contagious emotions that swirl about the marketplace. In my own efforts to stay insulated, I have found it highly useful to keep Ben's Mr. Market concept firmly in mind.

Following Ben's teachings, Charlie and I let our marketable equities tell us by the operating results— not by their daily, or even yearly, price quotations–whether our investments are successful. The market may ignore business success for a while, but eventually will confirm it. As Ben said: "In the short run, the market is a voting machine but in the long run it is a weighing machine." The speed at which business's success is recognized, furthermore, is not that important as a long as the company's intrinsic value is increasing at a satisfactory rate. In fact, delayed recognition can be an advantage: It may give us the chance to buy more of a good thing at a bargain price.

Sometimes, of course, the market may judge a business to be more valuable than the underlying facts would indicate it is. In such a case, we will sell our holdings. Sometimes, also, we will sell a security that is fairly valued or even undervalued because we require funds for a still more undervalued investment or one we believe we understand better.

We need to emphasize, however, that we do not sell holdings just because they have appreciated or because we have held them for a long time. (Of Wall Street maxims the most foolish may be "You can't go broke taking a profit.") We are quite content holding a security indefinitely, so long as the prospective return on equity capital of the underlying business is satisfactory, management is competent and honest, and the market does not overvalue the business.

However, our insurance companies own three marketable common stocks that we would not sell even though they became far overprices in the market. In effect, we view these investments exactly like our successful controlled businesses — a permanent part of Berkshire rather than merchandise to be disposed of once Mr. Market offers us a sufficiently high price. To that, I will add one qualifier: These stocks are held by our insurance companies and we would, if absolutely necessary, sell portions of our holdings to pay extraordinary insurance losses. We intend, however, to manage our affairs so that sales are never required.

A determination to have and hold, which Charlie and I share, obviously involves a mixture of personal and financial considerations. To some, our stand may seem highly eccentric. (Charlie and I have long followed David Ogilvy's advice: "Develop your eccentricities awhile you are young. That way, when you get old, people won't think you're going ga-ga.") Certainly, in the transaction-fixated Wall Street of recent years, our posture must seem odd: To many in that arena, both companies and stocks are seen only as raw material for trades.

Our attitude, however, fits our personalities and the way we want to live our lives. Churchill once said, "You shape your houses and then they shape you." We know the manner in which we wish to be shaped. For that reason, we would rather achieve a return of X while associating with people whom we strongly like and admire than realize 110% of X by exchanging these relationships for uninteresting or unpleasant ones.

8. View on other side are selling and I am buying?

Both investors have appositive view, a reason to buy and sell. The reason you are buying stocks meaning investing in general: This is simple, Investment as a concept is considered good for various reasons like achieving financial independence, second source of income, retirement planning or in some cased means to get rich.

Reason to sell when you are buying is the herd instinct explains why people tend to imitate others. When a market is moving up or down, investors are subject to a fear that others know more or have more information. As a consequence, investors feel a strong impulse to do what others are doing.

Herd instinct in finance is the phenomenon where investors follow what they perceive other investors are doing, rather than their own analysis. In other words, an investor exhibiting herd instinct will gravitate toward the same or similar investments based almost solely on the fact that many others are buying the securities.

In behavioral finance, herd mentality bias refers to investors' tendency to follow and copy what other investors are doing. They are largely influenced by emotion and instinct, rather than by their own independent analysis. This guide provides examples of how investors may succumb to herd bias, as part of behavioral finance theory. If an investor selling the stock, then all the investors will follow the same.

25

The Intelligent Investor by Benjamin Graham Quotes

- The longer the bull market lasts the more severely investors will be affected with amnesia; after five years or so, many people no longer believe that bear markets are possible

- Those who do not remember the past are condemned to repeat it.

- But investing isn't about beating others at their game. It's about controlling yourself at your own game.

- The stock investor is neither right or wrong because others agreed or disagreed with him; he is right because his facts and analysis are right.

- On the other hand, investing is a unique kind of casino—one where you cannot lose in the end, so long as you play only by the rules that put the odds squarely in your favor.

- You must deliberately protect yourself against serious losses.

- The market is a pendulum that forever swings between unsustainable optimism (which makes stocks too expensive) and unjustified pessimism (which makes them too cheap). The Intelligent Investor is a realist who sells to optimists and buys from pessimists.

- You will be much more in control, if you realize how much you are not in control.

- While enthusiasm may be necessary for great accomplishments elsewhere, on Wall Street it almost invariably leads to disaster.

- With every new wave of optimism or pessimism, we are ready to abandon history and time-tested principles, but we cling tenaciously and unquestioningly to our prejudices.

- Many skeptics, it is true, are inclined to dismiss the whole procedure [chart reading] as akin to astrology or necromancy; but the sheer weight of its importance in Wall Street requires that its pretensions be examined with some degree of care.

- It requires a great deal of boldness and a great deal of caution to make a great fortune; and when you have got it, it requires ten times as much wit to keep it.

- Never mingle your speculative and investment operations in the same account, nor in any part of your thinking.

- The whole point of investing is not to earn more money than average, but to earn enough money to meet your own needs.

- The best way to measure your investing success is not by whether you're beating the market but by whether you've put in place a financial plan and a behavioral discipline that are likely to get you where you want to go. In the end, what matters isn't crossing the finish line before anybody else but just making sure that you do cross it.

- The intelligent investor realizes that stocks become more risky, not less, as their prices rise—and less risky, not more, as their prices fall. The intelligent investor dreads a bull market, since it makes stocks more costly to buy. And conversely (so long as you keep enough cash on hand to meet your spending needs), you should welcome a bear market, since it puts stocks back on sale.

- No matter how careful you are, the one risk no investor can ever eliminate is the risk of being wrong.

- The secret to your financial success is inside yourself. If you become a critical thinker who takes no Wall Street "fact" on faith, and you invest with patient confidence, you can take steady advantage of even the worst bear markets.

- By developing your discipline and courage, you can refuse to let other people's mood swings govern your financial destiny. In the end, how your investments behave is much less important than how you behave.

- The more a stock has gone up, the more it seems likely to keep going up. But that instinctive belief is flatly contradicted by a fundamental law of financial physics: The bigger they get, the slower they grow.

- Even when the underlying motive of purchase is mere speculative greed, human nature desires to conceal this unlovely impulse behind a screen of apparent logic and good sense.

- Successful investing is about managing risk, not avoiding it.

- To invest successfully over a lifetime does not require a stratospheric IQ, unusual business insights, or inside information. What's needed is a sound intellectual framework for making decisions and the ability to keep emotions from corroding that framework.

- At heart, "uncertainty" and "investing" are synonyms.

- Losing *some* money is an inevitable part of investing, and there's nothing you can do to prevent it. But to be an intelligent investor, you must take responsibility for ensuring that you never lose *most or all* of your money.

- Before you invest, you must ensure that you have realistically assessed your probability of being right and how you will react to the consequences of being wrong.

- The intelligent investor is likely to need considerable will power to keep from following the crowd.

- The intelligent investor should recognize that market panics can create great prices for good companies and good prices for great companies.

- Wall Street has a few prudent principles; the trouble is that they are always forgotten when they are most needed.